Enriqueta Vasquez and the Chicano Movement: Writings from *El Grito del Norte*

Enriqueta Vasquez

Edited by Lorena Oropeza and Dionne Espinoza

With a Foreword by John Nichols and a Preface by Enriqueta Vasquez

Arte Público Press
Houston, Texas

This volume is made possible through grants from the Rockefeller Foundation, the Charles Stewart Mott Foundation and the Exemplar Program, a program of Americans for the Arts in collaboration with the LarsonAllen Public Services Group, funded by the Ford Foundation.

Recovering the past, creating the future

University of Houston
Arte Público Press
452 Cullen Performance Hall
Houston, Texas 77204-2004

Cover design by James F. Brisson

Vasquez, Enriqueta
    Enriqueta Vasquez and the Chicano Movement: Writings from El Grito del Norte / by Enriqueta Vasquez; edited by Dionne Espinoza and Lorena Oropeza; foreword by John Nichols.
      p.   cm.
    Articles originally written in the 1960s and 1970s for the newspaper El Grito del Norte.
    ISBN-10: 1-55885-479-7
    ISBN-13: 978-1-55885-479-6
    1. Mexican Americans—Social conditions—20th century. 2. Mexican Americans—Social conditions—20th century. 3. Mexican Americans—Politics and government—20th century. 4. Vasquez, Enriqueta—Archives. 5. Grito del norte (Española, N.M.) 6. United States—Race relations. 7. Southwest, New—Race relations. I. Espinoza, Dionne. II. Oropeza, Lorena, 1964- III. Title.
    E184.M5L65 2006
    305.868′72079—dc22

            2006042660
            CIP

6 7 8 9 0 1 2 3 4 5   10 9 8 7 6 5 4 3 2 1

With love to Ruben, Ramona, and Bill

Dedicated to

Gloria Anzaldúa,

a mestiza who could weave words

of serpentine grace to form

vision and song of

mystical sounds carried in the divine breath

of Ehecatl

now echoing in the *más allá*

creating new worlds on

both sides of the border

Contents

Foreword by John Nichols   ix

Preface by Enriqueta Vasquez   xiii

Acknowledgements   xvii

Introduction by Lorena Oropeza: "*Viviendo y luchando*: The Life and Times of Enriqueta Vasquez"   xix

Conclusion by Dionne Espinoza: "Rethinking Cultural Nationalism and La Familia through Women's Communities: Enriqueta Vasquez and Chicana Feminist Thought"   205

Enriqueta Vazquez and the Chicano Movement: Writings from *El Grito del Norte*

I. Land, Race, and Poverty

Introduction 3

Discrimination 5

Los Pobres y Los Ricos 8

This Land Is Our Land 11

Racism 14

"Communism," Just a Word 17

Welfare and Work 20

More Abuses at Santa Fe Pinta 24

II. Culture and History

Introduction 31

Teach True Values, Says La Raza Mother 33

'Tis the Season, Fa La La 36

Let's Be Seen and Heard 39
16 de septiembre 43
The 16th of September 47
La Santa Tierra 53
La Voz de Nuestra Cultura I 57
La Voz de Nuestra Cultura II 60
La Historia del Mestizo 64

III. Nation and Self-Determination
Introduction 83
Somos Aztlán! (English) 85
¡Somos Aztlán! (Spanish) 88
Our New Nation Is Born 90
Se Nace Nuestra Nación 96
Let's Take a Look at the Political System 101
New Levels of Awareness 106

IV. Chicanas, Organize!
Introduction 111
La Chicana: Let's Build a New Life 113
The Woman of La Raza, Part I 116
The Woman of La Raza, Part II 122
Chicana Resolution 127
¡Soy Chicana primero! 129
National Chicana Conference, Houston 134

V. Corporate Institutions and Industrial Society
Introduction 141
The Church Has Made Us Slaves 143
Values Lost 146
Apollo IX 149
Smog and Money Politics 152
The Church and the People 155
Money, Money, Money 158

The Atomic Age 162
Railroads and Land 163

VI. International Politics
Introduction 169
Draft and Our Youth 171
Tío Sam Says: "Gimme!" 174
¡Qué Linda Es Cuba!: Part I 178
Raza, Nos Están Matando. They Are Killing Us,
   Did you Know? 182
¡Qué Linda Es Cuba!: Part II 186
Kent State 190
El Soldado Raso de Hoy 194
El Soldado Raso Today 197
Third World Women Meet 201

Foreword

These articles, written in the late 1960s and early 1970s, are as relevant today as they were many years ago. The issues have not changed, and the United States seems to have regressed into a time that incorporates the worst of the McCarthy period and the Vietnam War together. We need Enriqueta Vasquez's wise and passionate voice now more than ever.

The columns are disarmingly straightforward, often conversational. They read like steel tempered by a gentle and courageous humanism. The manner of address is often touched by humor. The message is sophisticated and vitally important to all struggles for human rights and environmental sanity.

The writing teems with folk wisdom presented as part of a radical call to awareness. Although the articles are often focused on revolutionary concepts connected to the militant Chicano Movement, their intent is always universal.

Enriqueta insists on reason and hope, and she has a fierce determination to open our eyes and our hearts to the possibilities of a better future on earth.

Her columns speak to all issues of social justice, ethnic pride, environmental well-being, a skewed economy, poverty, and feminist issues that were (and still are) important within La Raza's call to forge Aztlán, and also within the wider need of all women on earth to be treated as co-equals.

Many of the columns are serious history lessons presented concisely in just a sentence or two. In a direct and comprehensive way they may also deconstruct complex economics so that the core issues are beautifully revealed. Her analysis of American "interests" in Latin

America captures in a couple of pages the entire history of U.S. Imperialism in this hemisphere.

A strong environmental message underlies many of Enriqueta's observations. Well ahead of the times, her brief protest against insecticides elucidates a major ongoing problem threatening this planet. And her three-page dissertation on cars and smog could well be a chapter from a current *State of the World* report.

Repeatedly, I was reminded of this fact: her vision that is ostensibly for the future of La Raza is a vision that *all* humanity must soon realize if the natural and human ecology on earth is to endure.

Many articles contain an ongoing discussion of racism discussed with blunt honesty yet seldom shrill polemics. Enriqueta's powerful writings might be compared to the native herbs of a *curandera*: occasionally bitter yet always part of the healing whole.

Which reminds me that this collection also includes several lovely and sensible forays into natural healing the indigenous way.

Without raising her voice, Enriqueta can lambaste the U.S. educational system, urging her readers *not* to accept the skewed academic values that attempt to program our children with a sense of cutthroat competition above all else.

Included in every column, implicit or explicit, is the history of those times. As such, the collected essays are very valuable as historical documents of a volatile and evolutionary as well as revolutionary era.

Some columns also provide a fascinating specific history of Mexico and the Southwest and the origins of mestizo/Chicano history.

And much of the writing is both in English and Spanish, emphasizing the living culture it is speaking about.

Enriqueta shies away from no subject matter: one brief, yet very perceptive commentary on hypocrisy within the Catholic Church must have taken great courage to write.

And there is a gentle yet powerful and touching cry to restore the unselfish spirit of Christmas before capitalism crams it into the cash register of market greed.

The article on Chicana activism is an important liberation document pertinent to all women of the USA, Afghanistan, Guatemala, Brazil. The essay "Soy Chicana Primero" is a forceful analysis on how general exploitation must not be allowed to destroy the liberation struggle between men and women of an oppressed minority.

Enriqueta can speak on the most serious subject, yet her commentary is often touched with a smile, maybe a wink, and an endearing underlying tolerance for humanity and its foibles that makes her voice friendly no matter how heavy the topic under discussion.

Sometimes I am reminded of the wonderful cartoons of Rius, who could explain Marxism or Capitalism or oil development in Mexico with a sardonic chuckle and an amazing ability to highlight the complex problem (and the complex answer) in just a handful of expert strokes.

"*Híjole*," Enriqueta more than once remarks, "how stupid do they think we are?"

In the end, each analysis is simple and direct and wise, presenting the heart of the matter in just a few clear paragraphs, no adornments.

Her columns, entitled "¡Despierten Hermanos!," can be read as fables, morality tales, and recipes for a more organic life. And although the columns always speak directly to La Raza, at the same time they really speak to us all. This entire collection is a call for the more humane, sustainable, and egalitarian lifestyle that the earth needs for life to survive.

Always, the gist is a strong radical politics couched in a quiet humanity.

And the bottom-line message is that we must learn in order to empower ourselves, which will enable us to feel much joy about being alive.

Yes, the voice of Enriqueta Vasquez was truly important thirty-five years ago . . . and it is just as truly important today.

John Nichols
October 2005
San Cristobal, New Mexico

Preface

The publication of these articles, written over thirty years ago, resulted from the encouragement from my friend, Lorena Oropeza, who together with Dionne Espinoza made such a publication possible. It has been an honor to have known Lorena and Dionne who came to my home to interview me. Both are now profesoras at universities. That we have scholars and Chicana PHDers of this caliber teaching in our educational institutions fulfills a vision of what we hoped would come out of the Chicano Movement. Even more extraordinary is the fact that most scholars do not forget "La Causa Chicana," thus watering the *raíces* of the ancient past and living the Chicano epic.

El Grito Del Norte, a Chicano newspaper based in Española, New Mexico, was born from the revolutionary flames that engulfed the Southwest in the late 1960s and early 1970s. It began as the official newspaper for Reies López Tijerina's La Alianza Federal de Pueblos Libres, an organization with a membership of 6,000 heirs representing descendents of fifty Mexican and Spanish land grants. With the help of Beverly Axelrod (RIP, June 19, 2002), we formed a cooperative of editors who came together as volunteers, community peoples and political activists. Elizabeth (Betita) Martínez led the pack, so to speak, by holding down the fort of *El Grito* headquarters in Española as it became a beehive of movement and activism. The variety of skills and people from all walks of life that united in producing this newspaper generated a phenomenal power of and with the people. *El Grito* reported Alianza demonstrations, courtroom battles, injustices and the growing militancy of the Spanish/Mexican population, Black Power, American Indian movements and national and international issues. The presentation of history and culture in the form of poetry, stories, recipes, and songs made *El Grito* appealing to everyone and it soon grew to be a very successful member of the Chicano Press Association, an organization of the time that included some fifty newspapers.

Doing a newspaper became an important part of our lives and a priceless education to those creating it. One cannot separate *El Grito* from the Civil Rights Movement which empowered Raza with political knowledge and experience. Evolving with the activism of the times, we embraced a new literary form, breaking all conventions regarding proper English, language purity, and word usage. Intellectual development grew with the use of bilingual lyrical abilities in a unique, creative, self-refined way, a people's way. This new Spanglish, as some call it, gave such freedom so that even my words and expressions in writing came from childhood family conversations as well as experience in community meetings and political conferences across the country.

I learned to listen, not only to words, but to the hearts of people; thus capturing the passion, anger, outrage, and indignation when discussing racism, greed, repression and exploitation. These sentiments became an eruption of hundreds of years of repressed thought now set free. This reflection of the past revealed who and what we had become and what we had lost, "por eso estamos como estamos." It deciphered the difference between "Justice" and "Justus" and in the process of activism, we envisioned a humanitarian way of governing by putting people before profits; a way to make people proud with honor and dignity.

During this time, the newspaper and our homes were under constant surveillance and we were followed by local, state, and federal authorities. Many of us are in the congressional record with telephone, car license numbers, and personal information openly targeting us to whomever. Despite all of this, our home in San Cristobal, where we had moved to help start La Escuela Tlatelolco which would be based in Denver, became a hub of activity and a source of inspiration in reading, studying, discussing, and learning with family and friends. Our neighbor, Craig Vincent, became a mentor to many of us, as did Cleofas Vigil. They joined our home circle when visitors stayed with us and we learned of activists and activism across the country. Our kitchen table became the heart and axis of movement secrets, laughter and discussion. My children always listened and marvel saying, "Wow, Mom, if these walls could talk."

My articles and column, "Despierten Hermanos," today I would also say Hermanas, became a regular in *El Grito del Norte*, a *grito* that could be read and heard from New York to Mexico, Cuba, Latin America, Puerto Rico, and all over the Southwest. I named the first column "Despierten Hermanos" and when I sent the next article, Betita called me to ask what I wanted to name it and without thinking I said, "Oh, call it 'Despierten Hermanos.'" And so the column became Despierten Hermanos.

I am but one of many who walked this path of change: it took a movement to change what this place called North Amerika had become. These essays represent labor and thought at a time when we even debated what to call ourselves. They are non-professional, most unplanned, some with logic and some with no logic, some great, some not so great and although diverse in subject, they remained consistent in taking racial attitudes, institutions, and ruling powers to task. I never claimed to be the best; actually I never even thought of myself as a writer or columnist, other people said that, not me. I just rambled, wrote my opinions my way, and ideas took shape flooding my mind with new ones. People either liked them or if they didn't like them, it made them think and pay attention to what took place in the country. A new dawn opened for La Raza.

Of all of my writings probably the article that created the biggest whoooraah turned out to be "The Woman of La Raza." This lost me friends and made me a target for the renowned "Malinche" label. But, like so many of my writings, the rewards were many and this article opened centuries-old flood gates that poured forth in women's words and thoughts. I knew "This is very important," and from this article came a whole women's history book, *The Women of La Raza,* hopefully to be published soon. This women's book begins to define the side of that mestizo face medallion we wore so proudly, La India.

The Chicana/o Movement is a vital chapter of Southwestern history, a history needed to inspire new dreamers as activists become the elder generation. As we recall this chapter in Chicano history, we reseed the harvest of the Civil Rights Movement and cultivate the harvest of "La Revolución Chicana" remembering that our ancestors planted the first resisting seeds of non-defeat. This Revolución is the foundation of today's evolving issues, the metamorphosis of activism that makes all movements more important than ever. It will take more than thirty years to change 500 years of colonial racist exploitative attitudes, changes which only you can make possible as we live the sun of justice, The Sixth Sun.

ᘓᘓᘓ

As I look back I remember, "To think that at one time even my mother accused me of being a communist and threatened to report me to the government as such." I always respected her and had never answered her, but this time I answered:

"Go ahead, I will call the FBI for you and you can turn me in. Who do you think I learned to be a revolutionary from? Remember when you would say: 'Si yo supiera hablar inglés, ¿ya me hubieran echado a la prisión?' Pues yo sí sé inglés, y ahora, ¿usted me acusa de ser comunista? Ándele, entrégueme.'"

Her little eyes blinked and after a long silence we both laughed, hugged and cried as she said, "Hija de tu nana, me ganaste." I thought, "Of course, I won, what do you expect from the daughter of the Mexican Revolution?"

Later, in 1968, I brought her to visit me in New Mexico and took her to hear Reies Tijerina when he spoke at Española High School. I will never forget the incredible look that came over her face as she drank up every word. After he finished, my mother walked right over to Reies, talked to him and hugged him, tearfully saying, "Nunca creí que oyera en este país las palabras y verdades que ha dicho usted."

After we left, I smilingly hugged her and reminded her that now, she too was a communist. ¡VIVA LA REVOLUCIÓN, SIEMPRE!

Enriqueta Vasquez
August 14, 2005
San Cristobal, New Mexico

Acknowlegements

Many people helped in preparing this anthology for publication. Fittingly, many of them were strong women, that *buen barro* that Enriqueta Vasquez celebrated in her columns. Foremost, we would like to thank Betita Martínez, the editor of *El Grito del Norte*, for her interest in this project over the years and for allowing us to use Rini Templeton's art in this work. Thanks also to Herminia S. Reyes, Delia V. Sarabia, and Bertha S. Figueroa, the translating *tías* of Lorena Oropeza. Just as the wisdom of Doña Faustina was a resource for Enriqueta Vasquez, our mothers, Audrey Espinoza and Celia S. Oropeza, also pitched in with expert advice. Without the aid of a crew of first-rate students who transcribed and chased footnotes, putting together this anthology would have taken even longer than it did. We would especially like to thank Elisabeth Ritacca, Kim Davis, Lia Schraeder, Fernando Purcell, and Julia Kehew, all University of California, Davis graduate students, and Emily Erickson, an excellent undergraduate research assistant. Most of the funding to pay these students came from Chicana/Latina Research Center on the UC Davis campus. Special thanks are owed to Inés Hernández Avila and Beatriz Pesquera for their long-time support of this project. Finally, we wish to thank Jorge Mariscal, who played a critical role at the inception of this project.

Viviendo y luchando: The Life and Times of Enriqueta Vasquez

Years later, Enriqueta Vasquez still remembered how whenever she visited the local hamburger joint in the town of La Junta, Colorado, she was handed her order in a paper sack. The restaurant's policy was to accept her money but not allow her to eat it inside. As the sign on the front door clearly read: "No Mexicans Allowed." Born in 1930 in nearby Cheraw into a family of farmworkers who traveled the southern portion of the state, Vasquez had often experienced blatant discrimination against people of Mexican descent. After World War II began, however, the restaurant's segregationist policy suddenly struck her as intolerable. Was not this war being fought in the name of freedom and equality and against a regime that embraced a creed of racial superiority? And did she not have three older brothers serving in the U.S. military fighting on behalf of American democracy? Although just barely a teenager, she decided to write a letter to the local paper in La Junta in which she railed against an injustice noted by many Mexican-American civil rights activists at the time: although apparently good enough to risk their lives overseas, Mexican Americans were not good enough to be treated as equals at home.[1] Faltering only at signing her name, she used the initials "HV" for "Henrietta Vasquez" having been renamed by a teacher upon entering the first grade. Then without telling anyone in her family, she mailed the letter and shortly afterward saw it in print.[2] Long before she had become a well-known columnist for *El Grito del Norte*, a leading Chicano Movement newspaper, Enriqueta Vasquez was taking up the pen against injustice.

Continuing that crusade as an adult, Vasquez's columns for *El Grito del Norte* showcased a distinctive voice of protest that was fierce yet always hopeful. The main aim of her columns, entitled "¡Despierten Hermanos!" [Wake up, Brothers and Sisters!], was to rouse an ethnic population that had long been described as a "sleeping giant." Toward that end, Vasquez employed equal parts anger and humor to offer a Chicana perspective on such weighty topics as racism, sexism, imperialism, and poverty. As a columnist, she drew upon her own life experiences to insist upon the primacy of the Chicano struggle. Yet during an era of tremendous political dissent, Vasquez consistently situated the Chicano Movement within a broader, even global, effort to advance equality. Candidly and even bluntly speaking truth to power, her columns traveled beyond New Mexico, where *El Grito del Norte* was published, and beyond the Chicano Movement. In the hope of allowing a new generation to reflect upon and perhaps find inspiration in her call for justice, this anthology has collected Vasquez's writings as they appeared in *El Grito del Norte* from 1968 to 1972.

An anthology of Vasquez's work serves another purpose: to underscore the contributions and complexities of the Chicano Movement more than thirty years after its height. Vasquez was an ardent champion of Chicano cultural nationalism, or *Chicanismo*, the main guiding philosophy of the Chicano Movement. In the words of the 1969 *El Plan Espiritual de Aztlán,* a foundational blueprint for the Chicano Movement that Vasquez strongly endorsed, nationalism was "the key" to advancing "total liberation from oppression, exploitation, and racism."[3] For more than a century, Mexican Americans had battled against discrimination in education, housing, employment, and the administration of justice. Yet during late 1960s and early 1970s, activists who called themselves "Chicanos" and "Chicanas" promoted a politics of cultural identity that challenged long-held assumptions about the history and contemporary role of the racial-ethnic group within U.S. society. Rejecting any notion of themselves as newcomers or immigrants, Chicano Movement participants like Vasquez insisted instead that Mexican-origin people in the United States were indigenous to the continent and therefore were residing in their homeland. Aware of the difficulties of making that claim a reality, advocates of

Chicano cultural nationalism insisted that a critical first step was to promote cultural pride, which, they hoped, would lead to ethnic unity and, in turn, greater political clout for all Mexican Americans. Proud to be a participant in what proved to be the most intense and widespread struggle for social justice by Mexican Americans in the history of the United States, Vasquez nevertheless grappled with the dilemmas posed by this prescription. Many of her columns revolved around the same set of implicit questions: How might Chicano Movement participants foster unity with those Mexican Americans outside the movement? What was to be the relationship between a politicized Mexican-American population and the majority society? And given the stated goal of "total liberation," what practical steps could Chicanos— and Chicanas—take to improve their status day-to-day? Her search for "answers" in her columns was revealing. Certainly, Vasquez's cultural nationalism never precluded her interest in feminism or socialism or coalition-building in general. Although the angry criticism that Vasquez directed toward majority society was one notable feature of her columns, her vision of a better future ultimately included Anglo Americans and Mexican Americans alike. Unwavering in her conviction that change was both possible and necessary, on the pages of *El Grito del Norte* Vasquez crafted a unique pedagogy of hope.

That hope endured despite Vasquez's intimate familiarity with the pain of violence, poverty, and discrimination. For the past several decades, scholars have employed the categories of race, gender, and class as tools of analysis. Under these circumstances, much of Vasquez's life could be read as a textbook study in subjugation. To reduce her life story to victimization, however, omits her remarkable resilience. For Vasquez, multiple confrontations with inequity simply strengthened her resolve to fight against oppression. Yet in contrast to her written work, and in sharp contrast to the academic attention paid to several male leaders of the Chicano Movement, Vasquez's biography is not well known. It deserves to be. A chronicle of both suffering injustice and triumphing against it, Vasquez's personal narrative provides tremendous insight into her published work, just as the work itself profoundly enriches our understanding of the Chicano Movement's significance overall.

᷃᷃᷃

Even as a child, Enriqueta Vasquez was always more inclined to speak out than bow down. As she once matter-of-factly observed, "I just had a strong sense of justice [from] somewhere." An intense personality was apparently hers from the start: her baby picture shows a serious-looking Vasquez with her arms outstretched as if she were orating on some pressing matter. Also true, however, was that her experiences as a person of color, as a low-paid worker, and later, as a single mother and as an abused wife sharpened and refined Vasquez's innate sense of justice. Through much struggle and determination, Vasquez finally arrived as a member of the Mexican-American middle class at the age of 38. Yet personality and personal experience had by then forged a political activist. Not content to rest upon her accomplishments, Vasquez decided to abandon the comforts of a conventional life and devote herself full-time to the Chicano Movement instead.

A child of the Great Depression, one of the defining experiences of Vasquez's life appropriately enough was financial hardship. Her parents, Faustina Perez and Abundio Vasquez, were among the estimated one million Mexicans who entered the United States during the first third of the twentieth century.[4] Like many of their compatriots, they left desperate to escape the violence, chaos, and poverty of the Mexican Revolution. Traveling separately from the state of Michoacán, both found low-paid work as farm laborers in Colorado where they met and fell in love. Soon they were the proud parents of a rapidly expanding family that joined them in the fields, the oldest children working alongside their parents harvesting tomatoes, green beans, beets, and onions, the next oldest watching over the youngest ones. With only one younger sibling, Vasquez recalled pitching in with odd jobs and then caring for her little brother. Yet despite the economic contributions of parents and children alike, the Vasquez family, like many Mexican-American farmworkers at the time, still could not afford basic medical care: only seven of Vasquez's 12 siblings reached adulthood.

Given the strained economic circumstances of the family, one bright spot was making music. Thanks to a traveling music teacher named Bonifacio Silva, Vasquez learned to play the mandolin by age five. Eventually, she also became proficient on the violin and guitar. In fact, some of her happiest memories of her childhood against the bleak backdrop of Cheraw, Colorado—muddy and cold in her recollection—were of song and dance. The family formed part of a village band organized by *el profesor* Silva that traveled to neighboring towns to celebrate such events as Mexican Independence Day, the 16th of September. Later, when Vasquez would use her columns to extol the richness of Mexican culture, her knowledge of traditional music buttressed this sense of pride.

As a young girl, Vasquez was closer to her father than her mother. Part of the reason was that she was an unrepentant tomboy who loved sports and the outdoors. While her sisters called her "Henrietta," the name she had to use at school, her brothers called her "Henry" or "Hank." Given the choice between embroidering with the girls and helping the boys fix a car, Hank preferred the latter. Indeed, she learned to drive by the age of 12 in order to help her family with errands once her three older brothers had joined the military service and her eldest sister had gotten married. By then, Vasquez also knew how to shoot. The year before, her father, telling her stories of the Mexican Revolution the whole time, had taught her how to fire a 22-gauge rifle. Only half-joking, her mother warned that, given her daughter's quick temper, teaching her to use a gun was probably a bad idea. Nevertheless, both parents fueled Vasquez's innate sense of justice—as well as her sense of Mexican identity—by telling her various times as she grew up, *"los gringos se robaron esta tierra* (The gringos stole this land)".

Her mother, a *curandera* (a healer), also imparted knowledge of Mexican—and indigeneous Purépecha—culture. As Vasquez recalled, her mother helped deliver dozens of babies in the Cheraw area. She was a talented *sobadora*, having been taught by Vasquez's great-grandfather the art of indigenous therapeutic massage. Later Vasquez would pay tribute to the wisdom of her mother in such columns as "La Voz de Nuestra Cultura," which favorably compared the curative powers of traditional healing practices to Western medicine. By then, the two women had grown closer in part because they shared a similar political outlook.[5] As a youngster, however, Vasquez was painfully aware that she was not her mother's favorite. That designation went to an older sister who Vasquez years later described as beautiful, well behaved, and fair-skinned. Vasquez, in contrast, was dark-complected.

Racism, another frequent theme in her work, consequently played a part in her political evolution as much as poverty. Encountering subtle racism within her own family, she was assaulted by it outside her home. At school, children were punished for speaking Spanish. When Professor Silva arranged for the Cheraw *banda* to play at the school— "and we were good," recalled Vasquez—band members played to an empty auditorium. During a decade when deportations and repatriations to Mexico were common, Spanish-speaking parents preferred not to venture into the English-only school setting, Vasquez recalled; Anglo parents were apparently not interested. Only the school janitor who was responsible for opening the doors for the event showed up. Official segregation, as was the case with the hamburger joint and most other restaurants in neighboring La Junta, was also commonplace. In La Junta, barbershops were also segregated. Closer to home, the elementary school in Cheraw had two swings, one for Anglos and one for Mexicans. Even if no Anglos were on the playground, Vasquez remembered, the ethnic Mexican children would dutifully line up to wait their turn on the swing designated for them.

Subsequent years provided ample evidence of how poverty and racism were intertwined. As a teen, Vasquez landed a job at the local cannery where she noticed that during the height of the harvest season, employees, virtually all Mexican-American women, were expected to work through the day and most of the night. Yet they did not receive overtime pay. True to form, Vasquez wrote another letter, this one to the U.S. Department of Labor, prompting government investigators to pay a call. Later, after she graduated from high school,

Vasquez, an excellent typist, moved to Denver hoping to land a secretarial job. To her dismay, she was told at the state employment office that most businesses were not ready to hire "Spanish American" girls for office work. Especially, one might assume from the comment, dark-skinned ones.

Vasquez's move was accompanied by dreams of a better future. For a while, those dreams came true. After a tough month of searching, she found a job doing everything from janitorial to clerical work in a furniture store owned and operated by a Jewish American man and his son, neither of whom evidently minded hiring a Mexican American. The wages were low, but the job had other benefits: Vasquez learned a lot about running a business, and the father trusted her to use the company car on weekends. She was young, happy, and independent. As someone with access to a car, she was also popular, with a wide circle of friends. Through this social circle she was introduced to a friend's cousin, a New Mexican man named Herman Tafoya. They married in 1951. His parents struck her as "real nice people," Vasquez recalled. "I always thought that if you came from a good family, you were a good person."[6] She was wrong. Five days after the wedding, her husband beat her. Called to service in Korea, he came back a heavy drinker and "even meaner." Vasquez thus came to know violent injustice directed against her as a woman.

For several years, despite the beatings and her husband's alcoholism, Vasquez attempted to make the marriage work. A son, Ruben, was born in 1952 while Tafoya was in Korea. Vasquez hoped that a child might bring the couple closer together, but recalled that her hope died once Tafoya returned unchanged. Nevertheless, in 1954, in another attempt to foster family unity, Vasquez relocated the family to Kentucky for several months so that Tafoya might pursue a job-training opportunity there. "I tried to do what he wanted," Vasquez explained years later.[7] Like many women during the 1950s, she also explained, she was convinced that the role of wives was to obey and respect their husbands, and that divorce was not only unthinkable, but also a personal failure on the woman's part. For several years, therefore, Vasquez devoted the strength of her personality toward trying to make the marriage work. Nevertheless, by the time Vasquez was pregnant with a second child, the unthinkable appeared as her only salvation. Deciding to separate from her husband, she returned to her parents' home in 1955, a single mother with one young child to support and another on the way. After the birth of her daughter, Ramona, she moved to a housing project in Pueblo where there was a medical specialist for Ruben, who had been born with a clubfoot.

Vasquez was a single mother for more than a dozen years. In her columns, when Vasquez wrote about the endurance and strength of Chicanas and the contributions they could make to the Chicano Movement, she spoke from experience. After the divorce, Tafoya had little contact with her or their children. He rarely sent child support payments. For nearly two years, Vasquez was dependent upon welfare to survive. Years later Vasquez remembered how stretched financially she was during the mid-1950s, a full decade before Lyndon Johnson's Great Society and War on Poverty initiatives bolstered such federal programs as food stamps and Aid for Families with Dependent Children.[8] Her welfare check barely covered the rent. The supply of food offered by community pantry scarcely lasted the month. Without health insurance, whenever Ruben, who was also sickly with asthma, needed to be rushed to the emergency room, Vasquez had to borrow money to pay the doctor.[9] Even making a phone call was difficult, she recalled, as she had to look for a neighbor's phone to borrow. But Vasquez eventually landed on her feet. Her typing skills secured her a secretarial job in a law office in Pueblo. Later in Denver, Vasquez found a well-paying civil service job with good health insurance. By then a divorced woman, she still feared her ex-husband and with good reason. In 1960, Tafoya found her in Denver and beat her for the last time. Overnight, she decided to pack up the family's belongings—three suitcases full—and move to the Los Angeles area, where her older brother lived.

During the three years she spent in Culver City just outside of L.A., the Catholic Church proved a refuge. Vasquez had been baptized Catholic not as an infant but at the age of 11. Part of the delay was logistical: Cheraw did not have a local Catholic Church; the family attended mass in La Junta no more than once a year. But part of the delay apparently stemmed from her parents' reluctance to make this commitment on behalf of their daughter. Vasquez described her father as especially "open-minded." "He encouraged me to attend the Mennonite church [in Cheraw] and whatever tent services came around so that I could learn as much as I could about the Bible for myself."[10] Once in Culver City, however, Vasquez became deeply involved in the affairs of the local parish even teaching catechism and taking her children and herself to mass and confession weekly. Years later she remarked that her sense of Catholic guilt was so refined that she used to make things up just to have something to confess to the priest. During this time, Vasquez worked at Hughes Aircraft as an executive secretary, but given the high cost of childcare, the family once again could only afford to live in a public housing project. Certainly, Vasquez's church involvement was accompanied by the hope that the church would provide a positive influence for her children, a counter to the negative environment of the housing project, which was increasingly plagued by gang- and drug-related problems. In fact, the danger posed by these problems prompted Vasquez to return the family to Colorado in 1963. Her now lengthy resume, embellished by community college courses she had taken in California, quickly secured her more civil service work, first at an air force base, then with the Internal Revenue Service, and finally with the U.S. Attorney General's Office in Denver.

The 1960s also marked Vasquez's introduction to political activism. Her involvement in Chicano activism was largely a result of her friendship with Rodolfo "Corky" Gonzales, an emerging Chicano Movement leader. She had first met Gonzales in 1950 in Denver, when he was already a well-known personality around town, a prize-winning boxer whose bouts she sometimes would attend. By the time Vasquez returned to Denver, Gonzales was also an established businessman, a seller of bail bonds. Although Vasquez technically worked for the prosecution, whenever she noticed a judge treating a defendant unfairly, she would call Gonzales to see what help he could offer the defendant. In 1964, Gonzales invited Vasquez to join the American

G.I. Forum, a Mexican-American civil rights group founded by World War II veterans. The following year, her Forum membership, commitment to racial equality, and strong administrative skills earned her a position as one of the directors of Project SER (for Service, Employment, and Redevelopment; in Spanish "ser" means "to be"), a War on Poverty program funded through the Forum. As a director, she visited corporations in the Denver area such as Coors Beer and asked them to start hiring Mexican Americans or face an economic boycott. For Vasquez, as for many Chicano Movement participants, the Great Society's reform programs marked the opportunity to deepen their political involvement.

Yet the Chicano Movement also represented, in the words of Ignacio M. García, "the rejection of the liberal agenda."[11] Along with rejecting traditional party politics, activists doubted the ability of federal government programs to deliver upon their promises. In the case of Gonzales, a political dispute hastened this rupture. Like Vasquez, Gonzales had been active in local Great Society programs: he had chaired the city's local War on Poverty board and headed an agency called the Neighborhood Youth Corps. His career as a Democrat Party loyalist, however, came to an end in 1966 when the city's conservative paper, the *Rocky Mountain News,* accused Gonzales of favoring Mexican-American groups in the dispersal of federal funds. The dispute concluded shortly thereafter when Denver's mayor fired Gonzales and Gonzales, in turn, announced his intention to form a new Chicano advocacy group called the Crusade for Justice.[12] Throughout, Vasquez had been among many Denver residents who had rallied to Gonzales' defense. She had joined picket lines outside the newspaper office and written letters of support on his behalf. She immediately joined the Crusade for Justice.

That was when Vasquez said she went "crazy," crazy for the Chicano Movement. She strongly believed that there was a need for an organization like the Crusade, that there was a need for change. "I didn't want my kids to go through what I went through," she later said. She was also impressed by Gonzales' leadership ability. "He was everybody's hero," Vasquez recalled. "I always had a tremendous amount of respect for him. I just felt that this man was going to do something."[13] As a result, Vasquez was willing to lend her secretarial skills to the organization when a task needed to be done. When Gonzales decided to run for mayor as a means of encouraging voter participation in Denver's barrios, for instance, Vasquez was one of two notary publics who collected signatures to get him on the ballot. Understanding that Gonzales' chances of actually obtaining office were slim-to-none, she nonetheless went door-to-door and set up registration tables everywhere from churches to bars. Along the way, Vasquez found herself falling in love with a close friend of Gonzales, an artist named Bill Longley, who was also deeply political. At the time, Longley, who had served for a long time as a personal bodyguard for Gonzales, was also working as an artist for the Crusade. When she decided to marry him after nearly 13 years as a single parent, Vasquez said, "Then I knew I was crazy. Artists don't even have jobs!"[14]

The union ushered forth a series of dramatic changes. First, both partners changed their name. Dropping "Tafoya," Vasquez reverted to her birth name. Born in Wyoming and of French ancestry, her husband legally changed his "William" to the Spanish "Guillermo" (within movement circles he became known as "Yermo"); "Longley" to the original French "Longeaux." Committed to the Chicano Movement, he added "Vasquez." Longeaux y Vasquez became their shared name. Second, Vasquez broke from the Catholic Church. As a divorced woman, she was not allowed to re-marry according to church teachings. Even before meeting Bill, she had inquired about an annulment but found the cost prohibitive for a single mother earning a secretary's salary. (For his part, Vasquez recollected, Bill was insistent that her first marriage was a "bunch of hogwash" not a life-long commitment before God.) Unable to resolve her dilemma, Vasquez went to talk to a liberal priest in Denver who told her to go ahead and re-marry and be happy. "At that point," she said later, "I saw through the church."[15] Although she remained spiritual, Vasquez went on to write scathing critiques of the Catholic Church as an institution. Yet a third change occurred in April 1968 when Gonzales asked her and Bill to run a cultural school for the Crusade in northern New Mexico on a ranch owned by Jenny and Craig Vincent, a couple long active in progressive politics.[16] At the time, Vasquez had made a down payment on a house and had a secure job with a retirement fund. She gave up both and headed south toward the village of San Cristobal just a few miles north of Taos. A new chapter was about to open in her life.

ᏩᏩᏩ

Dedicated to the Chicano Movement, Vasquez's conception of social justice had nevertheless always been inclusive: as early as 1963 she marched in Denver with her children in commemoration of Medgar Evers, the Mississippi head of the NAACP (National Association for the Advancement of Colored People) who had been assassinated by a white supremacist.[17] New Mexico expanded her political horizons even further. During the 1960s, the northern portion of the state was home to hippies, Red Power advocates, and activist Hispanos who sought the return of land deeded to their ancestors by Spain and Mexico but seized by the U.S. government after the war with Mexico. A few months after her arrival, moreover, Vasquez began writing for *El Grito del Norte,* a newspaper that soon proved to be unrivaled among Chicano Movement publications for the attention it paid to other struggles across the nation and around the world. Influenced by her neighbors as well as by the ethos of the newspaper, Vasquez in her columns seamlessly linked Chicano Movement activism to other issues of the days from the War on Poverty to the war in Vietnam, from environmental degradation to women's equality. Although declaring her first loyalty to the Chicano Movement, Vasquez also encouraged her readers to consider coalition politics across racial lines, gender divides, and national borders.

Her first assignment, however, was entirely local. With her husband, Vasquez helped establish a Crusade school for urban youth on the Vincent Ranch. A former vacation spot spread across more than 100 acres, the ranch boasted several buildings, including dormitories, a huge barn-like structure that contained a stage, and plenty of smaller edifices ideal for classroom teaching. Young people came from

Denver to explore Chicano culture through music, art, poetry, and the-
ater. They also read as much as they could about the history of greater
Mexico, including what is now the U.S. Southwest, tested their physical endurance by hiking in the mountains, and, on occasion, worked
as junior ranch hands on the land of Cleofas Vigil, a native New Mexican and Vasquez's neighbor across the road in San Cristobal.[18] The
school's mission soon affected Vasquez in her role as a behind-the-
scenes organizer: she too found herself reading more history, starting
to make music once again, and, with Bill's encouragement, picking up
a paintbrush. As a columnist Vasquez repeatedly encouraged Mexican
Americans to foster a greater appreciation of their cultural inheritance
through art and music.[19]

In addition to operating the school on behalf of the Crusade, however, Vasquez and her husband had another immediate task. They
hoped that by moving to the state they would help forge stronger links
between the Crusade for Justice and La Alianza Federal de Pueblos
Libres, a New Mexico organization dedicated to the return of land
grants taken from Spanish-surnamed people by the U.S. government
and American citizens through legal and extra-legal means after
1848.[20] Founded in 1963, the Alianza had catapulted to notoriety in
June 1967 when about twenty members of the organization including
its leader, Reies López Tijerina, conducted an armed raid of the courthouse in the tiny town of Tierra Amarilla. Even before the courthouse
raid, Corky Gonzales and Bill Longeaux, driving Vasquez's car, had
visited Tijerina and his associates in New Mexico. Gonzales and Tijerina agreed to cooperate despite their organizations' differences.
Increasingly youth oriented, the Denver-based Crusade tended to
focus on problems of the inner city such as police abuse and poor
schools whereas the Alianza, whose membership was multigenera-
tional and overwhelmingly rural, devoted itself almost exclusively to
the land issue. Nevertheless, according to one Crusade activist, members of the two groups shared "a spirit of common struggle (Vigil, 30).
For that reason, in the wake of courthouse raid, Gonzales and Bill
Longeaux organized a Crusade motor caravan to New Mexico in an
immediate show of support.

Once moving to the state permanently, Vasquez and her husband took other steps to nurture the relationship. First, the Longeaux y Vasquez family embraced the precarious economic circumstances of many of their Aliancista neighbors. During the 1960s, and as a direct legacy of land loss, the average individual income in New Mexico's northern counties was just over a $1,000 compared to more than twice that for the state as a whole and almost three times that for the United States overall.[21] For their part, Enriqueta, Bill, Ruben, and Ramona scraped by on a $142 disability pension that Bill received every month for his military service during World War II. Their home, a 100-year-old adobe that Vasquez had purchased with her retirement savings upon arriving, became another means of fostering good relations. Nestled in the scenic Sangre de Cristo Mountains, the modest structure soon served as a popular gathering place for Alianza members as well as for other Chicano Movement activists who came from across the Southwest to rest and recuperate. In still another display of solidarity, Vasquez, although not a land-grant claimant herself, made it a point to attend Alianza meetings regularly.

The result for Vasquez was a deeper appreciation of the historical roots of Chicano protest. She credited Tijerina, whom she labeled a "brilliant" and "dynamic" leader, with bringing renewed attention to the 1848 Treaty of Guadalupe Hidalgo that had concluded the U.S.-Mexico War. According to the treaty, the property rights of Mexican citizens in the ceded territory were to be "inviolably respected."[22] Yet across the new U.S. Southwest, as Tijerina constantly pointed out, Mexicans experienced massive land dispossession through fraud, intimidation, and the imposition of new judicial and tax systems that favored the conquerors.[23] To Vasquez, Tijerina's insistence that a historical wrong had been committed reverberated with the childhood memory of her parents telling her that the Southwest had once belonged to Mexico. Strongly identifying with the land-grant movement as a result, Vasquez recalled that Tijerina had one central message for all Chicanos, whether they were the descendants of long-ago Spanish colonists or, like her, the offspring of more recent Mexican immigrants (as well as a migrant to an urban area). It was: "This is our land."

By the summer of 1968, Vasquez was among a group of Alianza supporters who were determined to get that message out by starting a newspaper. Stepping in as editor was Elizabeth "Betita" Martínez, who was then a full-time staffer with the Student Non-Violent Coordinating Committee (SNCC). At the time, SNCC was making the transition from civil rights to Black Power politics. Meanwhile, Martínez, a former editor with Simon & Schuster in New York, had just finished a book about the Cuban Revolution. With SNCC and herself both pursuing new directions, Martínez took an exploratory trip to New Mexico to investigate the possibility of starting a newspaper. Acutely aware she was an outsider to the state's politics and culture, Martínez first conducted a tour of the northern portion of the state to ask dozens of long-time Alianza supporters what was *their* vision for a paper. Her traveling companion was Beverly Axelrod, a San Francisco-based radical lawyer who had defended several Black Panthers before coming to New Mexico to offer legal advice to Tijerina.[24] This inclusive approach paid off: as Vasquez remembered, *El Grito del Norte* seemed to emerge organically from the region's circle of activists. Indeed, among the earliest supporters of the newspaper were several participants in the 1967 courthouse, including José Madril, Juan Valdez, Tobias Leyba, and Baltazar Martínez Other early supporters included Craig Vincent of the Vincent Ranch; Valentina Valdez, a young Alianza member originally from San Luis, Colorado; Anselmo Tijerina, an older brother of Reies and a committed organizer for the land-grant movement; Rini Templeton and John DePuy, both artists in the area; Maria Varela, like Martínez a veteran of SNCC; and the future novelist John Nichols, who contributed cartoons. Before long, such local personalities as Cleofas Vigil, Vasquez's neighbor, and Fernanda Martínez, a fiery land-grant activist from Tierra Amarilla among others had joined the list of regular contributors.

With a staff that featured Aliancistas and other activists, imported professionals and homegrown talent, as well as folks with Spanish-surnames and those without, *El Grito del Norte* soon emerged as one of the most distinctive and wide-ranging publications of the Chicano Movement. Unlike other Chicano Movement newspapers that were largely student-run and campus-based, *El Grito del Norte* constituted an authentic "cry from the north" of New Mexico through its dedicated coverage of the land-grant movement. Yet the paper also stood out for the consistent attention it paid to other matters of interest to political progressives not just locally, but nationally and internationally. On the pages of *El Grito del Norte*, articles about Hispano folklore followed updates on Black Power and Red Power, and coverage of the Alianza complimented articles on land struggles in such places as Vietnam, Japan, Palestine, and Hawaii. Equally important, the newspaper, whose day-to-day operations fell largely to women staff members, stood out as a self-consciously feminist publication.[25] No doubt Vasquez herself is best known for those columns that sought to reconcile women's liberation and Chicano cultural nationalism.[26] Exhibiting the newspaper's multifaceted approach, however, Vasquez broached many topics with equal passion.

From the first issue in August 1968, the newspaper was infused with a collective emphasis that encouraged staff members to develop their full potential as contributors. Testifying to that fact: while early editions of *El Grito del Norte* listed Betita Martínez and Beverly Axelrod as comprising the editorial staff along with nameless "contributors," a few years later, the list of named newspaper "workers" had expanded to nineteen.[27] A spirit of camaraderie united the group. Years later contributors still remembered the sheer excitement of making each issue a reality each month. As publication day neared, staff members from throughout northern New Mexico started to gather in Española where the newspaper had its offices. Then came a blur of activity: camping out in the office with sleeping bags to work through the night if necessary; racing to the printers once the pages were laid out and pasted; and then rushing to the post office to get the freshly printed newspapers out in time.[28] For her part, Vasquez immediately found herself contributing to the editorial side of the newspaper as well. Although she previously had written poetry and prose at times of emotional turmoil for her own comfort, these were never to share.

Certain that Chicanos had a role to play on the national and even global stage, a sense of political urgency now inspired her work for a larger audience.

Her first effort, an essay about discrimination, featured several characteristics that when repeated, both conveyed that sense of urgency and formalized her contributions as a regular column. Most noticeable was the title, which shouted, "¡Despierten Hermanos!" As Vasquez told her readers in that first essay: "You better wake up and see what is happening."[29] Although not originally planned as the first in a series, the essay's title succinctly captured her central aim: to incite political action. In addition, Vasquez ended that first essay with a final rallying cry in Spanish. A stylistic flourish in keeping with the Chicano Movement's goal of instilling ethnic pride, as Vasquez later explained, she also used Spanish whenever she sought to strike at the emotional heart of an issue. Having the final say in Spanish therefore was a way of not only summarizing but also amplifying her message. For this reason, several columns appeared entirely in Spanish including those that Vasquez wrote under her mother's name, Doña Faustina. For these observations on Chicano culture, Vasquez reverted entirely to her mother tongue.

Yet by far Vasquez's greatest resource in terms of conveying a sense of urgency was her own candid, conversational style. In fact, like her first essay, many of her columns had their origin in actual conversations that Vasquez had shared or overhead with Mexican Americans who were not participants in the Chicano Movement.

Clearly, one central goal for Vasquez was to turn the tables on the conventional wisdom promoted by mainstream society and adopted by many Mexican Americans. In her debut column, for instance, she disputed the belief that discrimination was on the wane because some Mexican Americans were accepted as "white." Instead of striving to "become white," she wrote, Mexican Americans should be proud of their "mixed Indian-Spanish culture."[30] Subsequent articles dismissed patriotism and Cold War priorities, subverted the meaning of "machismo" and, despite widespread poverty among Mexican Americans, strongly contested the notion that wealth could be measured in terms of material possessions alone. Along the way, Vasquez proved fearless in lambasting Anglo America. In one telling example, in a column promoting the richness of Chicano culture, she managed to challenge Mexican Americans and criticize Anglo Americans at the same time. Demonstrating her impatience with the long-standing notion among academics and Mexican Americans alike that ethnic group members suffered from an "inferiority complex," Vasquez instead denounced Anglo American "superiority problems." "You know, just studying the lifeless Gringo (heaven knows they have studied minorities enough) one can feel sorry for them and wish that one could help them with their superiority problems," she opined. "I think that minorities can do this and I think we should."[31]

When it came to race relations between Anglo Americans and Mexican Americans, Vasquez walked a fine line. On the one hand, Vasquez reserved her most acidic comments for a people and a lifestyle that she labeled "Gringo." As she flatly announced in another column: "80% of Gringo society is reported to be neurotic and 50% of the people are hypochondriacs."[32] Although Vasquez routinely incorporated material that she had gained from reading news magazines such as *Time* and *Newsweek* and from talking to friends like Craig Vincent, a few statistics used in her columns were clearly the product of artistic license as was the case here. To Vasquez, "Gringo" society was characterized by an unrelenting drive for profit, as she put it, the "DOG-eat-DOG concept whose total goal" was "named MONEY."[33] On the other hand, she made clear that her use of the pejorative term "Gringo" was meant to refer specifically to white privilege and the misplaced values of mainstream society and not to whites in general. "When we speak of Gringo, we do not particularly hate all white people," she explained in 1969, "but we refer to their social system as 'Gringo.' That is what we don't like."[34] Supporting this distinction was her frequent appeal for Anglo Americans to reconsider their priorities and learn from Chicanos. "Raza has a beautiful way of life and has a lot to contribute to the majority," Vasquez offered in one instance.[35] Or to rephrase her somewhat ironic suggestion, minorities could "help" members of the majority with their superiority problems and much more. Vasquez knew that discrimination was real but so too was the possibility of Mexican Americans and Anglo Americans working together for the benefit of both groups.

Just as important, Vasquez's negative portrayal of majority society was as reflective of the era's counterculture as it was congruent with the sentiments of Chicano cultural nationalism. When Vasquez suggested, for example, that Mexican Americans return to a "humanistic way of life" that was rooted in the land and environmentally friendly, her inspiration was her hippie neighbors as much as her indigenous ancestors. By 1971, the Taos area boasted nine hippie communes with names like Hog Farm, New Buffalo, and the Reality Construction Company.[36] To many Spanish-speaking New Mexicans, these "longhairs" represented only the most recent Anglo invasion—and with good reason.[37] Years later Vasquez remembered how the hippies used to swim nude at local watering holes to the dismay of more socially conservative local folks or, worse, use the *acequias*, the region's communal irrigation system that dated from colonial times, as their personal latrine.[38] Still, Vasquez was favorably impressed by the hippies' attempt to build a communal way of life. At a time when impoverished native New Mexicans were leaving the rural north of the state in order to look for a city job, she recalled, hippies were determined to support their communes by living off the land. As a columnist, she suggested that Chicanos attempt to do the same. "Let's start thinking in terms of feeding ourselves instead of feeding the grocery stores. Cooperatives are certainly a big answer for the people," Vasquez advised her readers in 1969. "Let's go back to being more self-sufficient. Why do we have to support Mr. Safeway, whoever or wherever he may be?"[39] Although most of the communes collapsed a few years later, at the time the utopian visions of her hippie neighbors informed Vasquez's ideas about land, a central theme within the Chicano Movement.

Even more influential in this regard were her Native American neighbors. The move to New Mexico had provided Vasquez the opportunity to reconnect with her indigenous inheritance. Living just a few miles away from the Taos Pueblo, she made it a point to attend festivals and ceremonial days there as much as she was able to as a non-

Pueblo Indian. These included the traditional foot races held every May, the festival in honor of San Gerónimo, the patron saint of the Taos Pueblo, held every September, and the *matachines*, a processional dance that merged European and Indian traditions, held each Christmas. These experiences, combined with her own continued reading of such authors as Carlos Castañeda, convinced Vasquez that, as she explained years later, "the basis of a lot of our own [Chicano] culture is indigenous." From this feeling of cultural connection, moreover, emerged a sense of political solidarity. Vasquez was supportive of another land struggle culminating in northern New Mexico at the time: the ultimately successful campaign by members of the Taos Pueblo to regain control of their sacred Blue Lake and surrounding acreage from the federal government.[40] Although Vasquez was not directly involved in that struggle, she did receive frequent updates about it from Craig Vincent, who was close to the main architect of the final 1970 agreement, a Taos elder named Paul Bernal.[41]

Her respect for Native American sovereignty soon complicated Vasquez's interpretation of Aztlán. Aztlán was the mythic homeland of the Aztecs that many Chicano Movement participants claimed as their rightful inheritance in 1969 when they endorsed El Plan Espiritual de Aztlán, which outlined a series of Chicano Movement political, economic and cultural objectives. Regarding Chicanos, the prologue to the plan also asserted: "We are a nation. We are a union of free pueblos. We are Aztlán."[42] In this dramatic appropriation, Chicano Movement participants thus extended their claim to the land back in time to not just before the U.S. invasion of Mexico's northern territories but to before the European invasion of the Americas. In attendance at the conference, Vasquez celebrated that point of view. "Somos Aztlán! [We are Aztlán!] Aztlán Is Reborn!" began her report about the gathering.[43] Or as she explained years later, by emphasizing the indigenous roots of Chicano culture, Aztlán: "brought us back to our beginnings . . . . It gave us a myth . . . . This made us a tribe." For a short while, Vasquez even considered the possibility of carving out a separate Chicano nation within the United States.

Two meetings, however, prompted her to reject the territorial notion as political infeasible and, equally important, hardly liberating for Native Americans. The first meeting occurred in the immediate aftermath of the Denver conference when Vasquez eagerly sought out a lawyer friend of hers to ask him a series of interlinked questions concerning the legal status of Mexican Americans, the concept of Aztlán, and the provisions of the Treaty of Guadalupe Hidalgo. As Vasquez recalled, the lawyer confirmed her opinion that Mexican Americans should rightfully enjoy treaty and tribal rights on par with Native Americans. Any heady sense of entitlement, however, soon crumbled before the grim realization, as she put it years later, that "there was no way that we were going to be allowed to take back this land" from the United States. A second important meeting for Vasquez occurred a few months later when she traveled to San Francisco to attend a conference in support of those Native Americans who had been occupying Alcatraz Island since November 1969. As she recalled, Native American activists at the gathering "felt threatened" by talk of Aztlán and "had a hard time grasping [the concept]." Their concerns, Vasquez remembered, "made me really think: what does nationhood really mean? Do we have in mind that this is our land and [that] we are going to fight for it?" Convinced the answer to the second question had to be "no" given the relative power of Chicanos within the United States, Vasquez next sought to reconcile Chicano land claims and Native American concerns. "This is where I really delved into our history," she later commented, and so found herself "on the road to spirituality." Specifically, Vasquez turned to indigenous ideas upholding the sacredness of the land and rejecting private land ownership. Aztlán, she concluded, had "to take hold in the deepest self" not emerge from a legal document. To Vasquez, the relationship between Mexican Americans and the land remained a fundamental cultural and political precept. Yet, influenced by interactions with Native American activists, she rejected the idea that Mexican Americans should seek sole physical possession of any part of the present-day U.S. Southwest in favor of the idea that Chicanos and Chicanas needed to nurture their sense of cultural and spiritual belonging to the land. That conclusion, however, did not mean Vasquez was abandoning political protest. To the contrary, her spiritual journey as a member of Aztlán proceeded concurrently with her political radicalization. While the move to New Mexico had plunged her full-time into a world of leftist organizing, a trip to Cuba during the summer of 1969 cemented Vasquez's commitment to revolutionary social change. She had gone upon the invitation of the Cuban government, which wished to advertise the revolution's accomplishments to foreign correspondents ten years after the 1959 revolution that had brought Castro to power. Traveling through Mexico (and returning via Canada), Vasquez arrived in Cuba as a representative of *El Grito del Norte*. She immediately liked what she saw: socialism at work. Cuba seemed like a "solution," she later recalled. "I saw all the things [that] we talked about . . . saw [that] . . . it's possible to have a country that is sharing. Many experiences really affected me."⁴⁴ Certainly, land reform in Cuba struck her as entirely consistent with the type of communal land use that she had been advocating. Yet Vasquez later recalled that she was probably most touched by a smaller detail: the racial composition of an orchestra that she had heard. Whereas in the United States, symphonic musicians were usually white, Vasquez, a lover of music, noted that in Cuba white people, black people, and every shade in-between were up on stage. Such positive memories lingered. Well past the fortieth anniversary of the Cuban Revolution, Vasquez remained a committed leftist. "I certainly embrace socialism. I can't see any other solutions," she noted in 2003. "This country (the United States) could feed the world if it wanted too."

During the Chicano Movement, the question of advancing sweeping social change inevitably raised the question of violence. Like many within the Chicano Movement, Vasquez refused to rule out its use. To the contrary, part of her admiration of the Cuban Revolution—and of the revolution in Vietnam—was that the Cubans and Vietnamese had actually taken up arms to achieve their goals. On occasion, Vasquez even pondered whether Chicano activists should do the same. "I guess people are supposed to be submissive and robot-like and take all of this crap," she wrote in one 1970 column that made clear that meek acceptance was not her style. Instead, as she confessed in this moment of frustration: "I do believe that the only thing that Tío Sam will listen to anymore is violence and demonstration, if you don't have power and money to be heard."[45] The implicit threat contained in the article, however, was an anomaly for Vasquez who generally dismissed violence as a strategy because it was unnecessarily dangerous for a vulnerable political minority.

The use of arms for purposes of self-defense was another matter. Vasquez not only strongly believed that Chicanos had a right to defend themselves if threatened, but she also was convinced that being able to do so, as she later explained, was "very important; it empowers people a lot." After all, she asked in 1969, "How can one guarantee complete non-violence when one lives in a completely VIOLENT country?"[46] Indicative of the tenor of the times, Vasquez, along with many other area activists, routinely engaged in target practice outside her home, everyone bringing their own weaponry. Notably, the article that Vasquez wrote encouraging Chicanas to become politically organized, featured a drawing by her husband of Vasquez holding one of their rifles.[47] Years later Vasquez stressed how deeply rooted and widespread was the conviction among Chicano activists at the time that violence might erupt at any moment.

Near constant police surveillance was a major source of tension. In New Mexico, Vasquez noticed what she assumed were unmarked police cars following her whenever she drove. Vasquez received unique confirmation of that suspicion in an article that appeared in the March 1969 issue of *American Opinion*, the publication of the ultra-conservative John Birch Society. Entitled "New Mexico: The Coming Guerilla War," the article's premise was that a grand conspiracy to wage war against the United States was about to burst forth among Alianza supporters. Studded with almost comical references to "Castroite terrorist Tijerina" and "Rudolpho *sic* 'Corky' Gonzales—the Red-nosed Mutineer," the article less comically also included mention of a "Ms. Henrietta Vasquez Tafoya," the make of her car, and the car's registration address, suggesting that the author had been in close contact with law enforcement officers who, in turn, had been closely monitoring Vasquez.[48] That June, Representative O.C. Fisher, a conservative Democrat from Texas, inserted the entire article in the *Congressional Record,* adding by way of explanation merely that it contained "some interesting information."[49] By then, Vasquez's politics apparently also had piqued the interest of the FBI.[50]

The late 1960s and early 1970s offered plenty of proof to Chicano Movement participants like Vasquez that protest carried significant risks beyond mere surveillance. Three months before she moved to the state, for example, the Alianza's headquarters in Albuquerque were firebombed, just one episode in a series of anti-Alianza attacks that was to continue for several years afterward.[51] Violence turned deadly in January 1972, when two Black Berets, one of whom had worked for *El Grito del Norte* as a photographer and reporter, were shot and killed by police in Albuquerque. According to police, the two men had fired first and were probably attempting to steal dynamite from a construction site. According to the newspaper, the deaths were highly suspicious, not least because the activists were about to expose the mistreatment of Chicanos in prison.[52] Indeed, Vasquez's article updating an abuse scandal at the Santa Fe state prison appeared in the same issue dedicated to the memory of Antonio Córdova and Rito Canales, the two slain Black Berets.[53] As a continuing member of the Crusade for Justice, Vasquez also observed relations between that organization and law enforcement deteriorate over the years. In 1972, for example, she was at La Raza Park in Denver when clashes between Chicano activists and police at the park sent teargas wafting through the crowd. The following year, Luis "Junior" Martinez, a 20-year-old Crusade for Justice member was shot to death by Denver police during a confrontation. Although Vasquez was not in Denver when the shooting occurred, she knew Martinez from the summers he had spent attending the cultural school that she and her husband had operated for the Crusade. During these visits, the teenager had apparently fallen in love with northern New Mexico. He was buried in the San Cristobal cemetery just a stone's throw from Vasquez's front door.[54]

For five years, despite an atmosphere marked by occasions of danger and uncertainty, a committed cadre of volunteers had kept the newspaper running from its offices in Española. As early as November 1968, the staff received a phone call from a person who, after receiving directions to the newspaper office in order to subscribe in person, shouted "Thank you, you communist!" before slamming the phone down.[55] In addition, although the vast majority of the letters to the editor were enthusiastic of the newspaper's efforts, in early 1973 one vitriolic exception appeared. The missive thanked the newspaper for confirming the writer's "beliefs about the overall idiotic stupidity of 90% of the scumy filthy wetback welfare paratites spicks that have invaded my country from the south." (The newspaper retained the original letter's misspellings.)[56] By then, *El Grito del Norte* had relocated to Las Vegas, NM in order to take advantage of an offer of free office space by one supporter and to be closer to several key volunteers. The final edition of the newspaper in August 1973 nevertheless made an oblique reference to mounting pressures. "To our enemies, we say: don't celebrate. The spirit that El Grito voices will never die," the announcement of closure read. "Hasta la victoria."[57]

Vasquez embraced the sentiment. After the newspaper stopped, she remained busy as an artist, activist, and author. During the 1970s, she painted murals in Taos as well as in El Mirage, Arizona, as part of a larger project to recognize the contributions of women farmworkers there.[58] She also co-authored with Elizabeth Martínez a Chicano history entitled *Viva La Raza!* published by Doubleday in 1974. In 1977, she traveled to China as part of a Taos-based U.S.-China friendship association whose members sought to secure that the entrance into the United Nations for the People's Republic of China. She also became more deeply involved in indigenous spirituality, meeting with Native American elders in the United States and Mexico. In 1992, five hundred years after the Spanish arrival in the Americas, Vasquez traveled to Spain as part of an intertribal indigenous delegation that provided through speeches and ceremony a counter-balance to the nation's festivities marking the anniversary. Since then, she has frequently participated in sacred *ceremonias* as an elder and has nearly completed another book—a sweeping history of the women of La Raza from indigenous times to the present. Still the traveler, she also visits college campuses to speak to students. Tellingly, during the days of *El Grito del Norte*, the headshot that usually accompanied her columns had showed Vasquez looking past the camera and seemingly into a brighter future. Although *El Grito del Norte* ended, Vasquez, like so many people associated with it, continued to work toward that better future.

ఌఌఌ

This anthology was truly a collaborative project. Of course, the heart of the volume is the 44 essays that Vasquez wrote for *El Grito del Norte*. The co-editors, Dionne Espinoza and myself, contributed the concluding and introductory essays, organized Vasquez's columns thematically into six chapters, and included short introductions to each chapter. We also decided to annotate the essays in order to clarify references to people and events that the passage of time had sometimes made obscure. In addition, in the hope of gaining Vasquez the broadest audience possible, we included translations of sections that originally appeared only in Spanish. At the same time, recognizing that Vasquez's use of two languages testified to her rich cultural background, instances of "Spanglish" in the text remained. Finally, in honor of the activist life of Rini Templeton, an artist whose work frequently appeared in *El Grito del Norte*, we selected six of her drawings, five of which originally appeared in the newspaper, to grace each chapter's opening page.[59]

The anthology's origins date back more than decade ago when the words of Enriqueta Vasquez first captured the attention of both of us independently. In 1994, Dionne, then completing a doctoral dissertation in English at Cornell University, interviewed Vasquez as part of her research exploring the ways in which Chicanas participated in the predominantly cultural nationalistic Chicano Movement.[60] Meanwhile, also completing a doctoral dissertation at Cornell in the field of history, I was impressed with Vasquez's incisive criticism against the war in Vietnam.[61] Although Dionne and I had known each other at

Cornell, neither of us knew of the other's interest in Vasquez or, more generally, the Chicano Movement, until we were both Chicana dissertation fellows and office mates at the University of California at Santa Barbara during the academic year 1994-1995. I interviewed Vasquez for the first time in 1997 after Dionne kindly provided the phone number. That same year, two of Vasquez's most well-known essays on Chicanas were reprinted in an anthology of Chicano Movement-era selections, entitled *Chicana Feminist Thought: The Basic Historical Writings.*[62] During my first interview with Vasquez, the first of many as it turned out, I remember almost casually mentioning that all of her work should be collected and published in a single volume. It was not long before all three of us agreed that this was a very good idea indeed.

Still, competing visions for this project soon surfaced. Most significantly, true to her activist spirit, Vasquez hoped to update all her articles so that they could speak more directly to current events. Aware that some were written quickly and in the thick of the moment, she also hoped to revise and polish them as necessary. Together Dionne and I convinced Vasquez that the columns as they were written at the time were invaluable primary sources. Except for correcting obvious typos and adding some accent marks, the columns therefore appear as they did in *El Grito del Norte* with the addition of the annotations and translations. It is impossible to over-emphasize the courage of Vasquez in accepting this format. If she had had her druthers, for example, she certainly would have tweaked some of her negative comments about technology circa 1969 to reflect her current great appreciation for her computer. Similarly, Vasquez would have sought to explain that her promotion of Chicano culture as a columnist was never meant to bind Chicanos—or Chicanas—to a static set of precepts, but to encourage them to explore their indigenous heritage as an unexploited resource. What ancient wisdom was possibly available to them in terms of medicine, spiritual enlightenment, and ideas on land use? Adding to her concerns was this introduction because Vasquez is fundamentally a private person. While she had shared the wisdom gained from experience as a columnist, she had always avoided revealing the details of those experiences with others for fear of seeming too eager to grab the limelight. A lot of convincing took place on this point, too. In the end, Vasquez trusted two scholars who were not participants in the Chicano Movement with not only contextualizing and analyzing her columns but also her life story.

That story is important. Although recent years have seen a flurry of publication about the Chicano Movement, the vast majority of these books are still focused upon four male leaders. Specifically, Reies López Tijerina, Rodolfo "Corky" Gonzales, José Angel Gutíerrez, a founder of the Raza Unida Party of Texas, an independent Chicano political party, and, most of all, the iconic César Chávez.[63] This new work revived discussion about the successes, failures, political strategies, and vision of the Chicano Movement. Still, many of these accounts, by virtue of their focus on male leadership, inevitably omitted or obscured the considerable efforts of thousands of other individuals, half of whom were women. To capture the political evolution of one Chicana through her own words, along with the related scholarship of two academics, therefore, specifically highlights the gender dimensions of the Chicano Movement. What prompted Chicanas like Vasquez to join the movement? What appeal did Chicanismo hold for them? What did they as women hope to accomplish? Unfortunately, this single anthology cannot do justice to all of the women of *El Grito del Norte* (never mind record the remarkable history of the newspaper overall). But, along with a handful of other writings about Chicana activists, it is a start.[64]

The aim of this volume, however, is to do more than fill a gap in the scholarly literature. The power of Vasquez's voice offers a corrective to the polarization of representations about the Chicano Movement that was occurring outside of academia at the start of the twenty-first century. On the one hand, one of the most celebratory interpretations suggested that the Chicano Movement was the Mexican-American version of the African American civil rights movement. Appearing often in high school and college textbooks, this interpretation naturally featured César Chávez prominently. After all, the labor leader was not only the most well-known Mexican American to emerge from a decade of protest, but also the one whose commitment to Gandhian non-violence most closely paralleled that of Martin Luther King, Jr. and other civil rights advocates. On the other hand and at the same time, a much more sinister view of Chicano activism could be found on the Internet, cable news shows, and even some newspaper pages. Conservative media personalities repeatedly attacked the Chicano Movement's emphasis on cultural pride and ethnic unity as inherently dangerous and divisive. They offered as conclusive proof of their point of view a line found in the Plan de Aztlán, *"Por la Raza Todo, Fuera de la Raza Nada,"* which these non-Spanish speakers insisted meant, "For the race, everything, for those outside the race, nothing."[65] Thus, the Chicano Movement was either applauded as a familiar form of protest in the civil rights mold or, conversely, condemned as a Nazi-like bastion of reverse racism.

Ironically *neither* interpretation directly addressed the complexities and nuances of the Chicano Movement, which often paired integrationist goals with militant language. Indeed, the on-going tension between seeking inclusion, in terms of removing barriers to equality, and endorsing separatism, in terms of affirming Chicano cultural and political unity—a tension that Vasquez consistently explored— became one of the hallmarks of the Chicano Movement. Emphasizing the political implications of cultural pride, including pride in the complicated racial inheritance of Latin America, one Spanish-speaker and former Mechista explained the meaning of *"Por la Raza Todo, Fuera de La Raza Nada"* this way in 2003: "By or through this mixed up mongrel of a race, everything. Outside, or without, them, I have/am/can do, nothing."[66] Veterans of the Chicano Movement meanwhile noted that the slogan of *el Movimiento Estudiantil Chicano de Aztlán*, the Chicano Movement group attracting the severest criticism, was actually *"La Unión Hace La Fuerza* (Unity Creates Strength)."[67] These correctives corroborate a central message found in Vasquez's writings a generation before, that Chicano solidarity was always a means to an end, the end being Chicano empowerment and not, despite the angry criticism that she and other Chicano Movement participants directed at Anglo America, white defeat. Writing at a time that celebrated revolution, Vasquez advocated radical social change. At the same time, her politics, filtered through her own experiences and tempered by circumstances, maintained a sense of what was politically possible. Fierce, funny, and full of faith in a better future, the writings of Enriqueta Vasquez perfectly exemplified the Chicano Movement's complex character. With great pleasure, we present her work here.

Lorena Oropeza

---

[1] For an overview of this civil rights strategy that World War II amplified, see Lorena Oropeza, *¡Raza Sí! ¡Guerra No!: Chicano Protest and Patriotism during the Vietnam War Era* (Berkeley: University of California Press, 2005), especially Chapter 1.

[2] This brief biography was compiled primarily using information gained through oral history interviews that I conducted with Enriqueta Vasquez on June 28, 1997 in San Cristobal, New Mexico, and on May 14, 2003 in Richmond, California. Additional quoted material was taken from a two-day oral history interview conducted by Dionne Espinoza with Enriqueta Vasquez on June 13 and 14, 1994 in Taos and San Cristobal, New Mexico. Several more details emerged from conversations between Enriqueta Vasquez and myself during the week of August 23-28, 2004, which I spent at her home in San Cristobal. In addition, I pulled some information from a January 13, 2001 autobiographical piece Enriqueta Vasquez wrote entitled, "Jumping through the Crossfire," a copy of which is in my possession. To clarify a few remaining matters, I also asked several follow-up questions over the phone. In some cases, the citations below list more than one interview source because Enriqueta Vasquez recalled the same events in the same way during different interviews. Finally, the taped oral history interviews that I conducted are in my possession; Dionne Espinoza's are in hers.

[3] "El Plan Espiritual de Aztlán," reprinted in F. Chris Garcia, *Chicano Politics: Readings* (New York: MSS Information Corporation, 1973), 170-172. The plan is also easy to find on the world wide web.

[4] Manuel G. Gonzales, *Mexicanos: A History of Mexicans in the United States* (Bloomington: Indiana UP, 1999), 113.

[5] After Enriqueta took her mother to hear Reies López Tijerina, the leader of a New Mexican land-grant movement, speak, Faustina became a great fan.

[6] Espinoza interview with Vasquez, June 13, 1994.

[7] Oropeza interview with Vasquez, May 14, 2003.

[8] Gareth Davies, *From Opportunity to Entitlement: The Transformation and Decline of Great Society Liberalism* (Lawrence: UP of Kansas, 1996), 158, 171.

[9] She was fortunate that the March of Dimes paid for his foot operations.

[10] Vasquez, "Jumping through the Crossfire," January 13, 2001.

[11] Ignacio M. García, *Chicanismo: The Forging of a Militant Ethos among Mexican Americans* (Tucson: U of Arizona P, 1997), 11.

[12] Ernesto B. Vigil, *The Crusade for Justice: Chicano Militancy and the Government's War on Dissent* (Madison: U of Wisconsin P, 1999), 26. Additional details about the origins of the Crusade for Justice can be found in Elizabeth Sutherland Martínez and Enriqueta Longeaux y Vásquez, *Viva La Raza: The Struggle of the Mexican-American People* (New York: Doubleday, 1974), 229-163. More information about Gonzales can be found in Christine Marín, *A Spokesman for the Mexican American Movement: Rodolfo "Corky" Gonzales and the Fight for Chicano Liberation, 1966-1972* (San Francisco: R&E Research Associates, 1977).

[13] Oropeza interview with Vasquez, May 14, 2003.

[14] Ibid.

[15] Ibid.

[16] Very little has been written about the Vincents, whose ranch had operated as a vacation spot for political progressives during the 1940s and 1950s. Among their many projects, they supported the filming of the banned 1954 film *Salt of the Earth*, a movie about a successful zinc mine strike in New Mexico four years before. See James L. Lorence, *The Suppression of Salt of the Earth* (Albuquerque: UNM P, 1999), 56, 140.

[17] In 1994, a Mississippi jury convicted Byron De La Beckwith, a white supremacist, with murder in connection to the Evers case.

[18] A member of the Hermanos Penitentes, a lay religious fraternity that the U.S. Catholic Church had tried to stamp out after 1848, Vigil shared and strengthened Vasquez's low opinion of establishment religion. Recent works on the Penitentes include Michael P. Carroll, *The Penitente Brotherhood: Patriarchy and Hispano-Catholicism in New Mexico* (Baltimore: John Hopkins UP 2002) and Alberto Lopez Pulido, *The Sacred World of the Penitentes* (Washington, D.C.: Smithsonian Books, 2000).

[19] See, for example, "Let's Be Seen and Heard," January 29, 1969.

[20] The original name of the organization was *La Alianza Federal de Mercedes Reales* (The Federal Alliance of Royal Land Grants). The name was changed in June 1967 in an attempt to avoid turning over membership rolls to authorities. Richard Gardner, *Grito!: Reies Tijerina and the New Mexico Land Grant War of 1967* (New York: Harper Colophon, 1970), 146.

[21] Gardner, 183.

[22] Pertinent passages of (and deletions from) the Treaty of Guadalupe Hidalgo can be found in David Weber, *Foreigners in their Native Land* (Albuquerque: UNM P, 1973) 162-166. See page 164 for "inviolably respected." A succinct history of the treaty and its significance is Richard Griswold del Castillo, *The Treaty of Guadalupe Hidalgo: A Legacy of Conflict* (Norman: U of Oklahoma P, 1990).

[23] In New Mexico, roughly 80 percent of Mexican-era land holdings were rapidly lost. Victor Westphall, *The Public Domain in New Mexico, 1854-1891* (Albuquerque: UNM P, 1965), 49.

[24] The editor of *El Grito del Norte*, Betita Martínez, provided information regarding the origins of the newspaper to me via an e-mail message in October 2004 and

again on August 26, 2005. She also related the origins of the newspaper during an oral history interview that I conducted with her on January 14, 1993 in her home in San Francisco. Interview in author's possession.

[25] The June 5, 1971 special edition on La Chicana captured *El Grito del Norte*'s feminist and transnational ethos. Highlighting the contributions of Chicanas to the Chicano Movement and the work of women members of the Black Panthers and Puerto Rican Young Lords, the special insert also credited the efforts of Japanese, Chilean, Vietnamese, and Palestinian women toward creating a global *"sociedad de justicia y paz, y una vida sin hambre o miedo* [society of justice and peace, and a life without hunger or fear]." The quotation can be found on the page lettered "O."

[26] Espinoza's concluding essay offers an analysis of Vasquez's writings on precisely this topic.

[27] See the back page of the February 18, 1972 edition, for example.

[28] In separate conversations over the years, both Martínez and Vasquez shared the mechanics of producing the newspaper.

[29] "Discrimination," August 24, 1968.

[30] "Discrimination," August 24, 1968.

[31] "Let's Be Seen and Heard," January 29, 1969. A contemporary example of the assumption that Mexican Americans suffered from an inferiority complex can be found in Dennis R. Bell et al., *Barrio Histórico Tucson* (Tucson: College of Architecture, U of Arizona, 1972), 48. The pamphlet is available on the web at http://southwest.library.arizona.edu/barr/.

[32] "La Santa Tierra," December 7, 1970.

[33] "Values Lost," March 10, 1969.

[34] "Racism," September 14, 1969.

[35] "Discrimination," August 24, 1968.

[36] Iris Kelz, *Scrapbook of a Taos Hippie: Tribal Tales from the Heart of a Cultural Revolution* (El Paso: Cinco Puntos P, 2000,) 17. Arthur Kopecky, *New Buffalo: Journals from a Taos Commune* (Albuquerque: UNM P, 2004) is a personal memoir of one local participant in the counterculture.

[37] Tensions between the two groups was a repeating theme on the pages of *El Grito Del Norte*, see "New Mexico Longhairs," May 19, 1969, 14; "Newcomers and Old Struggles," July 6, 1969, 13 (reprinted in Kelz's *Scrapbook*, 54-55); "More Views on the Hippy Question," July 26, 1969, 3; and "Peace, Love in Taos?", May 19, 1970, 15.

[38] In *Scrapbook of a Taos Hippie*, Iris Kelz recalled watching a naked mother washing her baby's diaper in a ditch. "Hey, that's our drinking water," was the response of a writer for *El Grito del Norte*, July 6, 1969, 13.

[39] "This Land is Our Land, " April 14, 1969.

[40] For more information about this land struggle, see R. C. Gordon-McCutchan, *The Taos Indians and the Battle For Blue Lake* (Santa Fe: Red Crane Books, 1995).

[41] Craig Vincent was part of a larger citizens committee dedicated to the return of Blue Lake to the Taos Pueblo. Members included John and Clara Evans, JoAnn Reed, and John Collier of the Bureau of Indian Affairs.

[42] "El Plan Espiritual de Aztlán."

[43] "Somos Aztlán," October 13, 1969.

[44] Oropeza interview with Vasquez, May 14, 2003; Oropeza interview with Vasquez, June 28, 1997. For more of Vasquez's view on communism, see "Communism, Just a Word," March 28, 1970.

[45] "Smog and Money Politics," January 17, 1970.

[46] "Racism," September 14, 1969.

[47] The article was "Women of La Raza II," which appeared in the July 26, 1969 edition of *El Grito del Norte*. The drawing can be seen on page 13.

[48] Alan Stang, "New Mexico: The Coming Guerilla War," *American Opinion* 12 (March 1969): 49, 52, 54, and 58.

[49] *Congressional Record*, July 17, 1969, E-6076.

[50] An older brother who was working for federal government in Puerto Rico told Vasquez that Federal Bureau of Investigation agents had once paid him a visit, probably in 1970 or so, asking questions about her.

[51] See "Dynamiters Hit Tijerina Home," *El Grito del Norte*, January 29, 1968, 3. The newspaper recorded other occasions of violence directed at Alianza supporters on October 31, 1968, 5; March 28, 1969, 1; August 10, 1969, 1; and September 14, 1969, 1.

[52] "Why Are They Dead?", *El Grito del Norte*, February 18, 1972, 1, 4-5. In 1999, a man named Tim Chapa swore under oath that he had been asked by New Mexican police to infiltrate the Black Beret organization and that a police conspiracy to kill Black Berets had resulted in the deaths of Córdova and Canales. Based upon this new testimony, the familes of both sought to reopen a wrongful death suit. They were turned down by the Tenth Circuit U.S. Court of Appeals in 2001 and by the New Mexico Court of Appeals in 2004. The court decisions regarding *Córdova v. Larsen* and *Canales v. Larsen* were available on the web at http://www.kscourts. org/ca10/cases/2001/02/00-2164.htm and http://www.supremecourt.nm.org/past opinion/VIEW/04ca-087.html, accessed October 21, 2005.

[53] "More abuses at Santa Fe Pinta," February 18, 1972.

[54] Vigil, 172-178.

[55] *El Grito del Norte*, November 28, 1968, 7.

[56] *El Grito del Norte,* January-February 1973, 13.

[57] The announcement appears on the back cover of the final edition of *El Grito del Norte*, July-August, 1973.

[58] "Vasquez lives creatively," *Taos News*, December 14, 1978, B2; Oropeza phone call to Vasquez, August 9, 2005.

[59] For more about Templeton, see *El Arte De Rini Templeton: donde hay vida y lucha/ The Art of Rini Templeton: where there is life and struggle* (Mexico: Centro de Documentación Gráfica Rini Templeton/Seattle, WA: The Real Comet, 1988). The image of the dove for Chapter 6 came directly from this book.

[60] Dionne Espinoza, "Pedagogies of nationalism and gender: cultural resistance in selected representational practices of Chicana/o movement activists, 1967-1972" (Ph.D. diss., Cornell U, 1996); Dionne Espinoza, "Revolutionary Sisters: Women's Solidarity and Collective Identification among Chicana Brown Berets in East Los Angeles, 1967-1970," *Aztlán* 26 (Spring 2001): 17-58.

[61] Oropeza, *¡Raza Sí! ¡Guerra No!*

[62] Alma M. García, *Chicana Feminist Thought: The Basic Historical Writings* (New York: Routledge, 1997).

[63] See for example, the personal diary of Reies López Tijerina, translated and republished as *They Called Me "King Tiger"* (Houston: Arte Público P, 2000), the selected works of Rodolfo "Corky" Gonzales' gathered in *Message to Aztlán* (Houston: Arte Público P, 2001); and a memoir written by the founder of the Raza Unida Party in Texas, José Angel Gutíerrez, *The Making of a Chicano Militant* (Madison: U of Wisconsin P, 1999). Recent books on César Chávez include Frederick John Dalton, *The Moral Vision of César Chávez* (Maryknoll: Orbis Books, 2003); Susan Ferriss and Ricardo Sandoval, *The Fight in the Fields* (New York: Harcourt Brace, 1997); and Richard Griswold del Castillo and Richard A. García. *César Chávez: A Triumph of Spirit* (Norman: U of Oklahoma P, 1995). Complementing works that focus on leadership are several works that focus on Chicano Movement organizations. See, for example, Ignacio García, *United We Win: The Rise and Fall of La Raza Unida Party* (Tucson: Mexican American Studies & Research Center, U of Arizona, 1989); Armando Navarro, *Mexican American Youth Organization: The Avant-Garde of the Chicano Movement in Texas* (Austin: UT P, 1995); and Ernesto Chávez, *¡Mi Raza Primero!: Nationalism, Identity, and Insurgency in the Chicano Movement in Los Angeles* (Berkeley: U of California P, 2002), a look at four L.A.-based Chicano Movement groups. As the above citations also make clear, very little has been written about the Chicano Movement in New Mexico.

[64] Early efforts include Martha P. Cotera, *Diosa y Hembra: The History and Heritage of Chicanas in the U.S.* (Austin: Information Systems Development, 1976), especially 168-178; Sonia Lopez Cruz, "Role of the Chicana within the Student Movement" in Rosa Martinez and Rosaura Sanchez, eds., *Essays on La Mujer* (Los Angeles: Chicano Studies Center Publications, U of California, Los Angeles, 1977), 16-29; Magdalena Mora and Adelaida R. Del Castillo, *Mexican Women in the United States: struggles past and present* (Los Angeles: Chicano Studies Research Center, U of California, Los Angeles, 1980); Dorinda Moreno, *La mujer en pie de lucha* (San Francisco: Espina del Norte Publications, 1973); and Adaljiza Sosa Riddell, "Chicanas and el Movimiento," *Aztlán* 5 (Fall 1974): 155-165. In addition to Dionne Espinoza's work mentioned above, other scholars who have researched Chicana activism within the Chicano Movement include Maylei Blackwell, "Geographies of Difference: Mapping Multiple Feminist Insurgencies and Transnational Public Cultures in the Americas" (Ph.D. diss., U of Santa Cruz, 2000); Marisela R. Chavez, "Despierten hermanas y hermanos!: Women, the Chicano movement, and Chicana feminisms in California, 1966-1981" (Ph.D. diss., Stanford U, 2004); and Dolores Delgado Bernal, "Grassroots Leadership Reconceptualized: Chicana Oral Histories and the 1968 East Los Angeles School Blowouts. *Frontiers: A Journal of Women Studies* 19 (1998): 113-142.

[65] "El Plan Espiritual de Aztlán." For an example of the criticism, see Valerie Richardson, "Chicano Group Denied Funding," *Washington Times*, May 9, 2004, on the web at www.washingtontimes.com/national/20040509-123652-1592r.htm; Frosty Wooldridge, "Swallowing a Scorpion from Mexico, NewswithViews.com, November 25, 2005, found on the web at www.newswithviews.com/Wooldridge/

frosty7.htm; Michelle Malkin, "Media Ignores Bustamante's Ties to Racist Group, Cybercast News Service, August 20, 2003, found on the web at www.cnsnews.com/ViewCommentary.asp?Page=%5CCommentary%5Carchive%5C200308%5CCCOM20030820d.html. The gubernatorial campaign of California's Ltn. Governor Cruz Bustamante in 2003 also coincided with frequent criticism of the Plan de Aztlán on the Fox-TV Network. Because websites are notorious for disappearing, I also printed out a copy of each website mentioned in these citations. They are in my possession.

[66] See www.englishfirst.org/bloggerarchive/2003_09_01_bloggerarchive.html.

[67] For the slogan and a defense of MEChA, see Ralph de Unamuno, "The Facts Behind the Myths: FOX News, the GOP, and MEChA" which can be found on the CSUS (California State University, Sacramento) MEChA website, www.csus.edu/org/mecha/mythsfacts.html. See also a commentary written by Rodolfo F. Acuña, "Fair and Unbalanced Racism," which appeared on the website of Latino Political Wires at www.voznuestra.com/PoliticalWires/_2003/_August/29.

Land, Race, and Poverty

Introduction
Lorena Oropeza

Fundamental to the Chicano Movement's re-envisioning of American society and to Enriqueta Vasquez's aspirations for justice, was the land. As the preamble to the 1969 Plan de Aztlán proclaimed, "Aztlán belongs to those who plant the seeds, water the fields, and gather the crops and not to the foreign Europeans." Similarly, in a column written the following month, Vasquez approvingly quoted the Mexican Revolutionary hero, Emiliano Zapata: "La tierra pertenece al hombre que la trabaja con sus proprias manos (The land belongs to the man who works it with his own hands)." Underscoring the importance of land to the Chicano struggle, she ended the column, appropriately entitled, "This Land is our Land," with an even more famous saying accredited to Zapata: "Tierra o Muerte (Land or Death)."

Woven throughout her writings was the idea that the Chicano claim to the land was cultural as well as legal. Noting that, "we can be proud that our forefathers were here while the Pilgrims were landing on Plymouth Rock," Vasquez asserted in "Discrimination" that "Raza is the heritage of the Southwest." To Vasquez, Raza enjoyed "a beautiful way of life" precisely because Chicanos still were deeply connected to the land. "We have these strong roots and our families have been here a long, long time," she offered in "Welfare and Work." In the same article, she emphasized that the Chicano cultural inheritance included not only centuries of Spanish rule but also millennia of indigenous settlement in the region. "It is we, who come from the earth, the poor, who know the real secrets of endurance." To be certain, Vasquez was not about to forget that following the U.S.-Mexican War many Mexican families lost legal claim to their land despite the promises of the 1848 Treaty of Guadalupe Hidalgo. In "This Land Is Our Land," she summarized the effects of war and dispossession: "I have heard the Southwest called a 'colony of the U.S.'"

To make matters worse, a century after conquest, Anglo Americans continued to view themselves as "superior," according to Vasquez. Addressing critics of the Chicano movement who labeled brown power "racist," Vasquez in "Racism" posed the rhetorical question: "And who separated us to begin with?" Chicano cultural nationalism was a response, she argued, to the pervasiveness of racism directed against Mexican Americans. In several columns, Vasquez admonished her readers to recognize the pervasiveness of this phenomenon. Racism demanded that Spanish names be Anglicized.

3

Racism impelled prison guards to beat prisoners. Racism ignored the Chicano cultural contribution to the U.S. Southwest. Racism kept the best jobs for Anglos. All in all, she argued, Chicanos experienced a "second-rate" citizenship, except, she noted, when the draft called.

The combined result of land loss and racism was poverty for many Mexican Americans. Yet Vasquez insisted that the future could be different. In "Los Pobres y Los Ricos," she endorsed a twenty-hour work week without any companion decrease in pay, a radical idea that, she believed, would instantaneously double the number of jobs and the wages they offered. Vasquez also advocated that the United States spend less on military projects and more on domestic social programs to aid the poor. Why, she asked in another article, did Americans despise welfare recipients as "leeches," yet pay no attention to the fact that big corporations enjoyed fat subsidies from the U.S. government?

Vasquez's radical politics were likewise showcased in "'Communism,' Just a Word." In this article and others, she encouraged her readers to identify with the poor. Even those Mexican Americans who had reached the middle-class were economically vulnerable, she argued, because western industrialized society encouraged unrestrained spending on such things as cars, homes, and colored TVs. Consequently, many people owed more than they owned. Returning to the theme of the land, she proposed that communism and communal living were closely related. Granted communism was a political idea conceived in Europe, "communal living," Vasquez contended, was "nothing new" for Chicanos because of their indigenous heritage: "It was here for about 20,000 years before the wetback (crossing the ocean) arrived."

In several articles, Vasquez rejected consumerism and questioned the concept of private property. In fact, as she suggested in "Racism," the slaying of the "monster" of acquisition might be the answer for all Americans. "Certainly we [Chicanos and Chicanas] feel that if we can retain a humanistic way of life and change those mad social values of the Gringo, everybody will benefit," she wrote. In her attempt to change the economic status quo, Vasquez sought to untangle the interlocking issues of land, race, and poverty. Along the way, she tended to romanticize rural life and idealize the poor as rich in culture. Still, her sharp criticisms of materialism and militarism, of corporate greed and the political scapegoating of welfare recipients, continue to resonate more than thirty years later. So too does her insistence that Chicanos and Chicanas should together work for a more economically just future.

Discrimination

It is interesting to see what some people will say when the question of discrimination comes up. The other day I was speaking with a woman in Taos and we began discussing the situation in the Southwest. She is very light complected and married to an Americano. She mentioned that she is not in agreement with the various groups that are involved in civil rights movements. She is definitely convinced that there is no discrimination.

In the course of the conversation, she mentioned that she has an uncle who has a music group that went to Denver to play. They changed their names and were booked under an Anglo name in order to get the contract to play in this one spot. Then she mentioned that she has a nephew who also went to Denver to play and again he changed his name in order to get some playing jobs.

Can you imagine having to change your name to get booked to play and having these incidents happen in your own family and still say that there is no discrimination? You better wake up and see what is happening even in your own families and start admitting that this is discrimination and injustice. I can't see having to change my name for anyone.[1] And I can't imagine not admitting that this hurts our people. There is nothing wrong with us as we are, and if we have to become white and change our names it just isn't worth it. There is something very wrong when one has to do this in a country that is supposedly free. Wake up and see what is happening to you. Look around you and see what is happening even in your own families.

Here in New Mexico, for example, we have but to look at the population of the state. Who is taking over more and more of our jobs and

---

[1] The irony, of course, was that Enriqueta's own name was changed to Henrietta when she started elementary school.

businesses? And where are these people coming (or running) from???
They think it is a quaint little place to live. They come here, but they
do not want to become part of this land and live like the people here.
They come here as superiors and are telling us that something is
wrong. They say that there are changes to be made and the people that
have lived here for generations are supposed to change to suit the
superiors. These changes are supposed to condition you to become
white. I think that if they want changes, they better stay where they are
and come here to visit only. They better learn to accept us as we are.

It is hard to see the Welfare Department hiring a social worker
from Los Angeles or some eastern city to come and work with the
people here. They do this, you know. If you don't believe me, just look
at the people that hold some of these jobs. Don't we have the qualified people here? Darn right we do, but our youth is forced to leave
the area and go to other cities and states to look for jobs while the people here have some outsider telling them how to cope with their problems and telling them that they should change their way of life and the
ways in which they believe. They tell us that we have problems but
believe me we don't have nearly the problems they have as people.
They are the ones with the problems and they push them off here and
try to shift them on to us.

The Raza has a beautiful way of life and we have a lot to contribute to the majority. Goodness knows that they are going to need it
more and more. If you don't believe this, watch them run around in
circles in their materialistic, fast world that is made to build a greater
tomorrow and they forget to enjoy today. They are so wound up building kingdoms all over the world that they forget about the kingdom
that is within them. They forget their very soul. They forget to be people. They forget to have feeling toward their fellow man.

We can teach them these things, we can teach them to look at
themselves for what they are and we can begin by teaching them that
the Raza is the heritage of the Southwest. When they admit that the
Raza is the founder of the Southwest and they put this in the books,
then and only then are they headed for a different way of life. When
they admit that Taos is not the town that belongs to Kit Carson, whom
we cannot identify with and who was the biggest Indian and Mexican

killer, and say that it belongs to our Padre Martinez and others that fought for the people, *then* we can have the pride that the truth is being recognized, that the truth can be taught to our children and that we have mixed Indian-Spanish culture here.[2] We can begin to see ourselves for what we are. We can be proud that our forefathers were here while the pilgrims were landing on Plymouth Rock.

This will be but the beginning, but it will be the start for a better Southwest and for a better way of life.

Despierten mis hermanos, ya basta de vivir vidas hipócritas con precios anglos. Es tiempo de darle valor a nuestro modo de vivir y no dejar que nos echen al lado del camino como algo inservible. La cultura e historia del suroeste es herencia de nosotros. Defiéndanla, eso no se vende ni se compra. Es nuestra.[3]

---

[2]A popular parish priest in Taos, Father Antonio José Martínez was an ardent critic of American land acquisition even before the 1846-1848 war between the United States and Mexico. He was suspected of participating in the Taos Rebellion of 1846, an uprising against the American occupation. Kit Carson was an American frontiersman and trader who in 1843 married Maria Josefa Jaramillo of Taos, where the couple raised their family. During his own lifetime, Carson was idealized in the pulp fiction of the era as a hero of the Old West because of his extraordinary career as an Indian agent, trapper, soldier, tracker, and rancher. More recently, academics have criticized Carson as a genocidal killer of Indians. Short biographies of both men can be found in Richard W. Etulain, ed., *New Mexican Lives: Profiles and Historical Stories* (Albuquerque: UNM P, 2002) 106-28, 163-190.

[3]Wake up, my brothers and sisters, enough of living hypocritical lives at Anglo prices. The time has come for us to value our way of life and not allow it to be thrown by the wayside as if it were something of no use. The culture and history of the Southwest is our inheritance. Defend it; it is not to be sold nor bought. It is ours. Translated by Herminia S. Reyes.

Los Pobres y Los Ricos

A while back, I attended a meeting where I heard a man speak about his experience in Washington on the Poor People's march. It was good to hear one of our Raza stand up and speak for the Raza and our life here and the way of the poor.

During the discussion there was a lady present (Raza) that spoke up and said, "I am not poor, I work." Here was a person who has a nice home (mortgaged), two cars (mortgaged) and many beautiful useless things (also mortgaged). If this woman's husband was to become sick and hospitalized for a few months and she was not able to work, you would end up with human beings who would lose all of their material wealth and find themselves quickly changed from "wishfully middle class" to the "poor class." The picture would be changed, but fast. . . . What would they be?

Let us first of all forget the idea that we will never be poor and by all means let us never look down on the poor. For that matter, the poor are often times better people in that, because they do not have money, they know what to do with themselves and their time. Those with money and things are useless and have no real purpose in life. Take away their money and livelihood (I don't wish this on anyone) and you would find them jumping out of windows.

Now we come to the question, just what is it that we want? Do the poor want money? Do we want to be like the Anglo? What do we really value?

Just looking at the different government machines, I believe that probably the Department of Defense has the provisions for life that the poor people need. Do you know that they take care of their armies from cradle to grave? The entire family of a soldier is taken care of. Now, why can't everyone in this country have this? Isn't this an abundant economy? We have food surplus. Anytime they want, they can solve the job problem by cutting the working hours in half. Really, the amount of money spent for the people of this country is very little. A drop in the bucket in comparison with that which we spend in war killing little people in little countries. Asking for a share of the wealth is not asking too much.[1]

We should also unite with our people, all of us. This stuff about "I made it, you can too," does not sound good to me. It sounds too much like the higher-up talking to the down-theres. This competitive (playing one human against the other) way of life is what the "Americano" has given us. They build their lives around competition. And if you don't know what I mean, just watch that lousy TV and see what advertising is all about. They can make you want more fancy junk you don't need than you would ever believe. They have a way of making you build your lives around things and this, Hermanos, is what it is all about. The Anglo society is built on a value system of things, not humans. Once you begin to value things more than humans, it is like an alcoholic that craves more and more and there is no end to satisfying the thirst that wants more.

The Raza in the Southwest is not asking for things so much as being ourselves. Being human. We want our history back. We want our language and culture to be our way of life. We refuse to give in and submit to a hypocritical way of life. This Southwest was built on Indian, Spanish, and Mexican history, not English. Our cities, our mountains and rivers were explored and settled by Indians and Spaniards, not pilgrims and wagon masters. The first cattle raisers, cowboys and farmers were Raza, we weren't waiting here to be saved by the great white fathers. In Mexico, the Indians had big beautiful cities, they had mathematicians and astronomers and they weren't waiting to be "civilized."

We want to be treated with the dignity that is ours. In matters of jobs, law enforcement and business we are now second-rate citizens.

---

[1] In 1968, U.S. defense spending constituted 46.0% of federal outlays, or $81.9 billion versus $96.2 billion on non-defense expenditures. See Harold W. Stanley and Richard G. Niemi, eds., *Vital Statistics on American Politics*, 4th ed. (Washington, D.C.: Congressional Quarterly P, 1994), 361.

The only place where we are first-rate citizens is in the draft call and I sure don't consider it a compliment to be part of a useless machine. Let's all stop and look at ourselves for what we are. Let's wake up and help each other. Let's look at the issues, let's look at our country, let's look at our communities, let's look at ourselves and our families, let's look at our law enforcement agencies and let's look at this thing called justice. Let's not sit back and give up. We need YOU now. The time is NOW. Let's all stand up, beautiful people. Let's all stand up. LA RAZA UNIDA.

Despierten mis hermanos, no nos podemos permitir perdernos en la rueda de la vida hipócrita con precios anglos. Para que triunfe nuestra cultura e historia tenemos que hablar y gritar y cantar nuestra historia. La tierra es de nosotros. Defiéndanla, ella no se vende ni se compra. Es de nosotros.[2]

October 5, 1968

---

[2]Wake up, my brothers and sisters, we cannot loose ourselves in the hypocritical wheel of life with Anglo prices. In order for our culture and history to triumph, we must speak out, yell, and sing about our history. The land is ours. Defend it, it is not to be sold or bought. It belongs to us.
Translated by Herminia S. Reyes.

This Land Is Our Land

"This land is your land, this land is my land, this land was meant for you and me," those are some of the words of a beautiful song written by Woody Guthrie. Then we have the sayings of Zapata, Mexico's beautiful Indian revolutionary, "This land belongs to those that plant the seeds, water the fields, and gather the crops," "La tierra le pertenece al hombre que la trabaja con sus propias manos."

Land is a beautiful part of man's relationship to nature. How does this refer to the Southwest? The Indians lived here in great freedom. The history books look upon them as primitive, I believe they were totally free humans living the way of beauty. Then the Spaniards came along. It was a turmoil, they made slaves of the Indians. They forced the Indians to work in the mines and then they would send the gold to Spain. The Spaniards did live near the Indian Pueblos and intermarry. From here come the mestizo.

The slavery of the Indian occurred all through the continent and Mexico fought for freedom from Spain. With this independence from Spain, the Southwest lived under the rule of Mexico. Mexico, having economic and internal problems after its war with Spain, was not able to defend its land and thus the Southwest became part of the U.S. I have heard the Southwest called "a colony of the U.S."[1]

---

[1]Influenced by events in Vietnam and elsewhere, scholars during the Chicano Movement, advanced a sociological and historical interpretation of Mexican Americans as constituting a colonized people. According to this internal colony theory, the long-term subjugation of Mexican Americans stemmed from the American conquest of the northern portion of Mexico. Although the internal colony theory had become less popular among academics by the mid-1980s, more recently, scholars have again incorporated some of its assumption into their work. See Mario Barrera, Charles Ornelas and Carlos Muñoz, "The Barrio as an Internal Colony," in Harlan Hahn, ed., *People and Politics in Urban Society* (Beverly Hills: Sage Publications, 1972); Juan Gómez-Quiñones, "Toward a Perspective on Chicano History," *Aztlán* 2 (Fall 1971): 1-49. Also see Linda Gordon, *The Great Arizona Orphan Abduction* (Cambridge: Harvard UP, 1999), 179-185, and María E. Montoya, *Translating Property: The Maxwell Land Grant and the Conflict over Land in the American West, 1840-1900* (Berkeley: U of California P, 2002), 9.

Many people in the past have questioned the individual owning of "land." And the more I see of people being forced to the city because of rich land owners wanting more land, the more I think and wonder about land ownership.

I see land as something that belongs to everyone. Land is like air and life. It is part of each and every one of us. It belongs to the *peoples*. Tribal ownership was very just and served the needs of the communities.

Did you know the government subsidizes big land holders not to plant their land because it will upset the economy of the open market? We have to have a "boom" in this country while people all over the world go to bed hungry. This subsidy thing is taking an interesting trend. For example, we have a senator of the U.S. that received $176,000 a year for holding land and doing nothing with it. Can you imagine? And in Colorado, a large rubber company bought a huge amount of land in southern Colorado and hasn't plowed one inch of it, BUT the company is receiving money from the government for owning it! Who gets a profit from these land laws? Not the little guy like you and I, but the rich landowners—this is how they get rich and powerful. They make their own laws and know how to use them for personal benefit. I don't know how you look at this, but it sure smells fishy to me. I believe that the little people are getting took again.

The worse part of it is that when we have a few people receiving welfare, etc. we are looked down on and called "leeches." We are supposed to feel guilty and inferior while the big landowners, the really rich guy, is getting richer from the government. But what he gets is not called a welfare handout—it's a SUBSIDY.[2] They can get all this money from the government and are looked upon as having—what do you call it, incentive and motivation, I think . . .

---

[2] Vasquez was not alone in her complaints. During the late 1960s, critics of the farm subsidy program pointed to the apparent moral failures of the system and hypocrisy of many beneficiaries. Congressman Paul Findley from Illinois, for example, noted that in 1968 "forty-six [Texas] counties refused to participate in any food program for the poor while the farmers of these same counties harvested $26,462,617 in subsidy payments." See "No Ceiling on Farm Subsidies," *New York Times*, July 8, 1969, 42. This article was accessed on the world wide web on August 12, 2004 through ProQuest Historical Newspapers, *The New York Times*, 1857-Current file. See also Nick Kotz, *Let Them Eat Promises: The Politics of Hunger in America* (Englewood Cliffs: Prentice-Hall, 1969).

You know this thing called money and business is really out of hand and we can see the monster more and more as it reveals itself. Let's expose every corner. Let's see what really goes. It looks like the big giant has problems.

One of the things that we can begin to do is to start planting our lands, instead of just letting them lay there. Let's start thinking in terms of feeding ourselves instead of feeding the grocery stores. Cooperatives are certainly a big answer for the people. Let's go back to being more self-sufficient. Why do we have to support Mr. Safeway, whoever or wherever he may be? Let's work our land. Then the land will come back to the peoples and it will belong to those who plant the seeds, water the fields and gather the crops.

Entre más y más vemos que los ricos se van apoderando de tierras y aunque no se ocupan en plantarlas y el gobierno les paga [solamente] por tenerlas en su poder. Hasta hay compañías que empiezan a comprar tierras con el fin de que les paguen nada más por ser dueños de ellas. Ya basta de esto, de mantener al hombre rico y darle dinero a los negocios. Vamos a empezar a trabajar nuestras tierras, vamos a juntarnos, ya sea en cooperativas o sea como sea. Ya dejemos de darle tanto dinero a las tiendas. El modo del indio era tener tierras para las comunidades y trabajarlas juntos para el uso de la gente. Ésta era costumbre de nosotros. ¿Por qué no lo podemos hacer de vuelta? Recuerden que "La tierra le pertenece al hombre que la trabaja con sus propios manos", eso decía Zapata y también decía, "Tierra o muerte".[3]

April 14, 1969

---

[3]More and more we see the rich take over the land and even though they do not see to cultivate it, the government pays them solely to have the land in their power. There are even companies that begin to buy the land with the objective of only being paid for being the owners of the land. We have had enough of this, of having to support the rich man and of having to give money to business. We are going to begin working our land; we are going to unite, be it in cooperatives or however we can. Let's stop giving so much money to the stores. The way of the Indian was to have land for the community and to work the land together for the community's use. This was our custom. Why can't we do this again? Remember that, "the land belongs to the man that works it with his own hands." That is what Zapata used to say. He also said, "Land or death."
Translated by Herminia S. Reyes.

Racism

One of the matters we have to consider as Raza speaking up is that of racism. We live in a racist society, we are victims of racism and many times people turn around and accuse Raza of being racists. From some of the Anglos one often hears how very much they would like to help us, but they feel that the Raza struggle does not include them. They are used to running the show and unless they can do this, it seems that many of them feel that they cannot contribute. They find it hard to accept our leadership and they feel that they are left out.

However, this should not be the case at all. It is as simple as the farm animals that were talking and heard that there was going to be a very important breakfast for the newly appointed governor. All the animals were excited and wondering what they were going to serve for the breakfast. The chicken was just tickled pink and jumping about with excitement. She said to the pig, "Oh, I am so excited and want to contribute to the breakfast, I hope that they serve ham and eggs." The pig looked at the chicken very seriously and said, "If that is what they have for breakfast you will be contributing, but to me it is a full commitment."

Let's face it, as Raza we need help and we need contributions, but to Raza the struggle for survival is still a full commitment. There is serious work and business at hand. When we talk of land grants, justice, bilingual education, civil rights, etc. we are talking of human survival and the heritage of the Southwest. We have found that by being ourselves as people of a different culture, a culture related to this land, we have been able to find self-identity. It is in this way that we have been able to look at ourselves. And who separated us to begin with? We certainly don't want to be racists, but then too, we must consider that we are born and live in a RACIST society. We have been educated in the Anglo way of thinking so much that we have looked upon ourselves with racist eyes. We have been racists against ourselves. We have been rejecting our very being, our own culture, our own parentage. If we learned to be racists it is only because that is what the Gringo taught us. And by the way, when we speak of Gringo, we do not particularly hate all white people, but we refer to their social system as "Gringo." That is what we don't like. We dislike their superior attitudes and their society that nurses those attitudes from cradle to grave.

I think there is room for everyone in the Mexican-American struggle. Certainly we feel that if we can retain a humanistic way of life and change those mad social values of the GRINGO, everyone will benefit. If the Gringo in the Southwest wants to find a better way of life based on true human values, he will listen to the minorities. This is the only way this country may be saved. The Gringo is kidding himself if he thinks that the whole world looks up to him. His glorious days are numbered and very few.

Another thing we hear quite often in our struggle is that question of nonviolence. Some people say, "Well, I do want to get involved but can you guarantee there will be no violence?" That is like asking the Gringo, "Can you promise me you will look at me with love and fairness, always?" How can one guarantee complete nonviolence when one lives in a completely VIOLENT country? How can I honestly raise a nonviolent family when I hear such things as "Join the Armed Forces and become a MAN"? They may flower the service up to look like a career, but basically everyone of our young men that goes into the service is completely BRAINWASHED and taught HOW TO KILL. With all of our youth viewing Vietnam and Latin America, and watching our troops there, we talk of NONVIOLENCE? The foundation of this country has been bloodshed. And with the violence committed against Raza, I cannot stand by and relinquish my right to violence when I may see my neighbors and friends beaten.

And yet some Raza don't want to face the issues. They don't want to look at all of the facts. They don't want to talk about some of the issues involved. Despite this, the problems are coming to light and we have to be honest with ourselves. We have to stop and think. We have to stop and take a look at ourselves. There are fewer and fewer places to hide. We have to stop and to face the cold facts sooner or later. They are all around us.

So, whoever you may be, remember that you can make a contribution in the Raza struggle. You owe it to yourself to look at our issues. Weigh them carefully and understand the Raza when we speak. In this way you will better understand yourself. Listen carefully. Listen to the people. It is like listening to life. Can you hear it? The Raza speaks, HARD, CLEAR, AND STRONG. The heartbeat of humanity is coming from the little people. If you find you can contribute in understanding and supporting the Raza, fine and dandy. TAKE YOUR PLACE AND BE COUNTED. If not, understand us and realize that we have a FULL COMMITMENT.

September 14, 1969

"Communism," Just A Word

Híjole, they're doing it again. Panic and hysteria are the order of the day for lawmakers and law-enforcers. I hear they are calling all kinds of people COMMUNIST. So, if you are a good Samaritan, and if you speak on issues, you are likely to get thrown into the pot with the rest under this COMMUNIST label, I am told. You have to be brave to practice your freedom of speech.

You know, I am getting tired of this label "COMMUNIST" being thrown around. I don't understand it too well. I guess that comes mostly because I need an explanation for things, I refuse to settle for just ONE word to justify persecution. But this particular word has been built into all of our institutions as a BAD word, a DIRTY word and a BOOGEYMAN. Hummmm, I wonder. Like they say, I smell, (con su permiso) PEDO.

The way I see communism, it was really a serious thing planned by two Europeans named Marx and Lenin to combat a class structure that oppresses people. In this country, we don't seem to have the same class structure that they wrote about.

We do have the controlling rich, who are scared to death of communism because they have a lot to lose materially. As a protection, they have this huge middle-class with a real big, well-developed EGO that makes them THINK they are rich. Now these people are told that they must fight communism in order to be able to continue to possess and acquire their wealth and freedom. So they are to fight like heck, against this enemy, in order to keep their small acreage, their cars, colored TV sets, etc., oh yes, and their mortgages. So with this in mind, the institutions are teaching everybody to shiver with fear at the mere mention of the word communism.

Now, why is Raza particularly afraid of this word? Why are we afraid it may make us look like BAD people? I think we know that the word communism can be confused with the word communal. The institutions have also placed a taboo connotation on the way of life called COMMUNAL. Communal living is nothing new, it was here for about 20,000 years before the wetback (crossing the ocean) arrived. The people of the Americas knew this kind of living long before white man (and their laws) set foot on this continent. The people of Raza have a way of life that is able to adapt to any environment. In the Southwest we have been self-sufficient under different governments during our history. We have survived living in colonies, barrios, and villages. Always helping each other as brothers. So even COMMUNAL has been given a bad connotation in order to destroy a cultural way of life. With this image of badness, the power structure tries to make people reject a way of life. A little like trying to teach Raza to be WHITE. And I do know some Raza that think WHITE, but they just don't look it.

Now, back to the words COMMUNISM, COMMUNAL, and the Panic. Well, it seems strange to me that there would be any confusion on a way of life. Why don't we see communal for what it is related to? To COMMUNION, the partaking of a spiritual body. This has to do with living as brothers, not a thing to do with some political slavery. The Hermandad was a very good example of BROTHERHOOD being a spiritual body.[1]

And while we are looking at a way of life, let's look at some beautiful people I know. I was born and raised in Colorado and lived among Mennonites. These are Protestants who also live a real brotherhood, much as the Hermandad here in New Mexico used to be. And you know what, I remember when I went to school we used to sing the "Oh, say can you see" song and place our hand on our hearts for the "pledge" and these beautiful Christian people would only stand with their arms crossed. When I asked them about it, and why they didn't

---

[1] Members of Los Hermanos Penitentes helped maintain Catholic traditions in northern New Mexico and southern Colorado starting when the region was an isolated part of Mexico. After the war with Mexico, the American Catholic Church sought to uproot the organization.

sing and say the pledge, they explained that they didn't swear or pledge to anything but to God. Not only that, but they don't have to go into the Army. They are called Conscientious Objectors and do not have to serve in the service of their country. I agree with their way of life, they have a brotherhood and help each other with their farms. AND, you know what? To this day I don't hear anyone calling them COMMUNISTS.

So why should anyone else be called communist? I don't fall for that label, no more. I don't wonder about that one, no more. . . . . .

And, by they way, I have seen signs saying "AMERICA, LOVE IT OR LEAVE IT." The way I see myself, Raza, and the Southwest, the European foreigners are the wetbacks (they who crossed the ocean) and they are welcome to stay. If they just remember we want them to stay as brothers and sisters to us. We don't need white fathers. We don't need saviors. We just need equal BROTHERS and SISTERS.

March 28, 1970

Welfare and Work

WORK, WORK, WORK, dice El Patrón en Washinton. This seems to be the latest phobia from the Washinton politicos as they discuss the Welfare state, welfare and workfare programs. The European concepts of work and its puritan values are showing and the White Anglo-Saxon Protestant (WASP) ethics are being legislated as a philosophy of life, a purpose for living, all for the almighty reward called MONEY.

To live for the joy of living and to work at home or anywhere for that matter, for pure joy is not recognized as honorable work. To the Gringo, work means leaving home, spending certain hours a day out of your house, being production-oriented and earning some kind of paycheck for your hysteria and ulcers. This is supposedly honorable and cleansing to the soul. That the work be perhaps meaningless and unfulfilling is unimportant.

This basic WASP concept is now getting to the point where it is being shoved down the throats of the poor. When legislation becomes a law to force the poor to go to work when there is no work, we must question the intent of this law. Is it designed to oppress the poor and make them guilty for not working, to make them get on their knees to beg for mere existence?

Let's look at the national figures on welfare recipients:

50% of the total welfare recipients are children under eighteen years of age.

25% of the welfare recipients are over 60 years of age. (Many of these are not eligible for old-age pension.)

15% are blind, disabled.

10% are mothers and other hardship cases.[1]

OF THE TOTAL WELFARE RECIPIENTS, LESS THAN 1% ARE ABLE TO WORK AND LESS THAN 1/4 OF 1% ARE CHEATERS.

After looking at the figures as to welfare recipients one could ask, ¿qué pasa? What are the patrones políticos barking about? Let's consider something else. It takes $133 to administer $1 of welfare![2] So somewhere between the big money and the poor there are people earning a living off the poor. When we take this into consideration, one can wonder why, when they speak of cuts to be made, do they pick on the poor to suffer the cutbacks? One could suppose that it is because: (1) You can control the poor, just threaten them with taking away their welfare; (2) They have the poor convinced that they are defenseless; (3) Most recipients are women, children and disabled people, that is, a safe group to whip into shape and make a lot of noise about.

The new welfare laws are called "incentive to work." Welfare recipients are required to go to work, whether the work be on-and-off jobs, or menial jobs with low wages (the minimum wage is not required).[3] It seems that this is geared to create cheap labor from peo-

---

[1]According to the National Center for Social Statistics, a data collection agency within the Department of Health, Education and Welfare, in 1972 a total of 15 million Americans received welfare. These included 7.7 million children (52%), 2 million old people (13%), and 1.1 million blind and disabled persons (7 %). In addition, about 3 million recipients were parents, although the data was not broken down into single-parent and two-parent households. NCSS Report A-2 (January 1972) was reprinted in Timothy J. Simpson, *Welfare: A Handbook for Friend and Foe* (New York: Pilgrim P, 1972), 68.

[2]In the wake of the War on Poverty and President Richard Nixon's announced plan to provide a guaranteed family income for the poor (never approved by Congress), social scientists in the late 1960s and early 1970s produced reams of materials studying welfare history and debating public policy. While we could not find the exact source of some of her statistics, Vasquez's vigorous defense of welfare recipients as being truly needy and her anger regarding the high costs of administration fit well within this broader context. See for example, Simpson, *Welfare: A Handbook for Friend and Foe*, 114; and Stanley and Glenn Esterly, *Freedom from Dependence* (Washington: Public Affairs P, 1971), 11-13.

[3]Congress passed the Work Incentive Program in 1967 in the hope of replacing welfare with "workfare." In December 1971, Congress passed a measure that "strengthened the more coercive features of the Work Incentive Program." Whereas before states decided which welfare recipients to refer to work or training programs, now participation in the program was mandatory for all recipients of Aid to Families with Dependent Children, with the single exception of mothers with children under six years of age. In addition, states faced a loss of federal funds if they did guarantee a sufficient level of employment among participants. See Walter I. Trattner, *From Poor Law to Welfare State: A History of Social Welfare in America* (New York: The Free P, 1979), 270.

ple who may need to stay home; they are being put on the market of humanity.

WHAT WOULD HAPPEN IF all welfare recipients demanded jobs, right now? A welfare strike in reverse would put a lot of people on the spot, NO? WHAT WOULD HAPPEN IF there was no welfare and they erased the $133 it takes to give $1 to the poor? What would that welfare bureaucracy do for jobs? WHAT WOULD HAPPEN IF everybody demanded "justice and equality" and said: O.K. you have cut my check down 10%, so let's do it all the way across the board. We begin with you big welfare recipient administrators setting the example. A 10% cut across the board for *everybody*. One could have petitions and a court case on this and I wonder WHAT WOULD HAPPEN?

It looks like the poor of the country have been had again by El Patrón de Washinton. This is getting to be the history of our life. The other day a young Chicano said, "I just went to Washington, D.C., it's great, we should send a lot of our people over there, that's where the bread is, man." I must say, I don't dig you, man, I have a suspicion that that is where the crackpots are too, and if you want to trained to serve El Patrón, pues, go to it, hermano mío, learn the hard way. Just remember while you echo the bark of the top dogs, some of us better get busy and go about the business of building our own nation of Aztlán. Aztlán means we want and need technology, we want nothing but the latest and the best for our people. And we want to work, but what counts is, FOR WHAT? I still believe in being a person of principle, to work for my people and serve La Raza, not just for myself and a big fat check. We can't ignore the big Patrón en Washinton monster, but that doesn't mean that we have to fall to our knees and serve it.

Let us develop a new way of life among us, let's pool what little resources we have and learn to cooperate and share. It is in this sharing that we form un carnalismo that cannot be broken. From here we will learn that three and four familias can cook a big meal together and feed their children much cheaper and better than one little familia. So we get together, build friendships and close-knit ties, to us that is not hard, because we have these strong roots and our families have been here a long, long time. Out of this will come interesting family living, learning, and singing together, enjoying life, traveling.

The pure spirit, the truths and philosophies of La Raza will come from Los pobres de la tierra. For it is we, who come from the earth, the poor, who know the real secrets of endurance; power with such potential that we have not yet begun to recognize it. We may be poor in money, but we have much wisdom that money cannot buy. It is this wisdom that we value so highly for ése es el corazón and the legacy of mi raza, y ése es el espíritu de Aztlán.

Ándele mi raza, despierte, viva, levante la cara con orgullo, aprenda a vivir sin temor a nada. Infórmese de todo lo que sucede con nuestra raza, ponga el oído a las voces de nuestra juventud y apoye a nuestros hijos e hijas. Vamos a unirnos. VIVA MI RAZA LINDA.[4]

February 18, 1972

---

[4]Come on Raza, wake up, live, hold your head up high with pride; learn to live without fearing anything. Become informed about what is going on with our Raza, lend an ear to the voices of the youth and support our sons and daughters. Let's unite. Long live my beautiful Raza.
Translated by Herminia S. Reyes.

More Abuses at Santa Fe Pinta

More and more the New Mexico state prison at Santa Fe is seen exposed to the news as the dirty linen is being aired and the secret skeletons are being dragged out of the closets. These skeletons and closets seem to range anywhere from personal kingdoms to sadism and vendettas. These skeletons seem to become more numerously tied in with social concepts of morality as to humanity, punishment, and rehabilitation.

The penal institutions throughout the country are falling apart at the seams as are many "long standing traditions." Attica in New York began by leaving thirty-one dead.[1] The Florida State prison is announced as closing its doors and saying it can't handle any more prisoners. It is already overcrowded. In New Mexico, however, it seems that there has been a smug history of the establishment, the politicos and the news media working in harmony with each other and trying to lie to its citizenry, to shield them from the truth and keep them wearing rose-colored glasses.

---

[1]The Attica prison riot of September 1971 and its subsequent investigation made the racism and violence of the U.S. prison system an issue of national debate. From September 9 to 13, twelve hundred inmates took control of New York State's Attica Correctional Facility and held thirty-eight hostages. The action ended violently when state troopers and correctional officers stormed in to retake the prison; the state's special commission to investigate the riot later found that, of the forty-three deaths during the riot, thirty-nine occurred during this fifteen-minute battle (eleven were prison staffers held as hostages). Additionally, over eighty prisoners were severely wounded. Although the commission found that the rebellion was not the result of careful planning, it pointed to the racism and insensitivity of prison guards, unfair parole policies, harsh punishment of prisoners, and uncompensated prison labor as having significantly contributed to an environment of resentment and frustration among the prison population. See New York Special Commission on Attica, *Attica: The Official Report of the New York State Special Commission on Attica* (New York: Praeger Publishers, 1972), xi-xxi, 105; and Richard X. Clark and Leonard Levitt, ed. *The Brothers of Attica* (New York: Links Books, 1973), v-vii.

Thus, on Feb. 3, 1972, when three prison guards came forward to testify as to the truth on the prison situation and to verify the beating of prisoners during the October riot, many good New Mexico citizens could hardly believe their ears. And many did not want to face the truth. The guards came forward to testify only after Gov. Bruce King promised that their jobs were protected.

Joe G. Montoya, 23, from Santa Fe, was the spokesman for the guards. Leroy J. Romero, 21, also from Santa Fe, testified and appeared with Mike B. Vigil, 35, from Española, who did not testify. Orlando Roybal decided not to appear. The essence of the testimony presented was to reveal what so many people feel to be undercurrent truths. The fact that prison guards were ordered to beat and tear gas prisoners during the October 7 riot at the New Mexico penitentiary.[2]

It was also made clear that Felix Rodriguez, prison warden, has given actual control of the prison to Eugene Long, Assistant Warden for Correctional Services and to Deputy Warden Horacio Herrera. Through all of the maze of what has happened and what has been revealed, it can be assumed that if before the riot there was fear and distrust which provoked action and brutality, it has probably doubled and tension runs rampant throughout cell blocks as well as throughout official administrative offices and certainly through questionably acquired political jobs and positions.

---

[2]See *El Grito del Norte* Vol IV #10, October 28, 1971. *El Grito del Norte* had run an article detailing the strike by prisoners at the New Mexico State Penitentiary earlier in the month. Whereas the prison administration and mainstream press presented the action as a childish and spontaneous imitation of the Attica riot, choosing to focus on property damage rather than on prisoner complaints, *El Grito* used testimony by a few candid guards to challenge this simplistic picture. According to the newspaper, prisoner support for the rebellion had been nearly unanimous, prisoner demands had articulated particular grievances with the Santa Fe prison and parole board, and excessive guard violence after the prisoners had surrendered had been the cause of most of the property damage. See "Hiding the Truth at the State, Prison Says: 'Only Necessary Force Used'," *El Grito del Norte,* October 28, 1971, 2-4. Long-term problems evidently remained. In 1980, the New Mexico State Penitentiary was the site of a riot that cost 33 inmates their lives. No guards were killed in what was the second deadliest prison uprising in U.S. history after Attica. See Roger Morris, *The Devil's Butcher Shop: The New Mexico Prison Uprising* (New York: F. Watts, 1983; reprint, Albuquerque: UNM P, 1988).

Prison officials have repeatedly denied that beatings took place and this denial continues even after the guards as well as the prisoners have testified as to the beatings. The fact still remains that ten prisoners were beaten and hospitalized from Cell block 4 on October 7, 1971. It would seem that they were either beaten or they were critically hurt as they stumbled about in their cells.

Herman R. Buzbee testified, "No one was resisting. I saw twenty-four guys clubbed. Most were knocked down, I knew what was going to happen." "I heard one of the officers shout . . . 'You SOBs . . . you started it . . . you're gonna get it'."

In a recent development, 198 of the penitentiary's 500 inmates signed their names to a petition which was included with a letter from prisoner John Naranjo to Dr. John Salazar. The petition asks release from isolation for seven inmates and dismissal of Long and Herrera. The letter states that tensions at the prison are now greater than ever; that seven inmates held in isolation since the October riots are mentally affected by daily harassment; that Long and Herrera have been using inmates as informers; and that Herrera has been trying, so far in vain, to buy off the prisoners who filed civil suits by offering them partial damage payments and immediate release. Naranjo said that nothing has yet been made public about an incident on February 9 which may cost one prisoner his life.

Naranjo says more fellow inmates would have signed the petition had not fear of administration interception forced them to forward it hastily to Dr. Salazar. The letter warns that there may be another riot if things are not changed. The majority of Chicano prisoners are treated like animals, it says.

What would seem to be some of the solutions to these problems? Probably the first big step to be taken is that people have to quit lying. At one time we had the attitude of officers and politicos being honest and respectful and this is something that people will not buy anymore. We know now that if our streets are crime infested, these are but mere symptoms of the people in power. Which can bring us to the question of, "who is the real criminal?"

The basic attitudes of all of us and our views as to crimes and criminals must be re-evaluated. What are prisons for? Oppression, punishment, or rehabilitation? Now, when we are speaking of rehabilitation it is not hard to know what the needs of rehabilitation are. Just ask the prisoners and they can more than adequately give the answers as to their needs. Surely this is just and humane, after all, they are locked up in a wall and wire fence. They are not going anywhere, so what is wrong with listening to what can better prepare them for the day they leave this confinement?

When speaking of rehabilitation we should also think of resources on the outside, people with answers. This is where an organization such as the Black Berets, which protested the prison situation and held a sit-in at the governor's office, is extremely valuable.[3] The "qualified" people to work with rehabilitation are community-oriented people, many of which may be ex-cons. A portion of the parole board should be composed of these same persons.

These are but a few of the things to be considered by the prisons of this country. These are but a beginning of what may become a reality. A reality that can lead to sanity and humanity as well as to truth.

February 18, 1972

---

[3]Less well-known than the California-based Brown Berets, the Black Berets of Albuquerque were another Chicano Movement organization with a quasi-military presentation. The organization combined an international focus with an attempt to organize such barrio-based programs as free health clinics and free breakfasts for children in need.

Culture and History

Introduction
Dionne Espinoza

During the Chicano Movement, activists became aware of how, as a result of the racism and the pressure to assimilate in U.S. society, their history and culture had been undermined and deemed inferior. Subsequently, cultural resistance—the maintenance of culture despite the majority's view of that culture as lacking in value—became a principal strategy of the Chicano Movement. The writings in this chapter illustrate how Enriqueta Vasquez went beyond merely adopting a stance deconstructing the dominant culture's view of mestizo and indigenous peoples to participating in the reconstruction of historical and cultural knowledges in order to validate them.

The first major step in the process of reclaiming culture and history was to show how mestizo and native populations had been systematically misinformed about their history. Vasquez argued that this was because these populations had been erased, stereotyped, or misrepresented as lacking a culture or a history. "Teach True Values" addressed the bias of an educational curriculum that masked the mistreatment of racialized others in the early formation of American society. Parents, she urged, should be involved in the educational process and should speak up against these biases so that their children would gain a critical knowledge of U.S. society. Ironically, Vasquez noted, even when people of the Southwest—American Indians and Chicanos—were a source of interest to mainstream society, the relationship tended to be one of appropriation. "Let's Be Heard and Seen" discussed the exploitation of native cultures by academics and artists.

After coming to understand the ways in which *la raza* had been undermined in educational curricula and cultural production, the next step, according to Vasquez, was to counter the lack of presence in the curriculum, negative stereotypes, and acts of appropriation. This would be accomplished in two ways: 1) by reviving existing cultural traditions such as celebrations of Christmas in which food, sharing, and the birth of Christ (*el nacimiento*) would be central (as opposed to buying into commercialism and accumulation of goods), and 2) by Raza's picking up the pen—*poner la pluma* in Vasquez's words—to create their own stories, plays, and artworks.

Many of the stories, she suggested, could be found by listening to the teachings of the elders whose way of life, she asserted, involved an intimate connection to the rhythms of the seasons and mother earth. Elders' knowledge, in particular that of her mother Doña Faustina, served as the basis for

31

the two columns entitled, "La Voz de Nuestra Cultura," parts 1 and 2. These pieces described the *remedios* and natural healing practices of elders and *curanderas*. The first column was a *cuento* from Michoacan about how an elder leper discovered the medicinal properties of *polvo de víbora* (snake's dust). The second column detailed the need to reclaim indigenous knowledge of the body and ways of healing as a complement to Western medicine rather than to simply place blind faith in Western doctors.

"Viva México! Vivan Las Américas!" and "La Historia del Mestizo" illustrate Vasquez, the grassroots historian, engaging a "pedagogy of the oppressed." For Vasquez, historical contexts were most important when they illuminated the ongoing struggle for social justice. To commemorate the Mexican Independence Celebration of September 16th, "Viva México! Vivan Las Américas!" narrated mestizo history from conquest to the present. Using history as a backdrop to interpret contemporary events, she drew parallels between the loss of land in violent warfare in Mexico and the rioting and violence that occurred at the August 29, 1970 Chicano Moratorium against the War in Vietnam.

In "La Historia del Mestizo," Vasquez continued her role as a historian of conquest and colonization of indigenous peoples. Here she outlined the colonization process by Spain over indigenous peoples that produced a mestizo population. Given the historical prejudice and racism toward *el indio*, Vasquez's historical overview made the important point that Chicanos, as mestizos, were also native to the land. In this regard, Vasquez's historical perspective was transnational in scope, not limited to the United States of America or even to *Los Estados Unidos de México. Mexicanos* and Chicanos, she insisted, shared cultural ties as a people outside of the demands of *los gobiernos* and nation-states.

Teach True Values, Says La Raza Mother

A while back I talked with a wonderful young man who told me about a dream he had. In this dream, he saw the small schoolhouse that he attended when he was a boy. The schoolhouse cracked and began to crumble. It crumbled until there was nothing but dust left there. He was very happy because he had at long last seen his schooling for what it really was. He realized that it was a process designed not to educate but to indoctrinate him for competitive living. As life went on for him, he realized that the real way of life was a way of beauty which the school had not taught him. He had learned that the answers to living with our fellow man and the world were things that he had to learn for himself, from outside the schoolroom.

What do we mean when we talk about education and where are the schools failing? I believe that one of the most important things in life is that the schools teach our youth to think and figure things out for themselves. They should teach the people who they are. They should teach respect for the beliefs and the way of life of peoples. And in this Southwest we should have much more material on La Raza.

For example, our history books are all slanted to glorify the Anglo and to make him look like a superior. Right in the schools, our children are taught a history they can't identify with. They learn all kinds of social things which they are not part of. Thus they don't even learn that they belong in this land. Their ancestors are not given credit or given a place for the many things they did. They don't learn that the pioneers would have died had not the Indian showed them how to survive and live from the land. They are not taught to think out the fact that while our literary document called the Constitution was being written, there were slaves being shipped and sold, even though the

Constitution said "no slavery."[1] And they are not taught that the Anglo taught the Indians to kill and betray one another.

These are but a few of the things that our children are not taught. They are also not taught that the peoples of the Southwest have a beautiful way of life. That they have a culture.

We parents must learn to look at our schools and question what they teach. We parents must sit and talk to the children and give them real education. If there is anything that we do not agree with, we must learn to go and talk to the teachers and the schools. We must speak up, we must back up our children, we must question the schools. The times are gone when we are to let our children be pushed out of the schools. The time is gone when we remain silent and say, "the teachers and the schools know best." They don't know the answers and they have turned the schools into a factory that conditions people into becoming machines.

Let's speak up and discuss the schools. Let's discuss our language and our history and our culture and way of life. Let's look at ourselves and see who we are and let's take pride in what we are. Because someone speaks English and makes good grades does not mean he is any better than you. It only means that he may be more brainwashed than you. Don't take a back seat for anyone. Don't let the schools *un*-educate you into thinking that you are a second-class citizen. Speak up and change things. Speak up for yourself, speak up for your people and speak up for your beautiful children. When we start to do this we will find peace and pride in ourselves once again. We must come forward and make ourselves heard, NOW.

We must keep our children in the schools but we must teach them that they can contribute in the classrooms. They are to speak up and question and discuss issues in the classrooms. Only in thinking and speaking up can they learn from each other. Remember that we can all contribute to a better education. We must read books, but we must also think and question them. And we must begin thinking in terms of writ-

---

[1]Although aspiring to secure the "blessings of liberty" to the people of the United States, the U.S. Constitution did not ban slavery. It did, however, allow Congress to end the slave trade in 1808, which it did.

ing them *ourselves*. Only this way can we push our kids on and teach the schools a thing or two about education and life.

La educación de nuestra juventud es de mayor importancia en este tiempo. Entre la raza se sabe cómo vivir y se sabe lo que es batallar en la vida. Las escuelas no nos enseñan a pensar, no nos enseñan nuestra historia, no nos enseñan nuestra cultura. Por eso, más y más la juventud se siente perdida en no saber quiénes son ni cómo vive la raza por el suroeste. Tenemos que hablar con nuestros hijos, tenemos que hacer preguntas en las escuelas, tenemos que insistir que se nos enseñe nuestra lengua para hablarla propiamente. Tenemos que acordarnos que las escuelas y los maestros no saben todo, que la enseñanza viene de la gente a la que sirven. Tenemos que aprender a pensar por nosotros mismos. Nuestro modo de vivir y nuestro pensamiento es cosa que no se vende ni se compra. Hablen y despierten, hermanos.[2]

October 31, 1968

---

[2]Nowadays, the education of our youth is very important. Among the Raza, it is known how to live and how to struggle. Schools do not teach us how to think, they do not teach us about our history, and they do not teach us about our culture. That is why, more and more of our youth feel lost in not knowing who they are or how the Raza lives in the Southwest. We must speak to our children; we must ask questions in school; we must insist that our language is taught so that we may speak it correctly. We must remember that schools and teachers do not know every thing and that the teaching comes from the people who are being taught. We must begin to think for ourselves. Our way of thinking and living is not something that is bought or sold. Speak up and awaken, my brothers!
Translated by Herminia S. Reyes.

'Tis the Season, Fa La La

'Tis the season to be jolly, fa la la, Jingle Bells y Feliz Navidad. Christmas is a beautiful time of the year. And this means a lot to us all. It means the celebration of the birthday of the greatest revolutionist known to man. A man who overthrew big powers and brought about social change.

So, how do we celebrate his coming? Our parents used to cook many foods. Tamales, buñuelos, capirotada, dulces, and many foods. Then on Christmas day they would send out plates of food to the neighbors and friends. Our mothers would say, "Anda, llévale a doña Bríjida y a doña Carlotita este plato." Take this here and take this there. It was a beautiful custom among our people. It wasn't so much the food but the thought and feeling that counted. It was a time of giving. A time of cooking. A time of making decorations and a time of family gatherings and enjoying each others' company.

And now, everywhere it is a time of "What am I going to get?" The friendly loan companies have Christmas loans, you can pay by the month. Real easy too. Your first payment isn't due until 1969. It's buy, BUY, BUY. Many of the toys may stand up for only a week and we are teaching our children to demand more and more. They don't want clothing or something useful, but now it is a watch, a stereo or even a car. We have commercialized it so much that I wonder if Christ approves when he sees us now? I wonder if he likes our Christmas trees and celebrating? I wonder if he likes our way of life? I wonder how our Santa Claus looks to him? You can have your child's picture taken with Santa for maybe $3.00. I wonder if this is why He came on the first Christmas day?

¡DESPIERTEN HERMANOS! Let's get the real Christmas spirit. Let's get our families together and make our little gifts. Let's make our

Christmas decorations. And why not make our own Christmas cards? These can have just as much meaning. Probably more. They would be more fun and really give us a good Christmas spirit. Let's learn that the spirit of Christmas is within each and every one of us. You can't buy it and you can't sell it and above all, you can't feel it more by going into debt for Christmas.

Why not set up a "nacimiento"? The manger scene. Remember that? That's Christmas. We don't have to have that cold, meaningless, expensive tree. We can cook and send out little plates of treats to our families and friends. Let's break that $MONEY$ commercial Christmas. Let's return to the spirit of Christmas. Let's teach our young ones to the spirit of Christmas. Let's love our brothers and neighbors all over the world and let's celebrate a real live spiritual Christmas.

Un año, pienso que era el '44, me acuerdo que se juntó la familia para la Navidad. Eran cinco años que no nos habíamos juntado toda la familia en este día. Ya habían vuelto mis hermanos del servicio y nos reunimos a platicar, cantar, tocar música y a comer tamales. Nos repartimos los presentes y nos sentamos a gozar del gusto. Recuerdo que mi padre nunca abría sus presentes y siempre lloraba con sentimento y gusto de ver a la familia toda junta. Ahora comprendo que los presentes para él no tenían ningún símbolo de felicidad. Su felicidad en la Navidad estaba en su familia, su cariño y su gusto era la riqueza en el hogar.

Vamos a hallar la felicidad de Navidad entre nosotros y amar a nuestras familias y amistades con cariño sin tener que gastar dinero para mostrar nuestro gusto. Vamos a darle honor a Jesucristo en el día de su santo con nuestro corazón y con riquezas que no se compran ni se venden. Feliz Navidad, mis queridos hermanos y hermanas.[1]

December 18, 1968

---

[1] One year, I think that it was in 1944, I remember my family got together to celebrate Christmas. It had been five years since we had all been together on this day. My brothers had returned from the armed services and we all gathered around to talk, sing, play music, and to eat tamales. We distributed gifts to everybody and we sat down to enjoy ourselves. I remember that my father never opened his gifts and that he always cried from sadness and joy as he saw all of his family united. Now, I

understand that gifts to him were not a symbol of happiness. His happiness at Christmastime centered on his family, his love for them and his joy of being with them.

We are going to find happiness during this season among ourselves and we are going to affectionately love our families and friends without having to spend money to demonstrate our joy. We are going to honor Jesus on his birthday with our heart and with riches that are neither sold nor bought. Merry Christmas, my dear brothers and sisters!

Translated by Herminia S. Reyes.

Let's Be Seen and Heard

You know, just studying the lifeless Gringos one can really feel sorry for them and wish that one could help them with their superiority problems. I think that the minorities can do just this and I think that we can do it by sharing of ourselves.

Then one thinks, "How can we share of ourselves?" Here again we get back to offering our culture and heritage that would give them a culture to relate to, as they have none. This is, I believe, the biggest challenge of U.S. history. First, I believe that we can start by writing *our* stories, writing our history ourselves and in writing what life is all about. Some people look at this as being impossible because they do not have the degrees and so-called schooling. Well, let me tell you that once you start thinking and figuring things out for yourself you will learn things that the schools and universities could never teach you. If you want to know what I mean, just talk to a social worker. You will see that what they learned out of a book and what we know from living are two entirely different things.

You can never imagine the number of studies that have been made on the Raza and the Indian. I myself think of the many times that I have been interviewed and talked to by so-called educated people who were making studies. The universities have been trying to figure us out. (And for large sums of money, I might add.) Well, the time has come when we should speak out for ourselves. We have a beautiful life and a beautiful culture to share, let's begin to write it down. You don't need the big fancy words. Sometimes when we hear those big words we look at each other in wonder and feel inferior. Well, just because you learn big words does not mean that you know it all. It may only mean that you have to use someone else's ideas from books and they come out, not like you, but like you memorized them out of a book.

Each and every one of us has something great to offer, our emotions, feelings and OURSELVES. Let's begin to write it down. Not for money, but for ideas and life. You may be surprised at what you can offer. Our simple lives are alive and brave and the well-organized Gringo has forgotten to think about being human anymore. He lets someone else think about these things because he is too busy making the almighty DOLLAR, fighting other little people and going to the moon.

I remember once a wealthy woman talked with me about many things: just little, personal incidents in my life. Then she said, "I plan to use these in a play that am going to write, is it alright?" I said, "Sure." And now I think back of how many people have gone through the same thing over and over. If it were presented and the profits would go back to our people it would be fine, but it won't. She thrives on recognition, publicity and money. She wants no part of our personal problems. Writing a play about us will make her a great deal of money and this, my friends, is being EXPLOITED. It has happened to us many times in the past and will continue to happen until we put a stop to it. Let's stand up and speak for ourselves. Let's pull off those white masks and contribute of ourselves as we are.

Then there is the matter of art. In Mexico, they have murals and paintings all over showing the history and suffering of the people in their struggle for freedom. People can relate to this, they can BELONG. And what kind of art have we here? Galleries all over the place. Who is doing the painting? NOT US. And who is getting PAINTED? That's right, US. That's being EXPLOITED. Well, it is time that we started painting. Not for money and competition, but for LIFE. This is what we must do. I hope to see paintings all over showing the history of the peoples here. Showing that we BELONG here. Showing that we are the very breath and life of this Southwest. The struggle will not be easy. This kind of work you don't sell and you don't buy. The only real reward is in giving of OURSELVES to our PEOPLE. I still have a vision of seeing murals, showing pictures of the great Taos Pueblo Indian Jose Gonzales and Padre José Martínez marching through the Rio Grande Canyon on their way to invade

Santa Fe. I think I would like that commemoration more than the Kit Carson memorial.[1]

Despierten, hermanos, es tiempo de que luchemos por nuestro modo de vivir tal como somos. Tenemos que empezar a escribir nuestras vidas, nuestras ideas y nuestra historia. El anglo escribe libros y nos estudia por donde quiera. Es tiempo de poner la pluma y el lápiz en nuestra mano y trabajar.

En el arte es tiempo de tomar el pincel y pintar nuestras vidas, nuestras costumbres y nuestras historias. Estas cosas las hacemos para dar de nosotros mismos. Éstas son herencias para nuestros hijos. Esto no se vende a precios anglos, no se da ni se compran. Se contribuye a la humanidad. No tenemos qué competir o criticarnos unos a los otros, pero tenemos que unirnos en la causa de la humanidad. Despierten y fíjense en lo que sucede en el mundo, en nuestra nación, en nuestras comunidades y en nuestros propios hogares. Despierten, hermanos.[2]

January 29, 1969[3]

---

[1]During an 1837 rebellion in New Mexico, mestizos and Pueblo Indians rose up against the government in Santa Fe in opposition to new tax policies and the centralizing powers of the national government of Mexico. During this rebellion Jose Gonzales, a *genízaro*, a detribalized Indian, emerged as the rebels' leader and served as the rebel governor of New Mexico for a brief period of time. Although Father Antonio José Martínez, a popular parish priest in Taos, was an early sympathizer with the rebellion, when it began to promote anticlericalism, he opposed it. See Andrés Reséndez, *Changing National Identities at the Frontier, Texas and New Mexico, 1800-1850* (Cambridge: Cambridge UP, 2005) 177, 194-195; and Fray Angélico Chávez, *But Time and Chance, The Story of Padre Martínez of Taos, 1793-1867* (Santa Fe: Sunstone P, 1981), 51-58. Kit Carson was the legendary American frontiersman. He is called both an American hero for his courage in battle against the Native Americans, and an "Indian killer" for his viciousness. See R.C. Gordon-McCutchan, *Kit Carson Indian Fighter or Indian Killer?* (Colorado. UP of Colorado, 1996), x-xi.

[2]Wake up, my brothers and sisters; the time has come for us to fight exactly as we are for our way of life. We have to begin recording our lives, our ideas, and our history. Anglos write books and do research about us. The time has come for us to put pen and pencil in hand and begin to write.

[3]The newspaper banner in which this piece appeared was dated January 1968, but the first issue was in August 1968.

In the field of art, we must use the paintbrush to paint our lives, our customs and our stories. We do these things to give of ourselves. This is the inheritance to our children. These recordings are not sold, or given or bought per American standards. They are a contribution to humanity. We do not have to compete with one another or criticize each other, but we have to join together in the cause for humanity. Let's awaken and become aware of what is going on in the world, in our nation, in our communities and in our own homes. Wake up, my brothers and sisters!

Translated by Herminia S. Reyes.

16 de septiembre

¡Viva México, viva! ¡Vivan las Américas, vivan! ¡Viva Aztlán, viva!

El 16 de septiembre está aquí y hace que cada miembro de la familia de la raza sienta el removimiento de la sangre de nuestros antepasados, de nuestra historia de más de 25,000 años en esta bella y misteriosa tierra que llamamos Aztlán. Ésta, la tierra de las garzas, según la llamaba el nativoamericano de esta nación.

Una de las cosas de mucha importancia para nosotros es nuestra historia siendo que historia es el conocimiento de eventos de dicha tierra y de su gente. El 16 de septiembre de 1810 es importante para la raza porque es el día de la independencia en la historia de raza indígena, raza en México y raza en el suroeste, tan importante cuando sucedió como ahora mismo.

La historia del suroeste comenzó hace más de 25,000 años cuando andaban muchas tribus por aquí como los chichimecas, aztecas, apaches y muchas más. Ellos le llamaban a esta tierra Aztlán y nosotros bien sabemos que lo que dicen de que el indio era ignorante y salvaje es nada más que un cuento. Para desengañarnos solamente tenemos que ver las ruinas y pirámides en Nuevo y Viejo México y reconocer quiénes fueron nuestros antecesores.

Después vino el conquistador, la España y su Cortés. Esto fue al principio de la historia transplantada en América. Para mucha gente, con esto empieza la historia, en ser conquistados, a muchos les gusta conquistar, pero realmente un espejo nos dice que el español no vino con su mujer o muy pocas mujeres vinieron. No era puro —Oñate, que vino primero a Nuevo México ya venía con sus 120 familias mestizas. Así es que el conquistador fue conquistado y se convirtió en mestizo. La sangre del europeo y del nativo.

43

El 16 de septiembre es la celebración de lo que nombramos "El grito de Dolores". Este es el grito del sacerdote Miguel Hidalgo y Castilla que en 1810 hizo sonar las campanas de su iglesia y con su armada de cuatro indios tomó la causa del hombre nativo, del pobre, del hombre oprimido de México y les ayudó a pelear por su independencia de España.

La revuelta se extendió pero fue rápidamente controlada por las tropas del gobierno que finalmente ejecutaron a Hidalgo. Pero ese día, el 16 de septiembre, marcó el comienzo de la larga lucha que finalmente triunfó, y ha sido desde entonces celebrada en México como el día de su independencia de España.

Desde la independencia, México ha tenido que pelear con muchas naciones extranjeras, naciones que esperaban robarse la tierra tan rica y bella, el suroeste. Durante todo este tiempo era todavía parte de México. México ha sido invadido por Inglaterra, por Francia y su emperador, Maximiliano, y por la marina de los E.E.U.U. Según los documentos oficiales del congreso de los E.E.U.U., México fue invadido por las fuerzas de los E.E.U.U. *sin el permiso del congreso*, en trece ocasiones. La más reciente fue de 1918 a 1919.

En el momento exacto en que México estaba debilitado para la lucha, los E.E.U.U. atacaron a México y México perdió sus tierras. Se firmó el Tratado de Guadalupe Hidalgo. Su firmante, Santa Anna, había sido en esos tiempos desterrado a Cuba y por lo tanto no era representante del gobierno mexicano y de su pueblo. Así fue que el presente suroeste, antes territorio mexicano, pasó a ser territorio de los E.E.U.U. El plan de agresión e invasión triunfó y con un golpe de la pluma se hizo E.E.U.U. a la ciudadanía del suroeste, que era mexicana, con antecesores mexicanos. Sin embargo, lo que este golpe de pluma no nos sacó fue nuestra sangre indígena. La sangre permanece siendo indígena, sea una gota o sea entera. El golpe de pluma no nos robó nuestra cultura ni nuestra sangre.

Y con esta historia podemos preguntar, ¿por qué queremos celebrar el 16 de septiembre? ¿Aún siente fe el méxicoamericano, el chicano, él de la raza hacia México? Vemos a los ciudadanos de México como nuestros hermanos porque sabemos que en cultura somos la misma gente. Es respetar parte de nuestra herencia cultural. Es reconocer lo que es nuestro, la historia que nos pertenece tanto como la sangre que corre en nuestras venas. Sabemos que somos la misma gente y que nos tenemos respeto cultural el uno al otro.

Sin embargo, porque es verdad esto, no quiere decir que reconoceríamos al presidente de México como el nuestro. Al mirar la historia de los dos países vemos a este país cometer error sobre error en que nunca respetó el Tratado de Guadalupe Hidalgo, y todavía siguen con insulto sobre insulto en acciones tales como el Chamizal, cuando los E.E.U.U. dieron a México un puñado de tierra, 600 acres, en pos de generosidad y buena voluntad.

Además, ese mismo año en agosto, Díaz Ordaz y Richard Nixon se juntaron en Puerto Vallarta y los dos presidentes llegaron a un acuerdo sobre un tratado para RESOLVER TODAS LAS DISPUTAS TERRITORIALES PRESENTES y futuras. Otra vez aquí los E.E.U.U. siguen tratando desesperadamente de calmar su conciencia y legalizar su robo de tierra —tratando de poner firma sobre firma.

El hecho de que Díaz Ordaz se encontró con Nixon en San Diego también es otro asunto. Cuando Díaz Ordaz anunció a su congreso que visitaría este país, recibieron el anuncio con silencio completo, mostrando así su desaprobación que el presidente se reuniera con Nixon. Irónicamente, al mismo tiempo de la visita, 10,000 chicanos en una reunión pacífica recibían gas [lacrimoso] y golpes de parte de la policía.

El 16 de septiembre ahora tiene un nuevo significado para el mestizo. Tiene un nuevo símbolo en nuestra historia; nos enseña una nueva crisis, con la Moratoria del Chicano que vimos en nuestras televisiones o allá mismo, la violencia y el derrame de sangre de nuestros hombres, mujeres y niños al ser golpeados y atacados. Cada uno de nosotros sentimos los golpes al ver a nuestra gente y al opresor tan claramente y tan abusivo, las máscaras, los uniformes, las pistolas aún están en nuestras mentes.

Ésta fue una demostración pacífica y en el pasado hubo en Los Ángeles, 5,000 chicanos que marcharon pacíficamente. Pero esta vez había violencia en la mente de los policías. 500 policías esperaban, y si los manifestantes no provocaban la violencia, los poderes estaban preparados para hacerlo y lo hicieron.

Sin embargo, raza, no veamos esto como la primera violencia a nuestra gente, no pensemos que la violencia es algo nuevo a esta tierra y a la raza. Recordemos que esta tierra en la que vivimos fue colonizada con violencia, de España y del gringo. Nosotros hemos, como un pueblo, sufrido violencia espiritual, hemos sufrido violencia política, hemos sufrido violencia económica y hemos sufrido violencia social y ahora estamos luchando la batalla de VIOLENCIA CULTURAL. La sangre del hombre indígena de las Américas aún está húmeda sobre la tierra del suroeste; siempre ha estado allí la violencia, y con la violencia policíaca en Los Ángeles, otra vez nos recuerda que nuestra sangre está fresca sobre la tierra del suroeste.

¡VIVA MÉXICO, VIVAN LAS AMÉRICAS, VIVA AZTLÁN!

16 de septiembre de 1970

The 16th of September

¡Viva México, Viva! ¡Vivan Las Américas, Vivan! ¡Viva Aztlán, Viva!

The 16th of September is here and every member of the Familia de la Raza feels the call of our ancient blood, the call of our ancestry, the call of our history, the call of over 25,000 years on this mysterious and beautiful land we again call Aztlán, la tierra de las garzas, the land of the heron, as the Native-Americans called our nation.

One of the important things to us is history, for history is the knowledge of past events of a land and its people. Thus the 16th of September, 1810, is important to Raza, as it is a very important day of independence in the history of Raza everywhere; Raza in Mexico and Raza in the Southwest. It was important when it happened and is important to us today. The history of the Southwest started over 25,000 years ago and we know that this land was once roamed by Chichimecs, Aztecs, Apaches and many other tribes. They called this land Aztlán and we know that for the Native American to be called "savage" is like an old wives' tale. We have but to look at the ruins and pyramids in New Mexico as well as those in Mexico to know our ancestors. Aside from being Aztlán, this land was also called Mexitli, which means Mexico.

Then came the colonizer, Spain and its Cortez. This was the era of the conquistador and this is often glamorized in books, as if it were the beginning of the history of humanity on this continent. Actually, it is the beginning of European history in America. After all, everybody likes to conquer somebody. However, the conquistador conquered and was conquered; he did not remain pure bred for he brought few women with him from Spain. He blended in with the Indian. From this we have the Mestizo Raza, a mixture of Spanish and Indian blood.

The 16ᵗʰ of September is the celebration of what we call El Grito de Dolores. This was the cry of the priest Miguel Hidalgo y Costilla in 1810, when he rang the bells of his church and, with his "army" of four Indians, took up the struggle of the indigenous, the poor, the oppressed peoples of Mexico to gain independence from Spain. The uprising spread but was soon put down by government troops and Hidalgo was executed. But that day, September 16, marked the beginning of a long fight that was finally successful, and it has always been celebrated as Mexico's day of independence from Spain.[1]

Since independence, Mexico has had to fight many vulture nations that waited to pounce on it for the land that was so rich. The Southwest at this time was still Mexico. Mexico has had on its soil the British, the French with their emperor Maximiliano, plus the U.S. Marines. As a matter of fact, according to the U.S. Congressional Record (see *El Grito del Norte*, Aug. 29, 1970), Mexico was invaded by the United States armed forces *without congressional approval* 13 times.[2] This happened as late as 1918-19, when in August of that year Mexican and American troops fought at Nogales.

When Mexico was weak and powerless to fight off invaders, the U.S.A. stepped in with its "manifest destiny" and the land rush was on under a plan of aggression and invasion with careful planning and

---

[1] Mexico finally achieved independence in 1821.

[2] In 1969, Republican Senator Everett Dirksen of Illinois entered into the Congressional Record a list of U.S. military actions abroad, including 13 separate instances of aggression against Mexico, specifically, in 1806, 1836, 1842, 1844, 1846-48, 1859, 1866, 1870, 1873, 1876, 1913, 1914-17, and 1918-19. Dirksen's list was extensive even though it excluded congressionally approved wars and some of the Indian wars. As *El Grito del Norte* had noted the previous month upon publishing a facsimile of Dirksen's list as it appeared in the Congressional Record, Dirksen's intention was "to show that invasions by presidential order were a traditional part of the American Way." See *El Grito del Norte*, 29 August 1970, 6-7, and U.S. Congress, Senate, "Use of U.S. Armed Forces in Foreign Countries in Instances of Use of U.S. Armed Forces Abroad, 1978-1945," *Congressional Record* 115, no. 103 (June 23, 1969).

timing.[3] After much fighting and bloodshed came the settlement: the Treaty of Guadalupe Hidalgo was signed in 1848 by Santa Anna, who had been in exile in Cuba and was not representative of the Mexican government or the Mexican people.[4] Thus, what was Mexico—what is the Southwest then and now—became part of the U.S.A. With a stroke of the pen the U.S. stole the Southwest from Mexico and with this same stroke of the pen acknowledged that we, that people of the Southwest, are all of Mexican descent, of Mexican heritage. For that stroke of the pen cannot drain the Indian blood from within us, whether it be just a drop or whether it be pure. That stroke of the pen cannot erase our blood.

We can ask, why do we wish to celebrate the 16th of September? Does the Raza, the Mexican-American, the Chicano still pay allegiance to Mexico?

---

[3] John L. O'Sullivan, a New York City editor, coined the term "manifest destiny." In mid-1845, he stated that it was American's "manifest destiny to overspread the continent." That same year, the United States annexed the Republic of Texas as a state of the Union. American immigrants to Texas had proclaimed their independence from Mexico in 1836. In an attempt to provoke a war with Mexico, U.S. President James K. Polk in 1845 ordered American troops into territory disputed between Mexico and Texas and then, in 1846, to the banks of the Rio Grande itself. An American blockade of Mexican troops in Matamoros, across the river, followed. When Mexican troops fired upon American soldiers, Polk delivered a war message to the U.S Congress in which he declared that Mexicans had "shed American blood on American soil." The vote for war was 174-14 in the House of Representatives and 40-2 in the Senate. Walter LaFeber, *The American Age: United States Foreign Policy at Home and Abroad*, 2nd ed. (New York: W.W. Norton, 1994) 94-95, 117. See also Polk's War Message, http://historicaltextarchive.com/sections.php?op=view article&artid=219, accessed August 20, 2004.

[4] During Antonio López de Santa Anna's dramatic career in Mexican politics he gained and lost the presidency eleven times and was exiled five times. In June 1845, having alienated Congress and much of the army, Santa Anna's sixth presidency ended with his exile to Havana, Cuba, where he stayed until September 1846. At this time U.S. officials, whose country was at war with Mexico, secretly facilitated Santa Anna's return to Mexico in hopes that he would agree to cede significant portions of Mexican territory. In September and October 1847, Santa Anna once again lost the presidency and control over the army. The war with the United States ended in January 1848 and the Treaty of Guadalupe Hidalgo was signed on February 2 by other Mexican officials; in April, Santa Anna withdrew to Jamaica, and then to Colombia. See Robert L. Scheina, *Santa Anna: A Curse Upon Mexico*, (Washington, D.C.: Brassey's, Inc., 2002), ix-xii, 45-50, 74.

To celebrate September 16 is to see Mexico's people as blood brothers, for we know we are culturally the same people. It is to respect part of our cultural inheritance. It is to recognize what is ours, the history that belongs to us like the very blood that runs in our veins. We know that we are the same people and have cultural respect for each other. However, this does not mean that we would recognize Mexico's president as ours. When we celebrate the 16th of September, we are not showing our allegiance to the government of Mexico, but to the people of Mexico, who are our brothers and sisters in culture and blood.

As we look at the history of the two countries, we see the U.S. making blunder on top of blunder as it failed to honor the Treaty of Guadalupe Hidalgo. The U.S. also keeps adding insult to insult by such actions as the return of the Chamizal in 1968, whereby the U.S. gave Mexico a small strip of land—600 acres—as a gesture of generosity and good will on the part of the U.S. of A.[5] To the Mexican of the U.S., this was just a gesture of pouring salt on the wound, for Mexico lost over half its land to the U.S.

Then, last month, Díaz Ordaz and Richard Nixon met at Puerto Vallarta and the two presidents reached agreement on a *treaty* to SETTLE ALL PRESENT AND FUTURE TERRITORIAL DISPUTES. Here again, the U.S.A. is till trying desperately to ease its conscience and legalize its land robbery, trying to get signature upon signature.

Again last month, Díaz Ordaz came to the U.S. and met with Nixon at a big banquet in San Diego. When Ordaz told the congress of Mexi-

---

[5] For nearly 100 years, both the United States and Mexico claimed the same 600 acres of land in El Paso called the Chamizal. The dispute arose because the Rio Grande River had shifted south since the 1848 signing of the Treaty of Guadalupe Hidalgo, which ended the U.S.-Mexican War. In 1963, the two nations ratified a treaty that granted the majority of the disputed territory to Mexico. In December 1968, U.S. President Lyndon B. Johnson and Gustavo Díaz Ordaz, the president of Mexico, met in El Paso to take the last step in ending the Chamizal dispute: they opened a dam which allowed the river to flow along a newly completed river channel built in accordance with the 1963 agreement. See "Chamizal Dispute," *The Handbook of Texas Online*, Texas State Historical Association, http://www.tsha.utexas.edu/handbook/online/news.html, accessed August 19, 2004. Also see "Lyndon Johnson, Remarks in El Paso at the Inauguration of the New River Channel Completing the Chamizal Boundary Change," http://www.presidency.ucsb.edu/site/docs/pppus.php?admin =036&year=1968&id=623, accessed August 19, 2004.

co that he was going to this meeting, the congressmen greeted his announcement with dead silence—showing their disapproval. And the fact that the San Diego meeting took place just when thousands of Chicanos were being tear-gassed and beaten at a peace rally in nearby Los Angeles is worse than ironic. The President of the U.S. and the President of Mexico had an elegant meal together when the corpses of Mexicans killed by U.S. police were barely cold.[6]

The 16th of September now has a new meaning to the Mestizo because of what happened in Los Angeles. Some of us were there. Others of us saw it on TV—the violence and bloodshed committed against our men, women and children as they were beaten and tear-gassed during a peaceful demonstration. All of us felt the blows, many of us cried to see our people hurt. The oppressor with his masks, uniforms, guns and guns, is still a clear image in our minds. The struggle which began on September 16, 1810, is still going on.

Let us not see the violence in Los Angeles as the first violence against our people. Let us not think that violence is something that is new to this land. Let us remember that this land upon which we live was colonized through violence, by Spain and again by the Gringo. We have as a people suffered spiritual violence, we have suffered political violence, we have suffered economic violence and we have suffered social violence and we are now fighting the battle against CULTURAL VIO- LENCE.

The blood of the indigenous human beings of the Americas is still damp on the land of the Southwest. The violence has always been there. With the police riot in Los Angeles, with the beating of our men, women and children, our blood is again fresh on the soil of the Southwest.

¡VIVA MÉXICO, VIVAN LAS AMÉRICAS, VIVA AZTLÁN!

September 16, 1970

---

[6] U.S. President Richard Nixon and Mexican President Gustavo Díaz Ordaz met in Puerto Vallarta on August 20, 1970 to discuss drug trafficking and border disputes between the two countries, including disputes resulting from the fact that the river-banks of the Rio Grande continued to shift. Nixon told reporters that the U.S.-Mexican border was "not a wall that divides us, but a bridge of friendship which unites us," but the feel-good rhetoric of the meeting was at odds with events in Los

Angeles on August 31, when police broke up an anti-war rally, a decision that ultimately cost three people their lives and prompted local Mexican Americans to demand that Díaz Ordaz cancel his upcoming visit to San Diego. Several articles in the *New York Times* trace these events. See Robert B. Semple, Jr., "Nixon, Diaz Ordaz Agree on Border," *New York Times* (August 21, 1970), 1; "U.S. Inquiry Urged for a Riot Victim," *New York Times* (September 1, 1970), 23; and Robert B. Semple, Jr., "Nixon Is Host to the President of Mexico in California," *New York Times* (September 4, 1970), 2. These articles were accessed on the world wide web on August 12, 2004 through ProQuest Historical Newspapers, *The New York Times*, 1857-Current file.

La Santa Tierra

Man comes/man lives/man passes on through earth/through time/man forgets/but the earth/the land/remains/the earth/the land/knows.

Times passes: Thanksgiving, Christmas, New Year's; it could be the cold that is in the air, the season, the coming of winter, the passing of fall. Perhaps it is the drawing to the end of the year and the birth of the new year that tends to remind us of the passage of time. It is healthful, necessary and beneficial for us to sit and meditate about ourselves, our families, our people: La Raza. We must give ourselves time to think, to stop and think of the passing of time; the making of history. Our history is important, for it shows us the present as the product of the past and the key to the future.

We can all remember some of the things that our viejitos and viejitas taught us, the things they showed us. I remember well the things that my father taught in regard to the earth, land and people. Many would say that it was the teaching of daydreams but you know, I now realize it was the teaching of humanity, the teaching of life. For in the wisdom of our viejitos we learned about human beings and the universe: we learned about the earth, the land, and we called it; la madre tierra; la santa tierra; la tierra sagrada (the mother earth, the holy earth, the sacred earth). Our viejitos taught us about nature and the creatures of the earth. We would sit for hours and study the sky, its vastness and the cloud formations that traveled and played games as they went by. We would study the birds and we learned the flow of the air currents, how the birds would ride the currents for miles and miles.

DAYDREAMS? No, mi Raza; let us never for an instant dismiss this beauty as only daydreams. We must learn to realize that these things are an important part of reality; of what life is made of. For it is in this

53

knowledge of the earth that we have a good balance of nature and the function of human beings. It is in this that we find a place for ourselves; it is in this that we know what we are.

I recall how I learned about mother earth. I would ask why it was called a mother and I was told that a female is productive of life and the male is not, therefore because the earth gives life to all living things, it is female. We learned that the earth gives life and feeds us. Thus, we learned to respect the food on our table and we learned to respect and love the laborer and the campesino. These are a special people, special, for they work close to the earth, to nature. And special for they harvest the products that go on our tables and into our bodies to be processed and return to the earth. (Outhouses are really very sensible when we think of ecology).

These teachings, which have been handed down to us, are very important for it is here that we see the failings of the Gringo society and his education system. It fails because in all of its technology it does not make a place for HUMANS in relation to NATURE. This is what we mean when we speak of the dangers of the Mechanized Man and of technology in the method the Gringo teaches. You see, we as people, with all of our beautiful daydreams (philosophies) know that it is through them that we respect and live in harmony with nature. And this is absolutely necessary for us to know if people are to exist at all because we are at the mercy of nature. We should live within the balance of nature.

We don't say that there is anything wrong with machines and technology. On the contrary, we need technicians in all fields. However, realizing that 80% of the Gringo society is reported to be neurotic and 50% of the people are hypochondriacs, we can realize that in the teachings of our viejitos we have the cultural beliefs necessary for the survival of people. We seek to apply and conserve our knowledge, in our own way. This is why Chicanos are making a stand for cultural survival.

One example of applying our knowledge: I recall the first time that I saw a weather map in a weather tower and I immediately remembered the birds riding the air currents, and you know what? My father told me about air currents and weather forecasting every bit as well as the weather man with all his maps. Our children should learn this too.

Now as we study about the earth, it is interesting to realize that our viejitos said that the physical make-up of the human body had a close relation to the earth. Nonsense? No, not long ago I read where the earth is composed of 2/3 water and, that's right, the human body is also composed of 2/3 water.[1] We learned from our viejitos of the balance of nature; that we should not kill birds, for they ate insects. That humans breath oxygen into the body and exhale carbon dioxide. That the plants use carbon dioxide and give off oxygen for us to breathe. That is a balance of nature; to know how all living things complement and harmonize with each other. That is how all things live from the earth.

These DAYDREAMS are the things that our viejitos knew, by instinct and by experience. These are the things that we must recall, respect and learn to apply. For this knowledge I have a special place in my heart for the viejitos de nuestra raza, I have a very special place for our elders as I recall going to school to get schooling. We must learn, we must study, but to memorize facts and not be able to apply them; to learn and not be able to relate to the realities of life; is criminal. It's like being castrated. Our real education, our realities and philosophies, come from our viejitos. We learn from them, we learn to apply our schooling. Our viejitos are our knowledge and we bury it every time we bury one of our people.

My viejitos never went to school, they were self-taught. Many of us thought we were cheated by not having the opportunity to go to college. But if we are striving to be knowledgeable people we must read, listen, apply and learn everyday of our lives for learning never stops. Perhaps we can begin by watching the birds and the clouds. We may be fortunate that we have been spared some of the higher education of the Gringo value system; the brainwashing of the Gringo non-thinking machines.

We can well understand why to a people who are capable of living in harmony with nature, it is very difficult to understand the concept of

---

[1]Vasquez was correct about the similarity in ratios even if her estimation was low. Seventy-five percent of the earth's surface is covered by water, while the human body is composed of 70 percent water. See Michael A. Seeds, *The Solar System 3rd ed.* (United States: Thomson Brooks/Cole, 2003), 435; and British Museum of Nation History, *Human Biology: An Exhibition of Ourselves* (Cambridge: Cambridge UP, 1977), 80. The other percentage figures in the column meanwhile were clearly the product of artistic license.

ownership and possession of land. We can understand what stirs in us when we talk of the land in New Mexico. And even further we can understand why there would be conflict over the control of land. We know why the controlling Gringo is playing with fire when he maneuvers politically with lands in the Southwest. The indigenous concepts of Aztlán still live here. The concepts of humanity and nature are very much part of everyday living here. If there is a whole truth, if there is an answer to the problems of the Gringos and their sick society, it must come from the people who have been able to endure for thousands of years.

La Raza is a Mestizo nation. Our Spanish blood predates 300 years in Las Americas; our Indian blood predates 25,000 years and we are the Mestizo nation of Aztlán, the nation of mixed bloods. In realizing this, we come home to our true selves, to our indigenous being, to our Indian family ties. We would place our life and fate there, alongside our Indian brothers and sisters, as a comrade nation. We cannot go the Gringo way. We choose; we go the way of the land; the way of the earth; the way of the water; the way of the wind; the way of AZTLÁN.

El espacio;
>El universo;
>>El mundo;
>>>la tierra es la madre de todo lo que vive
Da vida y alimento;
>>>da espíritu y conciencia;
El hombre, el ser humano;
>>>en cambio;
No es más que un grano de polvo en la historia del tiempo.[2]

December 7, 1970

---

[2]Space;
The universe;
The world;
The earth, is the mother of all living things
It gives life and nourishment;
It gives spirit and conscience;
Man, the human being;
In contrast;
Is but a grain of dust in the history of time.
Translated by Herminia S. Reyes.

La Voz de Nuestra Cultura I
Por doña Faustina

Es muy interesante saber de los remedios de nuestra gente. Hay que fijarnos que cuando llegó Cortés a México no halló gente salvaje e ignorante como nos quiere pintar el gabacho. Entre la raza hay remedios que existen y que son tan saludables como la medicina moderna. Posiblemente hasta más saludable con eso que entre nosotros no se acostumbraba a usar el cuchillo para cortarnos tanto como lo acostumbran los doctores ahora.

Estas medicinas indias y de la raza —que también somos parte indio, ¿verdad?— son lo que nombramos medicinas naturales. Esto quiere decir que las medicinas naturales se pueden explicar como el azúcar. El azúcar que compramos es dulce artificial y la miel de colmena es dulce también, pero dulce natural hecha por insectos con el proceso de las flores y así se produce la miel.

Así también es la medicina de nuestra cultura. Cuando tomamos alguna hierba, ayuda al cuerpo a ajustarse a su ritmo natural. Esto es lo que nosotros le decimos medicina natural. Las medicinas en píldoras que se venden son hechas de productos químicos artificiales y hechas en un laboratorio. Y entre nosotros tomamos remedios naturales, un ejemplo es el polvo de víbora, que aunque no sea hierba, es animal y también medicina natural.

La víbora y el polvo de víbora son unas de las cosas más saludables y se usan para curar muchas enfermedades, precisamente enfermedades de la sangre. Muchos granos y llagas son resultado de la sangre impura.

En la Plaza Puruándiro, que está en el estado de Michoacán en México, estaba un hombre que tenía una enfermedad de llagas. Era una enfermedad así como la lepra que deformaba la apariencia del cuerpo también. Este hombre tenía llagas por sus piernas, brazos y la cara. Después de verse tan asqueroso, él mismo dijo, —Yo creo que mis hijos me han de tener asco, por como me veo. Ya me voy a la sierra mejor que estar aquí, voy a morirme.

Como él conocía el terreno bien, conocía una cueva donde pensaba irse a morir. Se había llevado un cántaro grande, del cual tomaba agua, y una cazuela chiquita para cocer lo poco que hallara de hierbas y animales para comer.

Esto fue en la primavera y él sobrevivió comiendo tunas y raíces de camote y lo que había. Y todos los días tomaba agua del cántaro que había llenado de agua en un arroyo.

Pasó el tiempo y el señor no se moría, sino que hasta se sentía mejor y empezó a ver que sus llagas estaban desapareciendo. Entre más y más, se miraba mejor.

Durante este tiempo la familia lo hacía perdido, y no sabían de él. Pensaban que se había muerto por allá lejos. Y el hombre al fin de tener tiempo en su cueva se sentía más y más aliviado y dijo al fin, —Ya me alivié, pienso que será la voluntad de Dios que siga viviendo bien y sano. Me voy con mi familia.

Con esto, agarró su cazuela y vació su cántaro de agua para irse. Al vaciar el cántaro, cayó un esqueleto de víbora. Se supone que la víbora se había ahogado en el agua y se deshizo con el tiempo y el hombre al tomar agua del cántaro todos los días realmente se estaba tomando su propia medicina y alimento todos los días. A este hombre lo conocí yo.

El polvo de víbora se puede comprar en México por donde quiera y es saludable para los granos, la mala sangre, las úlceras del estómago. Purifican la sangre. Estos [los polvos] se hacen de las víboras. Se le cortan cuatro dedos (medida antigua) de la cabeza y cuatro dedos de la cola y lo de en medio se seca y se tuesta en el cocedor y se muele.[1]

7 de diciembre de 1970

---

[1]It is very interesting to know about the medicinal remedies used by our people. We must remember that when Cortez arrived in Mexico, he did not find savage or ignorant people as the *gabacho* (slang word for Anglo) would like us to believe. Among the Raza there are remedies that exist which are just as healthy as modern medicine.

It is possible that they are even healthier being that among us we were not in the habit of using the knife to cut ourselves as much as the doctors now.

These Indian medicines, and of the Raza too, are what we refer to as natural medicine. This means that natural medicine can be explained like sugar. The sugar that we buy is artificial, although the honey from the honeycomb is sweet too, but a natural sweet because it comes from the insects and flowers that produce the honey.

So, likewise is the medicine from our culture. When we take some herbs it helps the body adjust to its natural rhythm. This is what we refer to as natural medicine. Medicine in pill form that is sold is made from artificial chemical ingredients that are made in a laboratory. Among us, we take natural medicine, an example being snake powder, that even though it is not an herb, it comes from an animal and is also a natural medicine.

The snake and the snake powder are some of the healthiest things and they are used to cure many illnesses, especially those illnesses relating to the blood. Many pimples and sores are a result of impure blood.

In the Plaza Puruándiro, in the state of Michoacan, Mexico, there was a man who was suffering from sores on his body. It was an illness similar to leprosy that deformed the appearance of the body. This man had sores on his legs, arms and face. After seeing how disgusting he looked, he said, "I think that my children find me so repulsive that it is better if I go live in the mountains than stay here. I'll die there."

This man knew the area well, he knew where there was a cave that he thought would be his final resting place. He took a big water jar with him and a small pot to cook the herbs and animals.

This happened in the spring and he was able to live on prickly pears and the roots from sweet potatoes and whatever else he found. Everyday he drank water from the water jar that he had filled from the arroyo.

Time went by and the man did not die. Instead he felt better and he started noticing that the sores were disappearing. As more time went by, he looked better.

During the time that he was away, his family thought that they had lost him since they had no news from him. They thought that he had died far away from them. After having spent some time in the cave, the man saw that he was getting better and better and said, "I am well and I believe that it is the will of God for me to continue living, well and healthy. I am going back to my family."

He picked up the small pot and then he emptied the water jar. Upon emptying the water jar, a skeleton of a snake fell out. We assume that the snake had drowned in the jar filled with water and that it had disintegrated over time and that when the man drank water from the jar everyday that he was actually drinking its own medicine and nourishment. I knew this man.

Snake powder can be bought anywhere in Mexico and is used to treat pimples, unhealthy blood, stomach ulcers. It purifies the blood. It is made from snakes. The snake is cut four fingers from the head (an ancient measurement) and four fingers from the tail. The snake is set to dry, and then it is toasted in the oven and then ground into powder.

Translated by Herminia S. Reyes.

La Voz de Nuestra Cultura II
Por la consciencia de doña Faustina

En los conceptos medicinales de nuestra raza podemos fijarnos que estos conceptos sobre la función del cuerpo han estado con nosotros siglo tras siglo y viene siendo una herencia de la raza. Cuando tratamos con enfermedades, realmente tratamos con las filosofías que vienen del pensamiento del hombre indígena de las Américas, el mero indio.

El pensamiento cultural y tradicional de la raza viene siendo de seres humanos que viven en armonía con la naturaleza. Esta armonía viene siendo salud total y cumplimiento en facultades físicas, mentales y espirituales. Eso es el ciclo de la vida completa del ser humano.

Muchos de nosotros sabemos cómo curarnos unos a los otros. En nuestras familias hay casi siempre algún miembro que sabe curar cosas simples. Un ejemplo es "El empacho". También hay que reconocer que hay gente que porque pueden estudiar para ser doctores. Cierto que de a veces van al doctor de más y no se hacen la lucha y confían mucho en el doctor. Cuando ponemos mucha fe en el doctor perdemos mucho conocimiento de los conceptos de nuestra herencia cultural.

Esto no quiere decir que los doctores no sirven, pero más bien que si hay unas enfermedades que los doctores no conocen, ni pueden curar. Donde nosotros tenemos curaciones naturales, el doctor usa muchas drogas y confía mucho en el uso del cuchillo . . . operan demasiado.

Todos hemos oído y sabemos del empacho, ¿verdad? Muchos curamos a nuestras propias criaturas y nosotros mismos unos a los otros. El empacho viene siendo una enfermedad del estómago —realmente indigestión. Hay muchos grados de gravedad. Hay empacho que no es muy viejo, que se cura de una sobada y una purga pero también hay empacho que es ya de años y muchas veces se ha dejado a la desidia, y este es un poco más difícil.

Los métodos de curar el empacho pueden ser varios pero tienen básicamente el mismo concepto. El empacho viene de comida que no se digiere correctamente y se pega en las tripas del estómago. A veces es tan extremo el caso de empacho que los doctores, que no lo saben curar, operan a la persona enferma y le sacan pedazos de las tripas del estómago. Esto es necesario porque dejándose mucho tiempo se puede hacer vieja la enfermedad y se forma cáncer.

Para curar el empacho primero se soban las corvas. En sobarse las corvas se pueden sentir las bolitas colocadas en las corvas en relación con el lugar donde se encuentra el empacho en el estómago. Se soban las corvas hasta que ya no se sienten esas bolas, se corren para abajo, y se pueden sobar los pies también.

Segundo, se soba el estómago. Esto se soba con cuidado porque es posible que un empacho retaque la tripa llamada apéndice. Un apéndice infectado nunca se soba. Eso requiere doctor. El estómago está colocado más alto y no se necesita tener miedo de sobarlo. Se soba bastante para que pase la comida en curso natural. Cuando se soba el estómago, siente mucho removimiento el enfermo y se pueden sentir las bolas de comida que se despegan de las tripas y siguen su curso.

El último paso es jalar el espinazo. El espinazo es muy importante. Primero se soba la columna de arriba para abajo, se golpea, con una mano puesta al plano y otra en puño. Después de esto se pellizca y se jala. Lo importante al jalarse es que tiene que tronar. Se pellizca con las dos manos y se jala de repente, sin miedo. Cuando truena es buena señal que se aflojó el empacho y que va a pasar. Posiblemente truena dos, tres veces. Entre más veces, mejor.

¡Y ya se curó! Muchas personas se levantan buenas y sanas, otras requieren una purga, pero el resultado es igual, pasan aquello que estaba pegado en las tripas.

Hay que reconocer que unos doctores sí saben curar el empacho y unos creen y entienden el concepto. Lo importante es reconocer "la cura". Nosotros usamos mucho "Las sobadas". Las sobadas aflojan los nervios y nos permiten descansar totalmente. La curación del empacho tiene un contacto que es saludable física y mentalmente. Es una fuerza que se da de humano a humano; una fe espiritual, que es una fuerza tremenda, una fuerza humana. Así es que el alivio de empacho como de algunas otras enfermedades es un alivio total que ayuda a la función natural.[1]

5 de junio de 1971

---

[1]We need to be aware that the medicinal concepts about the function(s) of our bodies have been with us, our Raza, and century after century have become part of our heritage. When we deal with illness, we really deal with the philosophy, the way of thinking that comes from the indigenous man of the Americas, the Indian.

The way of thinking, both cultural and traditional of the Raza, comes from human beings that live in harmony with nature. This harmony comes from all-around health and fulfillment of physical, mental and spiritual abilities. That is the complete cycle of the human being.

Many of us know how to heal one another. In our families there is always someone that can heal simple things. One example is the *empacho*. We must also recognize that many become doctors because they have the economic means. Of course, many people go to the doctor very often and they don't put forth any effort to heal themselves, instead they confide in the doctor. When we rely heavily on the doctor we forget about what we already know about healing, about our cultural heritage.

This is not to say that doctors aren't any good, however, there are many illnesses that doctors aren't familiar with nor can they heal them. We have many natural ways of healing many things; doctors use many drugs and rely on the use of the surgeon's knife . . . they operate too much.

We have all heard and know about the *empacho*, right? Many of us heal our children, ourselves and/or one another. The *empacho* is in reality an illness of the stomach—really indigestion. There are many levels of severity. There are *empachos* that are not old and they are healed by a rub down and a laxative, but there are also *empachos* that are many years old and have been neglected and this is more difficult to heal.

There may be many methods of healing the *empacho*, however, all of them have the basic concepts. The *empacho* is a result of food that is not digested correctly. The food attaches itself to the stomach's intestines. At times, the case is so extreme that doctors do not know how to treat it; they operate on the sick person and they remove part of the intestines. This is necessary because if left for a long time, the illness can become old and cancer may form.

To heal the *empacho*, the backs of the knees need to be rubbed down first. Upon rubbing down the backs of the knees, the lumps in the back of the knees are felt and they show the relation to where the *empacho* is in the stomach. The backs of the knees are rubbed down until the lumps disappear. The rubbing may extend down the legs and to the feet.

Next, the stomach is rubbed down. This must be done very carefully, because it is possible for the *empacho* to fill the duct known as the appendix. An infected appendix is never massaged. This requires a doctor. The stomach is located higher up and there should never be any fear of massaging it. It is massaged a lot to allow the food to follow its natural course. When the stomach is massaged, the sick person may feel a lot of movement and he/she may feel the lumps of food being detached from the intestines and now they are able to continue their course.

The last step is to pull the spine. The spine is very important. First the spinal column is massaged from top to bottom; the tapping of the spine begins with a fist over the hand that was placed over the spine. After this, it is pinched and pulled. The important thing about pulling the skin is that it must pop. It is pinched with both hands and pulled suddenly without fear. When it pops, it is a good indication that the *empacho* has loosened or separated and will then pass. It is possible to pop once, twice or three times. The more times the better.

And it's cured! Many persons will get up totally healed. Others will still require a laxative, but the result is the same, they will pass whatever was attached to the intestines.

We must recognize that there are some doctors who do not know how to treat the *empacho* and some believe that they understand the concept. The important thing is to recognize the treatment. We use the rubbing down, the massage a lot. The massages relieve the tension and allow us to rest totally. The treatment of the *empacho* is physically and mentally healthy. It is strength that is given from one human being to another; it is spiritual faith that is a tremendous strength, a human strength. So, the curing of the *empacho* like other illnesses is a total curing that helps in the natural function.

Translated by Herminia S. Reyes.

La Historia del Mestizo

Hoy en día oímos mucho de "El Chicano," "La Raza", "El Nuevo Chicano", "la Raza Cósmica". Y también algo sobre "El Movimiento". Y muchos nos ponemos a pensar, "¿qué es esto?" "¿Quién soy yo?" Y hasta nos miramos en el espejo y empezamos a pensar, "¿Cuál será mi raza?" "¿Cuál será mi gente?" "¿Quién seré yo?" "¿Cuál será mi historia?" Y con estas preguntas nos ponemos a pensar y a entender de dónde vienen nuestras raíces y así se descubre la historia del mestizo. Y entendemos que nuestra historia realmente no la hemos estudiado, tal vez por que no está escrita. Precisamente porque la historia del indio nunca ha sido escrita. Al sistema educativo presente se le hizo más fácil eliminarnos en total, y tal vez por eso nos hemos creído inferiores como se nos ha insinuado en la mente. Nuestra raza madre ha sido llamada salvaje, y nuestra raza padre, nuestra lengua, ha sido llamada inmigrante y extranjera. Y el mestizo del sudoeste que hizo por pelear por justicia, fue nombrado bandido, rebelde y nos han [calificado] como ciudadanos de segunda clase, en nuestra propia tierra.

Para el fin de estudiar nuestra historia, para que por fin sepamos quiénes somos tenemos que empezar con sacarnos estas rayas que dividen territorios y tanta telaraña de bordes de la mente, y pensar totalmente en términos de gente. El indio, que es la gente indígena de las Américas, es el nativo, el primer ciudadano de las Américas. Esta gente indígena cree que vino del oriente y que cruzó sobre la tira de tierra llamada Bering Straits, que unía a Rusia y Alaska. La última ola fue el Apache Wave, llegó a las Américas hace más de 25,000

---

[1] José Vasconcelos, the Mexican educator and writer, in his 1925 work, *La Raza Cósmica*, celebrated the racial mixture of Mexico. The term became popular again during the Chicano Movement.

años.[2] Así es que la conciencia y pensamiento del Indio son relativos al oriental.

Esta raza indígena vino a las Américas, caminó de Alaska hasta la "tierra del Fuego", la esquina del sur de la América del Sur. Durante estos 25,000 años hubo mucho movimiento entre el indio, que se movía en tribus de distinguidos nombres. Las tribus apache y azteca actualmente vienen siendo tribus hermanas. El grupo de tribus del norte de México y del sur del suroeste, se llamó "la chichimeca". Hay poca información exacta para saber cuál tribu estaba dónde, porque caminaron por todo el territorio de las Américas.

Poco a poco se asentaron muchas de las tribus y se dedicaron a la agricultura. Hicieron estudios astronómicos, matemáticos, filosóficos, etcétera. Hay que reconocer que esta fue una gente muy avanzada y civilizada. El territorio fue tratado como tierra que era de todos por igual, como el aire, el agua y lo que es del mundo, ¿verdad?

En 1519 llegaron los españoles a lo que ahora se llama México. Entraron por la costa y llegaron a Tenochtitlán, la gran ciudad de los aztecas. Hay que recordar que no traían mujeres ni vinieron príncipes o

---

[2] More recent linguistic and genetic evidence suggested otherwise. In 1987, Joseph Greenberg, a linguist, proposed that all the indigenous languages of the Americas could be divided into three main groups, Amerind, the largest group that covered 90 percent of all indigenous languages, Athabaskan or Na-Dene, only found in the southwestern United States and western Canada, and Eskimo-Aleut. While Apaches are Athabaskan speakers, Aztecs speak Nahuatl, which falls into the Amerind category. Based upon these linguistic differences, Greenberg further hypothesized that while speakers who fell into the Amerind category crossed the Bering land bridge probably about 15,000 to 20,000 years ago, Athabaskan speakers may have arrived 6,000 to 8,000 years ago by following the Pacific Rim coast. Although controversial at the time, the prevalence of a specific genetic marker called *M130* among Athabaskan speakers and its relative absence among other indigenous peoples of the Americas lent support to Greenberg's categorizations. See Joseph Greenberg, *Languages in the Americas* (Stanford: Stanford UP, 1987). A summation of these findings and much more was available in 2005 through a fascinating interactive website maintained by the National Geographic Society. Entitled "The Genographic Project," the website incorporated the latest scientific evidence to trace the history of human migrations over the past 60,000 years, including migrations to the Americas, https://www3.nationalgeographic.com/genographic/atlas.html, accessed October 17, 2005. Many thanks to Audrey Espinoza for her help in finding and analyzing this information.

lo que le nombramos sangre azul. Eran hombres exploradores, aventureros y fueron acompañados por sacerdotes. Así es que el español llegó y conquistó con los cañones, el caballo y la cruz cristiana. Con el español vino la conciencia y el pensamiento occidental, europeo. Llegó el español a las Américas hace 300 años. Relativamente poco tiempo comparado con los 25,000 del indio, ¿verdad?

Lo importante aquí es reconocer el nacimiento del mestizo. El español mató mucho del hombre indio y las mujeres y criaturas fueron marcadas con quemaduras en la cara. Cortés y sus hombres (que no querían pecar como hombres) declararon en la "ley de las Indias" que la raza india era humana, así pudieron bautizar a las mujeres y se casaron con ellas. Dentro de las primeras 20 mujeres se encontró doña Marina, de nombre Malintzín, y el español la hizo su esposa. Esto fue la conquista de la raza india cuando a la mujer se la tomó como propiedad, fue bautizada, nombrada con papeles y dominada por el español y tratada como traidora por el indio. Hoy mismo en México lo de Europa a veces se llama "Malintzismo".[3]

Vamos a ver de que cuando llegó el español a México se asombró de ver ciudades bellas. No entendía el calendario azteca (que realmente es una combinación de varios calendarios de diferentes tribus) que es tan antiguo y más exacto que el chino.[4] Y además de eso es tan correcto que se puede usar hoy mismo. El español vio que el indio vivía en armonía humana y en relación con el universo y la naturaleza. Sentía los cambios de luna, la fuerza del sol y respetaba y reconocía la tierra, que hasta hoy todavía lo hacemos mucho, ¿verdad? El indio no era tonto, tenía sus marquetas y mucha comida que no se conocía en Europa. Piñas, cacao, frijol, precisamente el maíz, la papa, el camote, mucha comida que comemos ahora, viene siendo comida del indio de las Américas. Que nunca pensemos que el europeo nos vino a salvar, más bien llegó con hambre y aquí vivía bien. Se llenó de comida, oro y plata. También entre

---

[3] More commonly the term is Malinchismo after another of Doña Marina's names, la Malinche.

[4] The Aztec Calendar was superior to any of the calendars used by Julius Caesar of Cleopatra, and 103 years older than the Gregorian Calendar. It consisted of 18 months with 20 days and an additional five sacrificial days every year making 265 days a year. Francisco González Dávila, *Ancient Cultures of Mexico: The Aztec Calendar* (Mexico: Museo Nacional de Antropología 1969), 36-37.

el indio tenemos nuestros conceptos de la vida que son tan válidos como la literatura europea. Tenemos en México hoy mismo *El libro de Los Libros de Chilam Balám* y el *Popul Vuh* que son tan válidos como la Biblia,[5] son libros de consejos. Y los conceptos del hopi, del navajo, del apache y de otros tribus tienen básicamente creencias relativas a las del azteca.

La tribu azteca es muy conocida precisamente porque fue la tribu que estaba en poder al llegar el español, pero realmente había varias tribus grandes en México en ese tiempo y lo reconocemos por eso que de allí nació el mestizo. Y tenemos que fijarnos que Juan de Oñate que vino a Nuevo México en 1598, ya era sobrino de Moctezuma, y ya tenía sangre indiada, y su esposa doña Isabel Tolosa Cortés Moctezuma, era bisnieta de Moctezuma y también la nieta de Cortés.[6] Así es que hay que comprender que el español con su cultura, lengua y pensamiento, conquistó y fue conquistado y el europeo entró a las Américas por México, [y así] nació el mestizo y entró al sudoeste del sur de México. Y este territorio se declaró con la primera raya y fue llamado Nueva España en el nombre de la corona de España. Con la independencia de México, este territorio fue nombrado y era México.

Así es que nuestra historia de nacionalidad fue muy española, mexicana. Y de sangre es muy mestiza.

La historia de los peregrinos y el sistema del anglo sajón, protestante, ya es como otra conquista y ahora por eso es algo difícil de aceptar sobre nuestras raíces. Por eso es que hoy se ha oído declarado por alguna de la juventud la nación de Aztlán, "la nación mestiza." A nosotros nos enseñan una historia algo confundida cuando nos dicen que el padre de nuestra patria es Washington. Esto viene porque nosotros sabemos que la primera capital del U.S.A. fue aquí en Santa Fe en el año 1609, y exactamente once (11) años antes de que los peregrinos anglos

---

[5] Dating from the mid-sixteenth century, the *Chilam Balám* and *Popul Vuh* are both Mayan texts. The first recorded Mayan religion, folklore, customs, and prophecy, the second contained creation stories, mythology, and history. In another demonstration of mestizaje, the Mayans used the alphabet they learned from the conquering Spaniards to record their own stories.

[6] Although Juan de Oñate was himself a *criollo*, a person of Spanish descent born in Mexico, he married Isabel de Tolosa Cortés Moctezuma, who was a descendant of Hernán Cortés, the conqueror of Mexico, and Moctezuma, the defeated emperor.

llegaran a Plymouth Rock. Así es que la historia indohispana de cultura, mexicana de nacionalidad realmente fue la primera en el U.S.A. y nos reconocemos con sangre indígena. Ya nos llamamos, la Raza Cósmica, la Raza Nueva, el Mestizo y muchas más. Pero sabemos que tenemos raíces aquí. No somos totalmente inmigrantes o extranjeros.

Que reconocemos ser mexicanos muchas veces es porque nuestra nacionalidad fue realmente mexicana, declarada por la conquista del español, y también tenemos relaciones en común con México, nuestra cultura es de la misma raíz y nuestra lengua española nos vino del sur. Entró por México. Así es que se puede decir que nuestra relación es fuerte espiritual y culturalmente. Ahora estamos pensando y hablando de gente, no de bordes [fronteras], sino de la lengua, cultura y del espíritu. Y esta unidad nos da fuerza ahora en el espíritu del plan de Aztlán. Que tenemos que conocer quiénes somos, como una gente en total, de allí empezamos a sacarnos las telarañas de la mente.

Para la raza es importante tener un fuerte sentido de quiénes somos precisamente porque allí es donde está nuestra fuerza. Nuestra fuerza de la historia, nuestra fuerza de la cultura y de la lengua. Eso es lo que más puede unir, nuestra raíz. Nuestras raíces son muy viejas para olvidarse así no más y sólo nosotros les podemos dar fuerza, y así nos damos fuerza nosotros mismos.[7]

30 de marzo de 1971

---

[7] Nowadays we hear a lot about el chicano, *la raza, el nuevo chicano, la raza cósmica* and also about *el movimiento*. Many of us begin to think, "What is this?" "Who am I?" And we even look at ourselves in the mirror and begin to think, "Which will be my Raza?" "Who will my people be?" "Who will I be?" "What will be my history?" With these questions we start thinking and began to understand where our roots begin and thus, the history of the mestizo is discovered. And, we also understand that we have not studied our history, perhaps because it is not written, especially, because the history of the Indian has never been written. It has been easier for the present educational system to eliminate us totally and perhaps that is why we have felt inferior. Our mother race has been referred to as savage and our father race, our language, has been referred to as imported and foreign. The mestizo from the Southwest who attempted to fight for justice was called a bandit and a rebel and we have been categorized as second-class citizens in our own land.

If our goal is to study our history and finally find out who we are, we need to start by erasing the boundaries and the cobwebs that exist in our minds and think solely of our people. The Indians, who are the indigenous people of the Americas, are the natives, the first citizens of the Americas. This indigenous people believe that they came from the Orient and that they crossed the Bering Straits that united Russia and Alaska. The last wave was called the Apache Wave and it arrived in the Americas more than 25,000 years ago. Therefore the conscience and way of thinking of the Indian is relatively Oriental.

This indigenous race came to the Americas, walked from Alaska to the Land of Fire (Tierra del Fuego) that is in the southern corner of South America. During these 25,000 years there was a lot of movement among the Indians who moved in tribes of different names. The Apache and Aztec tribes are actually sister tribes. The group of tribes in the northern part of Mexico and the southern part of the [U.S.] Southwest was called the Chichimeca. There is not enough accurate information to know which tribe was where because they walked all over the territory of the Americas.

Little by little many of these tribes settled and became farmers. They conducted astronomical, mathematical, [and] philosophical studies, etc. One must recognize that these people were very advanced and civilized. The territory was thought as belonging to everybody, like the air, the water and whatever else belongs to the earth, right?

In 1519, the Spaniards arrived to what we now know as Mexico. They came in through the coast and arrived in Tenochtitlán, the great city of the Aztecs. We must remember that they had neither women nor blue-blooded princes with them. They were explorers, adventurers and were accompanied by priests. So, the Spaniard arrived and conquered with cannons, the horse and the Christian cross. With the Spaniard came the Occidental, European way of thinking. The Spaniard arrived in the Americas 300 years ago. Not too long ago relatively speaking in comparison to 25,000 years ago for the indigenous people, right?

The important thing here is to recognize the birth of the mestizo. The Spaniards killed many men; women and children were branded on the faces. Cortés and his men (who didn't want to sin like men) declared in the "Law of the Indies" that the Indian race was a human race. That is how they were able to baptize and marry the women. Among the first thirty women was Doña Marina, whose Aztec name was Malintzin. The Spaniard made her his wife. This was the conquest of the Indian race when the women became property, were baptized, were named officially on paper, were dominated by the Spaniard and treated as a traitor by the Indian. Today, actually, in Mexico what comes from Europe is referred to as Malintzinsmo.

Remember that when the Spaniard arrived in Mexico he was amazed to see the beautiful cities. He did not understand the Aztec calendar (that in reality is a combination of calendars from various tribes) that is so ancient and more exact than the Chinese calendar. It is so exact that it can be used today. The Spaniard saw that the Indian lived in human harmony and that they related to the universe and nature, and to the changes of the moon, the force of the sun and that he respected and recognized the earth. Even today we do the same, right? The Indian was not dumb; he had markets and a lot of food that was not known to the European such as pineapples, cacao, beans, corn, potatoes and the sweet potato. A lot of the food that we eat today came from the Indians of the Americas. We must never think that the European came to save us, better yet, he came hungry and here he lived well. He filled himself with food, gold and silver. We also have among the Indians our concepts of life that are as valid as the European literature. Today in Mexico we have the book of *Chilam Balám* and the *Popul Vuh* that are as valid as the Bible. They are books filled with advice. The concepts of the Hopi, the Navajo, the Apache and other tribes have basic beliefs that are similar to the Aztec.

The Aztec tribe is very well known because it was the tribe that was in power when the Spaniard arrived. There were also many other big tribes in Mexico at that time. We recognize them because from them the mestizo was born. Also remember that when Juan de Oñate arrived in New Mexico in 1598, he was already Montezuma's grandnephew. He already had Indian blood and his wife Doña Isabel Tolosa Cortés Montezuma was Montezuma's great-grandchild and Cortés' grandchild. We must understand that the Spaniard with his culture, language and way of thinking, conquered and was conquered. The European entered the Americas through Mexico and thus the mestizo was born and he continued to the Southwest of Mexico. This territory was established with the first boundary and was named New Spain in the name of the Spanish crown. With Mexico's independence this territory became known as Mexico.

So it is that our history of our nationality was very Spanish, Mexican and of mestizo blood.

The story of the Pilgrims and the system of the Protestant Anglo Saxon is like another conquest and that is why it is somewhat difficult to accept our roots. That is why today some of the youth from the Aztlán nation have declared themselves to be "la nación mestiza." We are taught a rather confusing history when they tell us that the father of our nation is George Washington. This is [confusing] because we know that the first capital of the United States was here in Santa Fe in the year 1609 exactly eleven (11) years before the pilgrims arrived in Plymouth Rock. So that is why the history of the culture of the Hispanic Indian, Mexican of nationality, was truly the first in the United States and we are recognized as having Indian blood. We are already named the Cosmic Race, the New Race, the Mestizo and many more. But we know that we have roots here. We are not totally immigrants or foreigners.

That we recognize ourselves as Mexican many times is because our nationality was really Mexican, as declared by the conquest of the Spaniard. We also have common relations with Mexico, our culture has the same root and our Spanish language came to us from the south. It entered through Mexico. So we can say that our relation is strong spiritually and culturally. Now we are thinking and speaking of people not about borders but of language, culture and spirit. And this unity fortifies us in the spirit of the plan of Aztlán. We need to recognize who we are, individually and as a group, from there we begin to remove the cobwebs out of our minds.

For the race it is important to have a strong sense of who we are because it is precisely what makes us strong. Our strength comes from the history, the culture and the language. That is what can unite us; these are our roots. Our roots are very old for us to forget them and we are the only ones that can keep them alive and strong. We are the only ones that can share them.

Translated by Herminia S. Reyes.

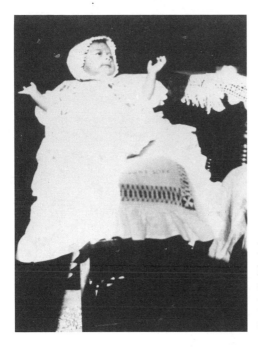

Enriqueta Vasquez's baby picture, 1930. Even before she could talk, she looked like she had something to say.

Vasquez dancing with a younger sibling in Cheraw in 1941 or 1942 according to the date written on the photo. The photo captures both the dusty bleakness of Cheraw and the joy the Vasquez family found in music.

The nameplate on the desk read Mrs. Tafoya, but Enriqueta Vasquez was already divorced and holding a civil service job at the Rocky Mountain Arsenal when this photograph was taken in the late 1950s. The secretarial skills ensured her family's economic survival in the decade that she spent as a single mother.

Vasquez and her children, Ruben and Ramona Tafoya, in a housing project in Culver City, California. Vasquez had moved to the Los Angeles area in 1960 to find a safe place for herself and her children far from her former husband. However, the gang-ridden projects did not provide the refuge she sought.

Enriqueta, her two children, Ruben and Ramona, and her new husband, Bill Longeaux, shortly before the family moved to New Mexico. Ramona is wearing her Catholic school girl uniform. Although Vasquez broke with the Church upon her remarriage, her daughter finished her school year in Denver.

Enriqueta Vasquez during her days as a contributor to *El Grito del Norte*. This photograph was taken outside the newspaper's Española office in 1969.

Faustina Perez and Abundio Vasquez, Vasquez's parents, outside their Cheraw home, sometime in the late 1960s. When Vasquez channeled the wisdom on her mother in her columns, she used her mother's name. Both her parents, however, instilled in her pride in her Mexican identity and cultivated her strong sense of justice.

Vasquez arriving in Havana, Cuba as part of a contingent of journalists and activists invited to report on the 10th year anniversary of the Cuban Revolution. She found the trip instructional. Behind her was Rafael Duran, long active in the land-grant struggle in New Mexico and a veteran of the 1968 Poor People's Campaign in Washington, D.C.

In 1972, Vasquez traveled to the People's Republic of China as part of a U.S.-China friendship association delegation from Taos. Here one of her hosts, the delegation's official translator, had taken her hand in a gesture of friendship.

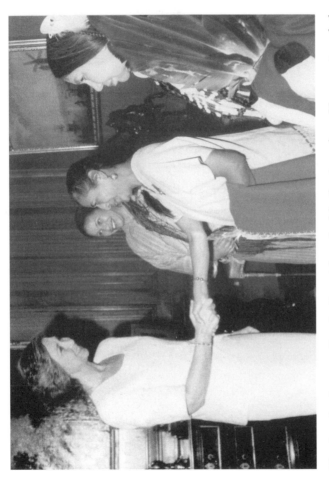

Five hundred years after the Spanish arrival in the Americas, Vasquez traveled to Europe as part of a group of indigenous leaders who presented through speeches and *ceremonia* a more critical view of the conquest. Here she is meeting the Queen Sofía of Spain in Madrid.

Vasquez has lived in the same adobe house in San Cristobal, New Mexico, since 1968. During the Chicano Movement, activists from New Mexico and elsewhere often gathered around her kitchen table prompting her children to remark on more than one occasion, "If these walls could talk . . ." Photograph by Rudy Gonzales.

In 2003, Vasquez traveled to northern California to give a talk at the University of California, Davis. The visit was also the occasion for a reunion with Betita Martínez, who was then recovering from a minor car accident. They are standing in Betita's backyard in the sunny Mission district of San Francisco. Photograph by Lorena Oropeza.

Nation and Self-Determination

Introduction
Dionne Espinoza

During the March 1969 Denver Youth Conference, *El Plan Espiritual de Aztlán* was adapted by the over one thousand attendees as a statement outlining the ideology and program of the Chicano Movement. Sometimes referred to as the "Chicano Declaration of Independence," El Plan Espiritual de Aztlán followed in a tradition of manifestos produced by historical liberation movements, most prominently the Mexican Revolution. Rejecting the "gringo" as an invader, the Plan called for a unification of Raza under the rubric of a common cultural heritage as *mestizos* and as descendents of ancient inhabitants of the land. As such, it inaugurated a new perspective of Chicanos as an exploited population whose history in the land provided evidence of their righteous claim to exist on it on their own terms.

Written after the First and Second Denver Youth conferences, respectively, the first two essays in this section and their Spanish translations promoted the ideology and programs of cultural nationalism as conceptualized and elaborated at the conferences. "Aztlán is Reborn/Somos Aztlán" emphasized two key points of El Plan Espiritual de Aztlán: (1) the need to acknowledge the ancient roots of the mestizo inhabitants of the Southwest and (2) the importance of "La Familia de la Raza" (a phrase oft-repeated in Vasquez's essays) as a model of unity. Vasquez also reiterated the hard line of El Plan, which insisted upon a complete rejection and opposition to the "European way of life" in favor of embracing Raza values and culture.

The 1969 Plan de Aztlán suggested that Aztlán as a nation represented a stance of autonomy and independence from dominant society and its negative influences and institutions, including governmental power, commercial marketing, and the two-party political system. By developing this autonomous stance, Chicanos proposed radical alternatives to the status quo. Written after the Second Denver Youth conference in 1970, "Our New Nation is Born" revised and updated the original agenda of the Plan de Aztlán. Noteworthy points in the revised program included the position that women should "strengthen la familia de la Raza" rather than separate (evidence of the growing concern over the development of a feminist movement among Chicanas); an announcement of the National Chicano Moratorium Against the War in Vietnam on August 29, 1970; and a statement critical of U.S. military interventions and supportive of international political prisoners.

In contrast to the programmatic tone of "Aztlán is Reborn" and "Our New Nation is Born," the last two columns in this section, "Let's Take a Look at Our Political System" and "New Levels of Awareness," adopted a reflective tone to address the issues of the capitalist system, political process, and cultural identity raised by El Plan. "Let's Take a Look at Our Political System" argued that the two-parties essentially represented a ruling class of capitalists whose main goal was to defend their financial investments in countries such as Vietnam. Given the power of this ruling class and the apathy of a large percentage of voters in the United States, Vasquez concurred with the need for a Raza political party. Such a party would serve for Raza as "real representatives of the people." As she wrote this piece, a full-scale effort to develop La Raza Unida Party was in full swing in rural communities in southwest Texas. By 1972, the effort foundered under the weight of internal divisions.

The final piece in this section, "New Levels of Awareness" reads as a corrective to one potential implication of cultural nationalism: that an individual's discovery and embrace of one's cultural heritage is an adequate social change practice. As the Movement developed, the "with us" or "against us" mentality of Chicano identity politics was accompanied by ideological debates regarding the best approach to large-scale social change. Responding to the ideological bickering and to the growing criticism that the exclusive focus on cultural identity obscured an analysis of the concrete situation of Raza in U.S. society, Vasquez maintained that a "new level of awareness" involved a political and economic analysis of society. For Vasquez, full politicization required that an individual become knowledgeable of the history of land dispossession. Cultural awareness, in this sense, went beyond a narrow knowledge of one's culture, as one became "open to many world ideas and world cultures." The integration of these levels—political, cultural, economic, and spiritual—provided a more sophisticated base from which to assess the project of social change.

Somos Aztlán!

Somos Aztlán! Aztlán is reborn! We have heard of "El Plan Espiritual de Aztlán," and now the time has come for us to stop and think about it and understand what it means to each and everyone of the peoples of this land of Aztlán.

"El Plan de Aztlán" came out of a youth conference which was held in Denver last Spring. Now we must take this plan and study it in order to understand the strong significance of this document of the Raza. We must all talk about it, and more than that we must think and search and know its deep meaning and how it affects all of us.

The *Encyclopedia Americana* states, "The name and national emblem of Mexico are derived from the Aztecs who, according to tradition, departed from Aztlán (thought to be in the northwestern part of the republic) in 820 A.D., and after a peregrination of many centuries arrived at what is today the valley of Mexico.

"It is believed that they chose this site on the banks of what was then the principal lake, in response to a prophecy which instructed them to settle where they saw an eagle holding a serpent in its claws.

"The name Mexico was derived from the word Mexitli—another name for the Aztec God of War, Huitzilopochtli—to which was added the suffix 'co,' signifying 'place'."

Through this and other books we learn that Aztlán is the name of the northern section of Mexico which is now considered the southwestern part of the United States. That's us! Archeological research tells us that the Aztec are believed to be part of the Apache migratory wave whose tribe is now in New Mexico and Arizona. This makes the Aztec and the Apache brothers.[1]

What does all this mean to us? How does this affect you and me? First, I will say it means that our ancestors go back a long, long way. It means that when we talk of culture it is not only something that we are born with and living today, but a deep spiritual awareness which cannot die.

Let us awaken to the fact that many of La Raza are lost and confused when trying to become Anglo and relate to the European way of life. And then let us ask, why is this? It is because we do not belong or relate to that way of life. Our ancestors have given us a cultural heritage too deep to be transformed and forgotten. When we understand this, we realize why we can and should relate to the Bronze continent. It is a matter of this being a continent de la gente de bronce with a Bronze culture.

And with this awakening of consciousness comes a call to our spirit and the revival of a too long dormant way of life. With Aztlán, we have the answer to the call of the spirit. We know that we will not let our culture die, we will not be defeated, for cosmic spirits do not die—they are the life that lives forever.

---

[1] More recent linguistic and genetic evidence suggested otherwise. In 1987, Joseph Greenberg, a linguist, proposed that all the indigenous languages of the Americas could be divided into three main groups, Amerind, the largest group that covered 90 percent of all indigenous languages, Athabaskan or Na-Dene, only found in the southwestern United States and western Canada, and Eskimo-Aleut. While Apaches are Athabaskan speakers, Aztecs speak Nahuatl, which falls into the Amerind category. Based upon these linguistic differences, Greenberg further hypothesized that while speakers who fell into the Amerind category crossed the Bering land bridge probably about 15,000 to 20,000 years ago, Athabaskan speakers may have arrived 6,000 to 8,000 years ago by following the Pacific Rim coast. Although controversial at the time, the prevalence of a specific genetic marker called *M130* among Athabaskan speakers and its relative absence among other indigenous peoples of the Americas lent support to Greenberg's categorizations. See Joseph Greenberg, *Languages in the Americas* (Stanford: Stanford UP, 1987). A summation of these findings and much more was available in 2005 through a fascinating interactive website maintained by the National Geographic Society. Entitled "The Genographic Project," the website incorporated the latest scientific evidence to trace the history of human migrations over the past 60,000 years, including migrations to the Americas, https://www3.nationalgeographic.com/genographic/atlas.html, accessed October 17, 2005. Many thanks to Audrey Espinoza for her help in finding and analyzing this information.

How do we strengthen and reawaken the past? It is time that we stop to see what is happening to our Raza everywhere. Let's look at Raza in California, Texas, New Mexico, Arizona, wherever they may be. Let's take notice and see what is happening and why.

We must raise strong children, children that know who they are and who their ancestors were. Let us remember that we are one big family. The Raza is a strong brotherhood. We are all brothers. When your neighbor suffers, it pains you also. The Plan de Aztlán is very clear and very strong. You are either for your brothers or you are not. You either live in the spirit of Aztlán or you do not. If you are a brother, your spirit will grow and live and enjoy life to its fullest, where it really means something. The old roots will have come to the surface and blossom again. If you are not a brother in spirit, then you are lost and have much to learn. You should want to learn.

We, the Raza, must wake up to Aztlán. We must know that as Aztlán we seek freedom—culturally, socially, economically and politically. This is our goal, we must live it, we must awaken. We must know we have many brothers in this, our homeland of the Southwest, and many brothers to the south in this continent. They, too, are a Bronze people; they too are people of the sun. We are not alone.

Here in Aztlán, we have been made to feel like strangers in our own homeland, but this is only because the intruders are rich and powerful exploiters. However, our strength lies with our Latin brothers. They are with us, they know us—we are one spirit, we are one heartbeat, we are Aztlán. With our hearts in our hands. Somos Aztlán.

October 13, 1969

¡Somos Aztlán!

¡Somos Aztlán! ¡Revive Aztlán! Hemos oído de "El Plan Espiritual de Aztlán" y ha llegado el tiempo en que tenemos que pensar y evaluar este concepto de la Raza. Vamos a pensar de Aztlán y ponernos a comprender lo que significa esto para nosotros, la Raza Cósmica de Aztlán.

"El Plan de Aztlán" es un plan que fue adoptado en una conferencia de la Juventud Raza que tomó lugar en Denver el año pasado. El Plan es un documento de la raza, un plan del pensamiento nuestro. Indica que nuestra raza anda en busca del espíritu que nos guie en una dirección positiva.

Según lo que la *Enciclopedia Americana* nos dice "El hombre y emblema nacional de México se sacaron de los aztecas quienes, según la tradición, salieron de Aztlán (se piensa que era el noroeste de la república) en el año 820 AD, y después de una peregrinación de muchos siglos llegaron a lo que ahora es el valle de México.

"Se cree que escogieron este sitio en la orilla de lo que entonces era la laguna principal, en respuesta a una profecía que les instruyó que debían establecerse donde vieran un águila deteniendo una serpiente entre sus garras".

En este libro y en otros, nos dicen que Aztlán es el nombre de la sección al norte de México que ahora se considera el suroeste de los Estados Unidos.

¡Eso somos nosotros!

Además, nos dicen que los aztecas, se piensa, fueron parte de la ola de los apaches; esa tribu ahora vive en Nuevo México y Arizona. Esto quiere decir que los aztecas y los apaches son hermanos.

¿Qué significa esto para nosotros? ¿Cómo nos afecta a mí y a usted? Esto quiere decir que cuando hablamos de cultura, no es nomás algo que estamos viviendo y con lo cual hemos nacido. Es más que eso, es un espíritu profundo y consciente que no puede morir nunca. El espíritu cósmico.

Mucha de la raza está perdida y confundida en desear una relación con el pensamiento europeo. Esto es algo difícil para nosotros. Nosotros no pertenecemos a ese modo de vivir o de pensar. Nuestros antepasados nos dejaron una herencia cultural muy valiosa como para olvidarla. Por esto mismo, ahora decimos que vivimos en el continente de bronce con una cultura de bronce. Nuestra raíz esta plantada aquí.

Y ahora con nuestra conciencia alerta viene la llamada al espíritu y se revive nuestra historia. Con Aztlán se oye la llamada de la raza. Sabemos que no morirá nuestra cultura, no conquistarán nuestro ser.

¿Cómo hallamos refuerzo en el pasado? Vamos a ver lo que le sucede a la raza en California, Texas, Nuevo México, Arizona y donde quiera que esté. Veamos qué sucede y por qué. Necesitamos gente fuerte, gente que sepa quiénes son y quiénes eran sus abuelos. Recordemos que somos una familia grande. La raza es una fuerte hermandad. Somos hermanos. Lo que sufre una raza le causa dolor al otro.

El plan de Aztlán es claro y fuerte. O somos hermanos fuertes juntos, o no. Vamos a vivir en el espíritu de Aztlán, ¿o no? Juntémonos como hermanos, renovemos nuestra fe y tengamos fuerza y motivo por el cual seguir en la causa de la raza. Nuestra raíz está aquí, nada más necesita salir al sol para florecer otra vez. Si algunos de ustedes no se sienten hermanos en espíritu, han perdido mucho y tienen mucho más qué aprender. Son como un coco, blanco por dentro y café de la cáscara. Despierten. Como la raza tenemos que saber lo que es Aztlán. Como Aztlán buscamos libertad cultural, social, económica y política. Éste es nuestro objetivo, lo tenemos que vivir, tenemos que despertar. Tengan conciencia.

Tenemos muchos hermanos en Aztlán, ésta es la tierra natal de la raza. Es la tierra del bronce, en este continente de bronce. Todos los seres de las Américas somos hijos del sol. No somos extranjeros aquí.

No estamos solos en nuestra lucha. El extranjero nos ha explotado pero no estamos muertos todavía. Nuestros hermanos latinos nos apoyan. Están con nosotros, somos un espíritu, un corazón, una raza. Con nuestro corazón en nuestras manos. Somos Aztlán.

11 de febrero de 1970

Our New Nation Is Born

With the stamping of feet, with the rhythmic clapping of the "Chicano hand clap," with fists in the air and the cry of CHICANO POWER, history was made for and by the Mexican American, or Chicano as we call ourselves. The homeland of Aztlán for La Raza is no longer buried in the past, it is no longer a myth, it is no longer a dream, but a necessity and a reality. In Aztlán, there is live, spiritual belief—a human revolution. A call for the reawakening and cultivating of human values. A call to make us whole again. And so, last month, a chapter was written in the history of a new society, a new nation.

On March 25-29, the second annual Chicano youth conference was held in Denver at the Crusade for Justice, whose chairman is Rodolfo "Corky" Gonzales. The Crusade used its own building and also paid for the use of the Coliseum for the conference. The Crusade's building is a symbol of a free people. It is not a government agency, another controlled institution. The services it provides FREE to the people could not be provided by a government agency for less than $250,000 a year.

In this vibrant building, over 3,200 of our people came together from throughout the nation. They began to arrive a few days before the conference. Everywhere there was Raza. The beautiful young faces were filled with enthusiasm, life and home. Over 100 organizations from 18 different states were represented. The people came in chartered buses, packed into cars and trucks, in any and all kinds of transportation. In Texas, one group had been promised chartered buses and found they had been cancelled at the last minute. But our people are not discouraged easily and our endurance is unending. The group from Texas arrived a day late but they arrived.

For five days our people met in workshops, in rooms and in hallways with the feeling of brotherhood and love for la Raza. We spoke of

90

our experiences in many parts of the nation. We expressed our ideas of what the Chicano people must do to create a new society. We met in a spirit of carnalismo and unity, to build our destinies—solid and strong.

The conference was well-inspired by creative people. Workshops were held in all creative fields. Poets, writers and musicians were all inspired by the nation of Aztlán. Actos were presented by the Crusade Ballet de Aztlán, El Teatro Triste and El Teatro Urbano, and many other people.

"I am Joaquín," a poem by Corky Gonzales, was presented on film and also enacted by a teatro group.

The original "Plan Espiritual de Aztlán" came out of the national Chicano youth conference last year. It is in effect a Grito de Independencia, for the rebuilding of a homeland that has been oppressed and exploited but never completely conquered. The conference this year brought out in more specific form just how the Plan is to be carried out. The conference made the following decisions:

A New Political Party

1. In politics, we have come to realize that the two-party system is one monster with two heads, and it is necessary to have our own party. We, the Chicano, a Mestizo, advocate the development of the Indian humanist concepts over and against European values. Thus we have established an independent "La Raza Unida" political party with El Plan Espiritual de Aztlán as its initial platform. This party will not be concerned merely with elections, but will work everyday with and for the welfare and needs of our people, as directed by our congress.

The congress of the nation of Aztlán will be the governing body for the party. It will be composed of Chicano delegates, two from each state to represent the people. The party and the congress will first and foremost maintain their activities within the U.S.A., and set an example for the rest of the world.

With the forming of the party on March 29, the chairman of the Democratic Party in Denver received a letter of resignation signed by 20 party officials. It said that the Democratic Party had been part of a double-standard party system as far as Chicanos were concerned. The 20 officials, it said, have joined the new independent party.

It has long been clear to the Chicano that the political machinery makes people think they are choosing something or someone when in reality they have chosen nothing. ¡BASTA YA!

2. Community control will come from the grass-roots people. We must provide the people with their basic needs: house them, feed them, clothe them. We must alleviate the needs of the people and become involved in meeting those needs.

Communities will be organized door-to-door, on the street, in the bars and home and everywhere, on the basis of the teaching of the brotherhood of Aztlán.

When we talk of Aztlán, we also prepare to fight and die for it.

Education

3. Having come to the realization that education has been a mere schooling built on an institution of dehumanization, we will educate all of our people at all levels. We will demand money from the institutions we have supported for so long—for example, the Church, H.E.W., etc.[1] Because we are predominantly Catholic, the Catholic Church will be asked for compensation for educational genocide under the present educational system.

4. Art will be an expression of Aztlán, of who we were—who we are—what we feel. Art is a weapon to strengthen the spirit and the unity of the familia de la Raza. The arts will bring out our values of life, family and home. This will help to fight the Gringo dollar-value system and encourage human love and carnalismo. Los artistas de Aztlán will refuse to sell to or in any way commercialize their work for the dollar system. The commitment of the artists will be to La Raza and humanity first, and ourselves as individuals last.

Professors and teachers employed in the schools of Aztlán will be required to know and teach Spanish. Community control of the schools will mean that the teachers, administrators and counselors will be ours and live among us.

We will form our own schools—and bring back the drop-outs!

---

[1] HEW was the acronym for the cabinet-level U.S. Department of Housing, Education and Welfare, which later became two separate departments, the Department of Education and the Department of Health and Human Services.

5. Economic control will come by the economic control of our lives and our communities. We will begin by driving the exploiters out of our communities, our pueblos and our land. We must develop and control our own talents, labor and resources. Our drive is to become more self-sufficient and independent. Develop cooperative buying and distribution of resources.

Land Banks

6. Lands rightfully ours will be fought for and defended. Land Banks will be set up immediately at the Crusade for Justice. Their purpose is to hold land communally by and for Chicanos.

7. The woman of Aztlán shall not be separate as a woman but strengthen the familia of La Raza. She now faces the responsibility with her brothers of forming our nation of Aztlán, and knows she must develop and function as a full human being. She is to participate according to her abilities in all aspects of the struggle. She must help to change the concept of the alienated, individualistic family to the concept of La Raza as a big united family. The love, care, and education of the children of Aztlán will be the responsibility of all Raza.

Anti-war resolutions were also adopted at the conference. Because we of La Raza have come to realize that we are providing the bodies for wars, we have said BASTA YA. We see Vietnams fermenting in many Latin American countries and we refuse to let our sons, brothers, relatives and friends, our very own, go to kill our bronze brothers on this continent only to protect the Gringo dollar. Our fatalities run much higher than our proportion of the population. We are no longer proud of the medals we receive. We have come to realize that our battle is here and now, building our nation of Aztlán. Our people treasure life, we have beauty for we are alive within and know love. The Gringo is dead and knows only war.

With these thoughts in mind, a national Chicano moratorium will take place on August 29, 1970 in Los Angeles, Calif. It is expected to draw 100,000 people from all areas.

Tijerina: National Hero

The conference declared that Reies López Tijerina is an official hero of the nation of Aztlán. June 5 was recognized as a national holiday in Aztlán, because it was on that day in 1967 that our revolutionary brothers armed themselves in an attempted citizens' arrest of District Attorney Alfonso Sanchez for crimes committed against our people and our lands.[2] This was a truly revolutionary act to regain our occupied lands.

The Denver meeting resolved to support the grape boycott as well as the boycott of Coors Beer.[3]

The conference declared that political prisoners in Aztlán, such as Los Siete in San Francisco and many others, will be supported.[4] Also, all Chicano prisoners in reform schools and penitentiaries who are there under the pretext of the due process procedure which we do not recognize. They are all political prisoners, having been arrested, prosecuted, tried and sentenced by a racist majority.

The conference declared the support of Aztlán for the political prisoners in Mexico. It demanded justice and liberty for them as well as for prisoners in Brazil, Puerto Rico, Bolivia, Santo Domingo, Peru and other parts of Latin America.

The conference protested the use of our tax dollars to support dictators in Latin America and demanded U.S. government withdrawal of military missions, troops and aid to those dictators.

One of the highlights of carnalismo during the conference came when two street gangs from Chicago, comprised of Raza and Puerto Ricans, were able to sit down and resolve their differences. They emerged from conflict with the warmest unity, under the concept of a free Puerto Rico and a free Aztlán as being one and the same goals of

---

[2] On that date, members of La Alianza Federal de Pueblos Libres, a land-grant group headed by Tijerina, conducted an armed raid at a courthouse in the New Mexican town of Tierra Amarilla. Intending to arrest Sanchez, they discovered he was not in the building. Frustrated, they fired upon a janitor and a deputy sheriff and for a brief while took hostages. For more about the raid, see Peter Nabokov, *Tijerina and the Courthouse Raid* (Albuquerque: UNM P, 1969), 81-92; and Richard Gardner, *¡Grito!: Reies López Tijerina and the New Mexico Land Grant War of 1967* (Indianapolis: Bobbs-Merrill Co., Inc., 1970), 1-5.

[3] At the time, the Crusade for Justice, charging discriminatory hiring practices. was leading a boycott against the Coors Brewing Company, located just outside of Denver in Golden, Colorado.

[4] Los Siete were seven Latino youths from the Mission District of San Francisco who in 1969 were charged with killing a plainclothes policeman. After a lengthy trial, all charges were dismissed. For more about Los Siete, see Jason Ferreira, "All Power to the People: A Comparative History of Third World Radicalism in San Francisco, 1968-1974" (Ph.D. diss, U of California Berkeley, 2003).

the family of La Raza Unida. They realized that brother against brother is suicidal and plays into the hands of the racist ruling class. This courageous decision stands as a living example for all Raza in all barrios, pueblos and villages of Aztlán, Puerto Rico, the world.

Love and unity were apparent in the people as they left the conference, embracing and taking with them a new spirit, a new hope, a new nation. As a poet of Aztlán, Lupe Saavedra, writes:

today,
history and time
as we have know it,
came to an end.
   today,
   is the birth of
   a new history of man,
      "AZTLÁN."

April 13, 1970

Se Nace Nuestra Nación

Atropellando pies, palmeando las manos al estilo chicano, con el puño cerrado en el aire y el grito de "Chicano Power" se hizo una página de historia nueva para y por la raza. La tierra natal de Aztlán para la raza no está enterrada en el pasado, ya no es un cuento, ya no es un sueño sino una necesidad y una realidad.

En Aztlán hay una creencia viva, espiritualmente viva, una revolución humana. Es una llamada a la renovación y cultivo de valores humanos, un llamado para que seamos humanos una vez más. Y así, se escribió un capítulo el mes pasado en la historia de nuestra sociedad, nuestra nueva nación.

En marzo 25-29 fue la segunda conferencia de la juventud chicana en la Cruzada por la Justicia de Rodolfo "Corky" Gonzales de Denver. La Cruzada usó su propio edificio para la conferencia y también pagó por el uso del Coliseo. El edificio de la Cruzada es un símbolo de la gente libre. No es una agencia de gobierno, ni una institución controlada. Los servicios que da GRATIS a la gente no los podría dar una agencia de gobierno por menos de $250,000 al año.

En este edificio vibrante, unas 3,200 personas se reunieron. En todas partes había raza. Las hermosas caras jóvenes estaban llenas de entusiasmo y de vida. Más de 100 organizaciones de 18 estados diferentes estaban representadas.

Por cinco días nuestra gente se reunió en talleres, en cuartos y en pasillos con un sentido de hermandad y amor por la raza. Hablamos de nuestras experiencias en la nación. Expresamos nuestras ideas de lo que la gente chicana tiene qué hacer para establecer una sociedad nueva. Nos juntamos con un sentido de carnalismo y unidad para determinar nuestros destinos —fuerte y solidariamente.

Presentaciones culturales fueron ofrecidas por poetas, escritores, músicos y artistas en general. Todos fueron inspirados por la nación de Aztlán. "Yo soy Joaquín," el poema de Corky Gonzales, fue presentado en película y también por el grupo de teatro.

El original de "El Plan Espiritual de Aztlán" nació de la primera conferencia de la juventud chicana el año pasado. Es, en efecto, un grito de independencia hacia la reconstrucción de nuestra patria que ha sido oprimida y explotada pero nunca completamente conquistada. La conferencia este año formuló en forma más específica cómo se llevaría a cabo el Plan Espiritual de Aztlán. La conferencia tomó las siguientes decisiones:

Un nuevo partido

1. Hemos llegado a la conclusión de que el sistema de dos partidos es un monstruo con dos cabezas, y, por lo tanto, es necesario tener nuestro propio partido. Nosotros, los chicanos, mestizos, advocamos el desarrollo de los conceptos humanistas indígenas en lugar de los valores europeos. Por lo tanto hemos establecido un partido político independiente, "La Raza Unida", con el Plan Espiritual de Aztlán como su plataforma inicial. Este partido no se concernirá solamente con elecciones sino que trabajará día a día por y para el bienestar y las necesidades del pueblo chicano.

El congreso de la nación de Aztlán tomará las decisiones políticas que gobernarán al partido. Estará compuesto de dos delegados populares por cada estado.

Con la formación del nuevo partido, 20 oficiales del partido Demócrata presentaron su renuncia para incorporarse al nuevo partido.

2. El control estará en manos de aquéllos que forman parte de la comunidad. Deberemos satisfacer las necesidades básicas: casa, comida y ropa. La organización se llevará a cabo en las calles, casas, los bares, dondequiera que se encuentre la gente, siempre basada en las enseñanzas de la hermandad de Aztlán.

Cuando hablamos de Aztlán estamos preparados a pelear y morir por ella.

Educación

3. El sistema educacional tal y como está hoy es una institución deshumanizada y por lo tanto nosotros mismos educaremos a nuestra gente. Formaremos nuestras propias escuelas e incorporemos otra vez los "drop-outs".

Porque somos predominantemente católicos, se pedirá compensación de la iglesia católica en pago por el genocidio educacional bajo el presente sistema educativo y por la destrucción psicológica de nuestra gente.

A los maestros y profesores de nuestras escuelas de Aztlán se les requerirá que conozcan y hablen el idioma español. El control de las escuelas estará en manos de la comunidad, lo que quiere decir que maestros, administradores y consejeros serán parte íntegra de ella.

4. El arte será una expresión de Aztlán de qué fuimos, de qué somos y de qué sentimos. El arte es un arma para revitalizar el espíritu y la unidad de la raza. Los campos creativos mostrarán nuestros valores culturales de vida, familia y hogar. Esto servirá como arma poderosa en contra del sistema gringo de valores monetarios y alentará el proceso humano de amor y carnalismo.

Los artistas de Aztlán se negarán a vender o comercializar sus trabajos por el sistema gringo del dólar. El compromiso de los artistas será con la raza y con la humanidad primero, y con ellos como individuos al último. Los trabajos serán exhibidos a y para nuestra gente, no como ventas de turismo u ornamentos para agradar al gringo.

El Teatro Nacional de Aztlán, que será establecido en California, tendrá por objetivo mostrar el orgullo de la raza, de nuestros poetas, dramaturgos, compositores y pintores.

5. En nuestras manos estará el control económico de nuestras vidas y nuestras comunidades. Comenzaremos por deshacernos de los explotadores de nuestras comunidades, nuestros pueblos y nuestras tierras. Debemos desarrollar y controlar nuestros talentos, trabajo y riqueza propias. Desarrollar la compra y distribución cooperativa de nuestras riquezas y productos.

6. Pelearemos por las tierras que pertenecen por derecho a nosotros, y las defenderemos. La Cruzada por la Justicia creará Ban-

cos de tierra con el propósito de mantener la tierra comunal por y para los chicanos.

7. Las mujeres de Aztlán no serán separadas por ser mujeres, sino que fortalecerán a la familia de la raza. Ella sabe que debe desarrollarse y funcionar como un ser humano completo. La mujer debe liberarse psicológicamente de la idea de sí misma como un ser humano inferior. Deberá participar de acuerdo a sus posibilidades en todos los aspectos de la lucha. Debe cambiar el concepto de la familia alineada por el concepto de la raza como una familia unida. El amor, cuidado, educación y despertar cultural de los niños serán la responsabilidad de toda la raza.

Resoluciones contra la guerra fueron también adoptadas. Hemos sido los proveedores de cuerpos para las guerras y ahora decimos BASTA YA. Nosotros vemos Vietnams fermentados en muchos países de Latinoamérica y nos negamos a permitir que nuestros hijos, hermanos, parientes y amigos, vayan a matar a nuestros hermanos de bronce en el continente, con el solo propósito de proteger el dólar gringo.

Con este pensamiento en nuestras mentes, se hará una moratoria chicano el 29 de agosto de 1970 en Los Ángeles, California.

Tijerina es un héroe

La nueva nación de Aztlán reconoce a Reies López Tijerina como héroe oficial de esta nueva nación. También reconoce a Reies como prisionero político y ha decidido concentrar sus poderes para liberarlo —utilizando cualquier medio que sea necesario para ello.

La conferencia reconoció el 5 de junio como día de fiesta nacional en la nueva nación de Aztlán. En este día de 1967 nuestros hermanos revolucionarios de la Alianza Federal de Pueblos Libres se armaron con la intención de llevar a cabo un arresto civil del "District Attorney" Alfonso Sanchez por crímenes cometidos contra nuestro pueblo.

Prisioneros políticos

La conferencia dio su apoyo a los prisioneros políticos de Aztlán como Los Siete de la Raza de San Francisco y muchos otros. También a todos los prisioneros chicanos en las prisiones juveniles, reformatorios y penitenciarias bajo pretexto de un proceso legal que no reconocemos. Porque todos son prisioneros políticos habiendo sido arrestados, juzgados y sentenciados por una mayoría racista.

También demandamos justicia y libertad para los prisioneros políticos de México desde Lecumberri a El Frontón, como para aquéllos en Brazil, Bolivia, Santo Domingo, el Perú y otros de Latinoamérica.[1] Nosotros simpatizamos con sus luchas contra la injusticia porque nos atan lazos de sangre.

Nosotros protestamos que los dólares que pagamos en impuestos sean usados para apoyar a dictadores en todo el territorio de Latinoamérica, y demandamos que el gobierno de los Estados Unidos retire sus misiones militares, tropas y toda ayuda a dictadores de Latinoamérica.

13 de abril 1970

---

[1] Lecumberri and El Frontón were infamous jails in Mexico and Peru respectively that held political prisoners.

Let's Take a Look at the Political System

That political machine has turned again and we are all left with the taste of the big snow job, part of the brainwashing. The politicos were all over the place, barking on TV, smiling like crazy, renewing acquaintances and making new ones. Shaking hands and beating the bushes for voters, slinging mud and lying through their teeth for all their worth. It wears one out just having to listen to the speeches over and over. I don't know when I have heard so much talk from people with so little to say.

Let's stop and take a close up view of this political system of ours and figure out HOW it has been working and for WHOM. Many of us remember that at one time it used to be said that the Republican Party was the rich man's party— it believed in BIG business, in making the rich man richer, so to speak. At the same time the Democratic Party was supposed to be the poor man's party. It believed in bettering the poor man's lot, they said, or in a more equal distribution of wealth. They used to say it was making the poor man as rich as the rich man. HUMMMM!!!

That was the philosophy that we used to hear. But let's look at some facts. As history shows us, instead of the poor becoming rich, the rich in this country have become super-rich and so very powerful that economics to the U.S. of A. is no longer a matter of economics mostly within the boundaries of the U.S. of A. The control of this country lies in the hands of about 33 ruling families [1] The INVESTMENTS of this country's rul-

---

[1] In his influential 1956 critique of the American "power elite," C. Wright Mills showed how various positions of economic, political and military power were often concentrated in the hands of a few very wealthy families, with the children of these families inculcated with a sense of entitled authority. Although he did not narrow down his elites to 33 families, Mills' thesis challenged the nation's self-image as a thoroughly middle-class society, a fundamental aspect of the American democratic ideal. C. Wright Mills, *The Power Elite*, (New York: Oxford UP, 1956), 94.

ing class are now all over the world. This country also has millions of the world's population working for it. And we know that this world-work is set up for making a profit for the U.S. of A.'s ruling class, otherwise it wouldn't be there. This, by the way, is called exploitation and imperialism.

Now all of this matter of money, expansion and economics is very important for us to know about, to sit back and figure out, because many of the issues of today are based on these very facts. You see, the holdings of this country are the very things that force it to CONTROL, PROTECT and DEFEND those interests on FOREIGN soil. This is the reason that we have 3-1/2 million (3,500,000) troops in foreign lands.[2] And this is also the reason for the 43,861 dead U.S. youth in Vietnam.[3] Did you ever stop to think or try to figure out just WHY we have millions of our young men in other countries? And exactly what are they doing there? Remember, they are not there as civilians or tourists, but as SOLDIERS. WHY? What are they protecting? The politico may have us believing that they are protecting you and me, but as far as I am concerned, I want the young men in my family to protect me here, ON MY OWN SOIL, ON MY OWN LAND; because I have a stinking suspicion that when we have our young men on foreign lands they are protecting the personal kingdoms of people like the Rockefellers, the Kennedys, the DuPonts, the Proctor and Gambles, etc. Now I don't think I want our young sons dying to protect rich people's holdings so that they can become richer. Do you?

Just the other day I was watching on TV a panel program of television and movie personalities that were talking about who was worth how

---

[2] This troop estimate was closer to the total number of U.S. servicemen and women overall. In 1970, U.S. military personnel on active duty totaled 2,875,000, with only 888,000 of those troops stationed abroad. However, Puerto Rico, Guam, and the Panama Canal Zone were considered domestic assignments. See U.S. Bureau of the Census, *Statistical Abstract of the United States: 1971*, 91st ed., (Washington, D.C., 1971), 252.

[3] The number of American war dead would exceed 58,000 before the war's end. Given the circumstances of the war, the estimated number of Vietnamese war dead, North and South, soldier and civilian, killed during the American phase of the conflict is a number that ranges wildly although even the lowest estimates place the number close to one million while higher estimates double and even triple that number. See "Death Tolls for the Major Wars and Atrocities of the Twentieth Century," http://users.erols.com/mwhite28/warstat2.htm, accessed September 22, 2005.

much money. And they talked about $200,000,000 as if it was $10. And they were competing to see who was worth more. It is very hard for me to understand rich people, I guess, because I know that it is impossible for a man to *honestly* during his lifetime EARN one million dollars. This is a fact. Therefore, as far as I am concerned, the millionaires in this country must have made their money DISHONESTLY and sadder yet is the fact that this DISHONESTY has been time and again LEGALLY REWARDED. We have even seen Internal Revenue pass special laws to protect the rich. To save them money. And these very people, the super-rich, are now screaming about law and order and no wonder; they are scared to death of losing their little empires. These people feel threatened with the world situation they have created. The world unrest is rocking their boats. And when we get right down to it, who really suffers from the enforcement of law and order? That's right, the little guy, the small-time criminal.

But you know what, after looking at all of these happenings, it could lead one to believe that the biggest blue-blood criminal of all is that rich guy with all of the legal money and power. And yet he is so clever that they have us believing that we have to protect ourselves and send our young people to foreign lands to PROTECT US. Híjole, how stupid do they think we are? All we have to do is sit back and figure these things out, you know?

Now, let's get back to politics and see how this all ties in and what is happening to people because of this O.K.? First of all, in the U.S. of A. only about 55.4% of the voters bother to vote.[4] Now it looks like this would mean that for the flag raisers to think that the silent majority in this country is solid behind the flag is one great big myth. Un chisme.

---

[4] Vasquez's voter participation estimate was generous. Of those Americans old enough to vote in 1970, only 46.60% voted on Election Day. Typically, voter participation is higher in years of presidential elections and 1970 was an off-year, but even by this measure voter turnout was low. Throughout the 1970s, moreover, voter turnout continued to decline, both for presidential elections and for off-year congressional elections. In 1972, the percentage of the voting age population that voted in the presidential election was down by more than 5% from 1968. See Federal Election Commission, "National Voter Turnout in Federal Elections: 1960-1996," http://www.fec.gov/pages/htmlto5.htm, accessed July 30, 2004. Additional data drawn from Congressional Service reports, Election Data Services, Inc., and State Election Offices.

And that is putting it nicely. Therefore, with such a large amount of people not voting, it seems that there are probably a lot of people that couldn't care less.

A look at the young people of this country is necessary when we speak of politics. There are more young people than there are old people, and with the eighteen-year-old being able to vote, the majority of this country's voters will be young people. Which means that we may see a change in the politicos of the Gringo, and rightfully so, because Washington is full of old goats that are still fighting the civil war. Among the young, we see many, many eligible voters that don't bother to vote. These include hippies, dissenters, and some that are still hoping for reforms but are losing hope.

So all of this looks pretty much like a sinking ship to me; Raza, it's time that we seriously start building our own people, that we open more doors to the building of our own nation of Aztlán. After all, look at the issues that the politicos avoided, that they did not give a specific solution to. These are the issues that need to be clarified for Raza as they have been around for years and years. We know it. We need solutions to land issues; this means everything from the Treaties of this U.S. of A. to the present-day grazing rights, the Blue Lake issues.[5] What are they waiting for to do justice? What holds up the fact that this land belongs to the Indians rightfully? Then we have civil rights and racism in every form, beginning with education. We have the most racist books, and we feed this very poison to our children in the schools every day. Unemployment, we can well imagine who suffers the most from unemployment, we know who loses their job first. Police brutality: we know case after case of this, without question; political corruption: need we say more; organized crime: that is where we need law enforcement, but they don't want to tackle that big problem, it might hurt a lot of respectable (?) people we all know. And another big issue that drains and kills our youth, WAR; they still don't tell us WHY our young people have to scurry around the globe, do they?

Politics has been treated like a sportsmanlike game; the same game, played with the same rules, everybody endorses everybody else and

---

[5] At the time Taos Pueblo Indians were engaged in an ultimately successful campaign to wrest control of their sacred Blue Lake from the federal government.

when the election is over, they shake hands and the whole machine is really ONE BIG FAT POLITICO. The destiny and the decisions of the U.S. of A. and the citizenry of the U.S. of A. in reality are already decided and dealt with. And you and I, Mr. and Mrs. Voter, haven't made a dent on this Republican and Democratic monster with two heads. All the monster wants from us is our tax money, not our voices.

We have, in the past, been used and reused in the game of politics and the feeling is again one of being used by a first-class hypocrite. What can we do about this two-headed monster? What can we, as a minority, do about this thing called majority rule —really a rich ruling-class? It seems to me that we better look seriously at this political animal and come up with our own party, a Raza party. A party that is committed to Raza, a party that is armed with the voice of truth, with a platform of El Plan de Aztlán, a plan of the people, for community control, to create our own leadership, to make our own decisions and to strengthen La familia de la Raza. A party to let us know that we all belong to la familia de la Raza. A party to bring us home to that familia.

A Raza political party can do much for organizing our people and creating an awareness as to what is happening to us. As to what our history is and who we are. All of this, plus showing us how our lives are affected today by politics. In Colorado, La Raza Unida party has been doing this very effectively. Hopefully, for the next election we can see Raza parties on every ballot in the Southwest. When a Raza candidate wins, it SHOULD mean that we will have people serving Raza without the concept of personal gain; we SHOULD have public officials that are willing to live among us; that are willing to live the same life style as we, the Raza, and can give their excessive incomes for the use of the development of the people. These SHOULD be real representatives of the people who will identify with us and with our needs.

This is our answer to the politico, this is the only way. And this will be done through the love for Raza; the love of our people; the love of *who* we are; the love of *what* we are; the love that makes us shout BASTA YA, for we are growing stronger in our familia de la Raza and this brings us and leads us to be a RAZA UNIDA.

New Levels of Awareness

Springtime and Eastertime are times of planting, times of searching and evaluating the mother earth—and ourselves. We as Chicanos, and as Aztlán, must also stop and look at la familia de la Raza, our family of millions, to see what is happening. As we have come to Chicanismo, to la Raza, some of us are at a level of awareness that says: "I want to be conscious of my culture, my language, brotherhood (sometimes sisterhood)—and nothing else."

Bueno, this is important, but if we only focus on me, myself and culture, we end up picking on each other with pettiness. If we don't like something, we just say "outsider," "white liberal," "Communist," "radical," or even "ese español es de Nuevo México." So instead of being open to learning, we shut off avenues of awareness, of growing. And while we bicker with each other, us little guys, the real powerful outsider, el Gringo político, el patrón de Washington, D.C. moves in y nosotros nos quedamos con la boca abierta. Then we see the young Chicano radical with real guts, raising cain and we say "¿qué pasa?"

I'd say it's about time we opened other levels of awareness and consciousness: economics, politics and spiritual life. How? We can begin with history. People history. We can begin learning who we are? Who are Americans? What is a Mestizo? What is el Chicano Movement, la causa, and what are they saying?

You see, the patrón en Washington is—por allá. The disputed land, the war on Mexico, the resulting Treaty of Guadalupe Hidalgo and its effects on Raza are here, in the southwestern U.S. of A. But never underestimate El político for he made it possible for land-grant land to be stolen and sold to individuals; he made it possible for Moly Mine (Canadian owned and run by U.S. easterners) to take minerals; and he made it possible for "speculators" to come here some years ago and buy second- and third-grade land, now bursting with oil wells.[1] This is why economic and political awareness is necessary because while we are focusing on cultural issues, we're getting taken politically and economically.

History and politics will also open our eyes as to what has been rammed down our throats in the name of "tradition" and is really colonialization.

Young people must be politicized, not just asked for a vote. Young people must be culturally aware—this means open to many world ideas and world cultures. Young people must be spiritually rejuvenated. The Church has collapsed and can no longer fulfill our spiritual needs. Unless we face this need and satisfy it, our youth will vanish and die in the non-cultured Amerikan nightmare.

The young Chicano is becoming aware of Raza needs. All of these needs tie in together, one is not separate from another. For us to think we can discuss brotherhood and come up with any kind of solution without discussing politics, economics, land and mineral robbers, etc., is not being truthful to ourselves or to la Raza. It's not being realistic. It's like saying "Peace, let's quit fighting (today)" while we know they are beating the hell out of us at home, in the schools, the courts, in the armed forces.

It is time to join la familia de la Raza. Quit wondering what's going on in the Chicano Movement, find out. Support our youth. Learn what ails the world and how El patrón dictates and controls the world. The Raza is learning and moving ahead. We're building our own nation of Aztlán, a nation of brotherhood and sisterhood that tolerates no patrones or dictators.

April 10, 1972

---

[1] In 2004, Molycorp, Inc. continued to operate a molybdenum mine near Questa, New Mexico, in the Sangre de Cristo mountain range of the Southern Rockies. The mine is located within the 1.7 million acres of land formerly designated as the Maxwell Land Grant by the U.S. government. Information about the company could be found on its website, http://molycorp.com/home_frameset.html, accessed August 13, 2004. Land use rights associated with the land grant continue to be disputed in court, most recently in *Espinoza v. Taylor* in 1998. See María E. Montoya, *Translating Property: The Maxwell Land Grant and the Conflict over Land in the American West, 1840–1900*, (Berkeley: U California P, 2002), 1-7, 208-11.

Chicanas, Organize!

Introduction
Dionne Espinoza

Enriqueta Vasquez examined how racial discrimination, poverty and sexism negatively affected Chicanas both in U.S. society and within the Chicano Movement. Despite the positioning of Chicanas at the bottom of race, class, and gender hierarchies, she refused to construct Chicanas as victims. Rather, she focused on how Chicanas' experiences of oppression positioned them as an untapped pool of activists and nation-builders for the Chicano Movement. In "The Woman of La Raza I," Vasquez pointed to women's cultural knowledge, personal strength, and survival skills in upholding family life as single mothers. For Vasquez, here was ample evidence that Chicanas would make ideal political actors within the movement family.

Although she couched many of her observations of women's roles in terms of la familia, in "The Woman of La Raza, Part I," "The Woman of La Raza, Part II" and "La Chicana: Let's Build a New Life," she questioned the idea that tradition equaled women's subordination. In each of these pieces, she criticized a static understanding of tradition and advanced alternative histories and models of family life that valued women's roles and contributions. For example, in contrast to the representation of the family as inherently and historically male dominant, Vasquez recounted a pre-colonial history in which women were revered for their contributions to tribal society. In "La Chicana: Let's Build a New Life," she presented a vision of communal life based on women's pre-existing networks and ties to each other. Simultaneously drawing upon ideas of radical feminism, the cooperative movement, and indigenous ways of life, Vasquez imagined a community that fostered women's flourishing.

Nevertheless, as she ventured into the terrain of alternative models of communal life, Vasquez continued to grapple with the contradictions of cultural nationalism. Written in the midst of a widespread rejection of Chicana feminism by men and anti-feminist women who accused feminists of selling out to the "white women's" movement, the column "Chicana Resolution," which reported on the Denver Youth Conference of 1970, underscored the position that Chicanas would maintain the familia of Aztlán rather than build autonomous women's groups. "¡Soy Chicana Primero!" called for a distancing of Chicanas from the women's liberation movement. She declared, "YOU MUST BE A CHICANA FIRST, for when you are a Chicana Primero, you can wander all over, you can relate to many struggles, for they must all someday

111

come together, BUT you will be home, in Aztlán, working with your own familia." Such a statement revealed her desire to affirm the value of certain nationalist impulses, which she conjoined to woman-identification, while also opening the door to coalition politics.

While many of Vasquez's columns had been reprinted in other newspapers, Vasquez's report on the First National Chicana Conference, a conference that was held on Memorial Day weekend in 1971 at the Magnolia Branch YWCA, is not widely known. A turbulent moment in Chicana/o politics, the conference was marked by conflict among women activists regarding the relationship between the male-defined agenda of the Chicano Movement and the agenda of an evolving Chicana feminism. The piece initially expressed a deep faith and joy in women's ties to each other. However, as she reported, Vasquez was among a group of women who walked out of the conference. The walkout and the divisions among women that emerged at the conference were a testament to the larger issues facing Chicanas of the time: How to both pursue the goals of the Chicano Movement agenda while demanding that the Movement contribute to women's empowerment and flourishing.

La Chicana: Let's Build a New Life

Bueno, Comadres, here we go again on the woman thing. The other day I was listening to a group of young people talking about how the Southwest is a homeland for the Chicano wherever he may be. They were saying this is an area where the Chicano can identify with the land, and how the culture is rooted here, and how it would be good to have our families move onto the land and raise our children here in OUR homeland of Aztlán.[1]

After listening to this talk for some time I sat back smiling and said, "There is only one group of Chicanos that I think would really be able to do what you are talking about." And guess who that is, "The CHICANA."

Having lived in housing projects in the city, I know many of the women there that were from small cities and farms and would love to go back to live in the country. Many of these women have anywhere from 2 to 6 children, live on Aid to Dependent Children, do not own homes, own very few belongings, have no jobs and truly have very little to tie them down to the city. Not only this, but in the city the problems of raising children are multiplied many times over and some of these Chicanos would welcome the chance to leave the city with their families.

---

[1] During the Chicano Movement, activists' understanding of the Southwest as a "homeland" derived from the fact that the territory that now comprises much of the southwestern United States had been acquired from Mexico after the U.S.-Mexico War, a war initiated when General Zachary Taylor crossed into Mexican territory. See John R. Chávez, *The Lost Land: The Chicano Image of the Southwest* (Albuquerque: UNM P, 1984), 35-42. Scholars have debated the precise location of Aztlán, but its symbolic significance as the "birthplace" of the Aztecs, said to be a "land to the north" of Tenochtitlán, fit well with the understanding of the Southwest as a lost territory.

Then, what would they do? Well, let's say that a co-op of about six such families would buy about ten acres of land. In a summer they could do their home repairs and building. For the Chicana, building is no problem. I have talked to many Chicanos in the area and they still remember the times when it was the woman who did the building. They did the home repairs and mudding of the walls, etc. Many of the old-timers say that the woman is every bit as capable as the man when it comes to building.

Once these families get themselves built-in, they could begin to think about planting and growing crops to help feed themselves and learn from the land. And this is the beauty of the whole thing, in that they would be cultivating themselves and also be teaching the young ones how to relate to the earth. These women could actually build a satisfying home life for themselves and their families. They could work and play together with the children and they could study together and learn about nature, crops, and life in general. There would be a deep spiritual relationship and bond there.

Not only could the children grow all strong and beautiful, Raza, but the woman could also lead full, fruitful lives. For example, I know of a woman who lives in the projects, who enjoys fixing cars. She can't do this in the city, but she does fool around fixing radios and electrical appliances. She really enjoys this kind of work. In a community such as this of which we speak, each woman could find the things that she really enjoys and they could all learn to do these things and do them as a contribution to the community. These women could teach and learn together, relate to each other and read and study together.

What are the advantages of this kind of life? Well, all throughout the Southwest, the Raza has been forced to move from rural areas to the cities to make a living. Many of these people leave and abandon entire homes here. Our Raza goes to the city to make more money, not realizing that it costs more money to live there in the dog-eat-dog rat race. Life there is a vicious circle. Meanwhile, on the land that they left behind, we find the young hippies that have just learned that the city destroys humanity and these young people are running away from the life of comfort that their parents gave them. They are buying many of these abandoned simple homes that Raza left and fixing them up while they live in them. They seem to manage somehow and are making the attempt at a new way of life.

The thing is that it should be Raza that is coming back to the land. We don't need a new way of life, we have a good way of life already. We know the land well. It is ours. We should be raising our children here, on the land. We should be teaching them to relate to the earth and to other humans. This is part of our culture. And I really think that the Chicana can come back and rebuild the society and homeland that the Chicanos need to relate to. This would be a community that would be giving itself to the people. It would be a community of children that belong to everyone, and the mothers would form the solid foundation of the strong spirit needed from which to draw strength for all Chicanos. This could be the rebirth of a truly tribal community and an example from which would come expansion and more communities like these.

You know, I really think this would be worth trying and I have a lot of faith in the Chicana making it work. So, you there in the barrios and the projects, you with OUR beautiful RAZA children to raise, what do you say? Start to talk about this and start to look into it. You may hold the key to the cultural rebirth of our beautiful RAZA de AZTLÁN. It is worth making this dream a reality, ¿qué no?

November 15, 1969

The Woman of La Raza, Part I

While attending a Raza conference in Colorado this year, I went to one of the workshops that were held to discuss the role of the Chicana. When the time came for the women to make their presentation to the full conference, the only thing that the workshop representative said was this: "It was the consensus of the group that the Chicana woman does not want to be liberated."[1]

As a woman who has been faced with having to live as a member of the "Mexican-American" minority as a breadwinner and a mother raising children, living in housing projects and having much concern for other humans, leading to much community involvement, this was quite a blow. I could have cried. Surely we could have at least come up with something to add to that statement. I sat back and thought, Why? Why? I understood why the statement had been made and I realized that going along with the feelings of the men at the convention was perhaps the best thing to do at the time.

Looking at our history, I can see why this would be true. The role of the Chicana has been a very strong one, although a silent one. When the woman has seen the suffering of her people, she has always responded bravely and as a totally committed and equal human. My mother told me of how, during the time of Pancho Villa and the revolution in Mexico, she saw the men march through the village continually for three days and then she saw the battalion of women marching for a whole day. The women carried food and supplies; also, they were fully armed and wearing loaded "carrilleras."[2] In battle, they fought

---

[1] Vasquez was referring to the women's workshop that took place at the Denver Youth Conference at the Crusade for Justice Headquarters in March 1969.

[2] "Carrilleras" are long belts with slots to hold bullets. For further information about women participants in the Mexican Revolution, see Elisabeth Salas, *Soldaderas in the Mexican Military* (Austin: UT P, 1985); Shirlene Soto, *Emergence of the Modern Mexican Woman* (Denver: Arden P, 1990) 43-46; and Andrés Reséndez, "Battleground Women: *Soldaderas* and Female Soldiers in the Mexican Revolution," *The Americas* 51 no. 4 (April 1995): 525-553.

alongside the men. Out of the Mexican revolution came the revolutionary personage "Adelita," who wore her rebozo crossed at the bosom as a symbol of a revolutionary woman in Mexico.

Then we have our heroine Juana Gallo, a brave woman who led her men to battle against the government after having seen her father and other villagers hung for defending the land of the people. She and many more women fought bravely with their people. And if called upon again, they would be there alongside the men to fight to the bitter end.

And now, today, as we hear the call of the Raza, and as the dormant, "docile" Mexican American comes to life, we see the stirring of the people. With that call, the Chicana also stirs and I am sure that she will leave her mark upon the Mexican-American movement in the Southwest.

How the Chicana reacts depends totally on how the "Macho" Chicano is treated when he goes out into the so-called "Mainstream of Society." If the husband is so-called successful, the woman seems to become very domineering and demands more and more in material goods. I ask myself at times, "Why are the women so demanding?" But then I realize: This is the price of owning a slave.

A woman who has no way of expressing herself and realizing herself as a full human has nothing else to turn to but the owning of material things. She builds her entire life around these and finds security in this way. All she has to live for is her house and family and she becomes very possessive of both. This makes her a totally dependent human. Dependent on her husband and family. Most of the Chicana women in this comfortable situation are not particularly involved in the Movement. Many times it is because of the fear of censorship in general. Censorship from the husband, the family, friends and society in general. For these reasons, she is completely inactive.[3]

Then you will find the Chicana with a husband who was not able to fare so very well in the "Society" and perhaps has had to face defeat. She is the woman that really suffers. Quite often the man will not fight the real source of his problems, be it discrimination or what-

---

[3] Noteworthy here was Vasquez's attention to class differences among Mexican-American women, a topic not often discussed in Movement circles of the time.

ever, but will instead come home and take it out on his family. As this continues, his Chicana becomes the victim of his machismo and woeful are the trials and tribulations of that household.

Much of this is seen particularly in the city. The man, being head of the household and unable to fight the system he lives in, will very likely lose face and for this reason there will often be a separation or divorce in the family. It is at this time that the Chicana faces the real test of having to confront society as one of its total victims.

There are many things she must do. She must: (1) Find a way to feed and clothe the family; (2) Find housing; (3) Find employment; (4) Provide child care; and (5) Find some kind of social outlet and friendship.

(1) In order to find a way to feed and clothe her family she must find a job. Because of her suppression, she has probably not been able to develop a skill. She is probably unable to find a job that will pay her a decent wage. If she is able to find a job at all, it will probably be only for survival. Thus she can only hope to exist—she will hardly be able to live an enjoyable life.

Even if she does have a skill, she must all at once realize that she has been living in a racist society. She will have much difficulty in proving herself in any position. Her work must be three times that of the Anglo majority. Not only this, but the competitive way of the Anglo will always be there. The Anglo woman is always there with her superiority complex. The Chicana will be looked upon as having to prove herself even in the smallest task. She is constantly being put to the test. Not only does she suffer the oppression that the Anglo woman suffers as a woman in the market of humanity, but she must also suffer the oppression of being a minority with a different set of values. Because her existence and the livelihood of the children depend on her conforming to an Anglo society, she tries very hard to conform. Thus she may find herself even rejecting herself as a Mexican American. Existence itself depends on this.

(2) She must find housing that she will be able to afford. She will very likely be unable to live in a decent place. It will be more the matter of finding a place that is cheap. It is likely she will have to live in a housing project. Here she will be faced with a real problem of being

able to raise children in an environment that is conducive to much suffering. The decision as to where she will live is a difficult matter as she must come face to face with making decisions entirely on her own. This, plus having to live them out, is very traumatic for her.

(3) To find a job she will be faced with working very hard during the day and coming home to an empty house and again having to work at home. Cooking, washing, ironing, mending, plus spending some time with the children. Here her role changes to being both father and mother. All of this, plus being poor is very hard to bear. Then, on top of this, to have a survey worker or social worker tell you that you have to have incentive and motivation and get ahead! These are tough pressures to live under. Few men could stand up under them.

(4) Child care is one of the most difficult problems for a woman to have to face alone. Not only is she tormented with having to leave the raising of her children to someone else, but she wants the best of care for them. For the amount of money that she may be able to pay from her meager wages, it is likely that she will be lucky to find anyone at all to take care of the children. The routine of the household is not normal at all. She must start her day earlier than an average worker. She must clothe and feed the children before she takes them to be cared for in someone else's home. Then, too, she will have a very hard day at work for she is constantly worrying about the children. If there are medical problems, this will only multiply her stress during the day. Not to mention the financial pressure of medical care.

(5) With all of, this, the fact still remains that she is a human and must have some kind of friendship and entertainment in life —and this is perhaps one of the most difficult tasks facing the Chicana alone. She can probably enjoy very little entertainment as she can not afford a baby-sitter. This, plus she very likely does not have the clothes, transportation, etc. As she can not afford entertainment herself, she may very often fall prey to letting someone else pay for her entertainment and this may create unwanted involvement with some friend. When she begins to keep company with men, she will meet with the disapproval of her family and often be looked upon as having loose moral values. As quite often she is not free to remarry in the eyes of the Church, she will find more and more conflict and disapproval and

she continues to look upon herself with guilt and censorship. Thus she suffers much as a human. Everywhere she looks, she seems to be rejected.

This woman has much to offer the movement of the Mexican-American. She has had to live all the roles of her Raza. She has had to suffer the torments of her people in that she has had to go out into a racist society and be a provider as well as a mother. She has been doubly oppressed and is trying very hard to find a place. Because of these facts she is a very, very, strong individual. She has had to become strong in order to exist against these odds.

And what usually happens to this woman when she tries to become active in the Causa? One would think that the movement would provide a place for her, one would think that the organizations would welcome her with open arms and try to encourage her to speak up for her Raza. One would think that because of her knowledge and situation the groups would think of liberation schools with child care for the victims of broken homes, in order to teach them culture and history so that they may find self identity. But, NO. Instead one finds that this woman is shunned again by her own Raza. When she tries to speak of Machismo, she is immediately put down and told "We know all about it, there are many many books written on the subject." She receives nothing but censorship again. She tries so hard to say, "Yes, there is much on Machismo, but can't you Machos look at the women and children who are the VICTIMS of your Machismo?" She tries so much to speak up and instead finds herself speaking to deaf ears and a completely closed mind.

Then she tries other ways, perhaps to offer her skills and knowledge in some way. This too is difficult. It she does do a good job, she will have to walk lightly around the men for she may find herself accused of being "Agringada" or "Agabachada" (Anglicized). To top this off, quite often the men will accept or allow an Anglo female to go in and tell them how to run things. The Anglo will perhaps be accepted and be allowed more freedom than the Raza woman. Through all of this, one sees a discouraged Chicana. One that hungers and bleeds to help her people and is being turned away and discouraged. What is to become of her? Will she be forced into being a skeleton in the closet that one does not want to see?

The Mexican-American movement is not that of just adults fighting the social system, but it is a total commitment of a family unit living what it believes to be a better way of life in demanding social change for the benefit of mankind. When a family is involved in a human rights movement, as is the Mexican American, there should not have to be a woman's liberation movement within it. There should not have to be a definition of a woman's role. We should get down to the business at hand. Do we want a liberation for the Raza? Is this supposed to be a total liberation?

The woman must help liberate the man and the man must look upon this liberation with the woman at his side, not behind him, following, but along side of him leading. The family must come up together. The Raza movement is based on Brotherhood. ¿Qué no? We must look at each other as one large family. We must look at all of the children as belonging to all of us. We must strive for the fulfillment of all as equals with the full capability and right to develop as humans. When the man can look upon "his" woman as HUMAN and with the love of BROTHERHOOD and EQUALITY, then and only then, can he feel the true meaning of liberation and equality himself. When we talk of equality within the Mexican-American movement we better be talking about TOTAL equality beginning right where it all starts. AT HOME . . .

July 6, 1969

The Woman of La Raza, Part II

When we look at and talk about the Raza woman, we have to really think seriously and realize that we are dealing with a real mixed-up side of the social battle. We must know that we again have a fairy tale to live with. How many times have we heard reference made to the "squaw" of the family? The woman has been stereotyped as a servant to the man and the Raza has come to accept this as a great TRADITION.

Well, Compadres, after doing some thinking and reading, I'll have to blow up that little dream bubble for us. It seems that before the Europeans came to the Americas, our highly cultured Indian woman usually held an honored position in the "primitive" society in which she lived. She was mistress of the home and took full part in tribal elections. The position of the woman was not only free, but honorable. She was a strong laborer, a good mechanic, a good craftsman, a trapper, a doctor, a preacher and, if need be, a leader. It seems that among the so-called SAVAGE people of this continent, women held a degree of political influence never equaled in any CIVILIZED nation. The woman of the Aztecs was far superior to that of Spain, then and now. And in Oaxaca, Mexico, the Mayan woman to this day is equal to her men.[1] As a matter of fact if there is some political issue at hand, it is the woman you will see PROTESTING. They won't take anything lying down. They even tell the government where to go.

So, after all of this, it looks to me as if this continent had a highly CIVILIZED way of life (and that is probably why the European

---

[1] The indigenous groups that populate the area around and including Oaxaca are the Zapotec and Mixtec. Scholars who have studied this area have shown that women do have a central role in social organization as merchants.

could not live up to it).[2] The Europeans certainly DESTROYED a good thing. ¿Qué no? And now we talk of the tradition of the woman and say, "No, we must not change the role of the woman, the woman must remain totally dominated in order to keep this tradition." Let's take another look at this family "tradition" the men say we have.

Remember we are Mestizos, a people of Spanish fathers and Indian mothers. Male domination over the woman is a thing of Spain and Europe. Destroying the Indian woman's freedom was necessary in order to conquer and destroy the Indian. It was also a tool used to make subject-wives of the Indian woman, who would have to submit to a European way of life.[3]

When we look at all of this and see our real history and heritage, we come to realize that a strong Raza woman is inevitable. If our Raza is to survive and endure, it seems that we have to prepare the woman once again to live a strong role in relation to her people. We can expect to see the Raza woman stand up and take more and more action in matters, for it is in doing this that she will be fulfilling the deep thirst of our Indian blood. Our Raza woman will take her place in the social and cultural struggle and this will be nothing new to her, it will be as natural as giving birth.

The woman of the Raza is becoming more and more aware and has been learning in her silent way. She has been watching her people suffer. She is watching her culture being raped. We see that our families are being destroyed, not only as families but also because our children are growing up without the human values we know as ours. We see many a Raza woman having to confront the Anglo world alone and trying to raise a family. She hasn't quite figured it out, but she knows something is wrong.

---

[2] During the Chicano Movement, activists often represented pre-colonial indigenous society as an ideal society that was destroyed by conquest. Vasquez used this discourse to argue that pre-colonial indigenous societies were either gender egalitarian or even, in some cases, matriarchal. To be certain, the ways in which indigenous groups organized gender categories varied widely because of regional differences and cultural diversity.

[3] The Spanish population in early colonial Mexico was composed predominantly of male explorers, the *conquistadores*. These men saw in the population of indigenous women wives, sexual partners, personal caretakers, and bodies open to sexual violation.

Look at the Reform Schools

And why should we be concerned? In order to see just one of the problems of our young people, we have but to look at the reform schools. For example in the state of Colorado where the Raza is 10% of the population, three reformatories have an average of 62% of the Raza. That's way over our population percentage, no? The biggest percentage of youth there come from broken homes. This alone, hermanos, means that there is a problem and that, my dear sisters, we are bearing the brunt of raising our families in this barbarous society.

One of the things we Raza women must do is to see just what it is that our families must contend with, and what we can do to prepare them for facing up to life. We must make them strong and unafraid in today's world. We must first talk to our children and examine just what it is that they are learning in school. I believe that one of the big problems we will find is the racism in education. We know that in school they are not given a culture that they can identify with. They are not taught who they are. Our way of thinking and our human values are, as a matter of fact, discouraged. Our own children are wandering away from Raza culture and this is mostly because they have been educated to feel inferior. Our own history books in the schools tend to wipe us out as a people. Our children don't know themselves. It is our obligation and responsibility to show them who and what they really are. We must realize that when educators speak of equality, it is in law and in writing but not in practice. And worse yet, what is being taught to our children is that the Americano as well as their history is superior and infallible. This is totally inhuman, and if you really want to see what this attitude does to people, just go to a foreign country and see the behavior of the American wherever he goes. And listen to what people from other countries feel about the Gringo.

Teach the Children to Question

At home we do not only have to learn what the family is being taught, we must teach them to question these things in order to learn. We have to teach them to discuss things, not just sit in the classrooms and accept everything as the "ultimate truth." They have to learn to relate to the teachers as fellow humans, humans who also have to learn. And we as women, have to support our children in the classroom, go to school and question too. Remember that the teachers and schools are there to SERVE you. You tell them what you think should be taught. Everywhere that our families walk the path of life we must question the things of man. The only thing in life we have to accept and take our place in harmony with is NATURE and its CREATOR.

These are but a few of the things that we have to contend with in the matter of raising the family. Now Chicanos, we must look at the things that are going to give us strength in raising our families. If we are to teach our families something of what is REALLY going on with the Raza, we have to look around and hope to find a strong and lasting bond for our people. We must look and see what is going on with our people. We have to start thinking about the land grant struggle. The Alianza has been in existence for many, many years.[4] Let's look at some of its claims and see what they are. The Crusade for Justice in Denver is confronting the educational system, the court system, the politicians and all the establishment and making them answer some questions.[5] They are teaching old schools some things they can't seem to find in books. How to THINK for instance.

Let's Talk to Each Other

And what about César Chávez in California? What's the history of the campesino and what is he fighting for? These are our people too. And in Texas our brothers and sisters have a struggle. Just what is this all about? What is happening to our people? We feel what is happening, let's learn about it and let's start speaking up. Let's talk to each other and let's not be afraid to be heard.

---

[4] The Alianza refers to the organization of land grantees headed by Reies López Tijerina For Tijerina's account of the organization and its evolution, see his memoir, *They Called Me "King Tiger": My Struggle for the Land and Our Rights* (Houston: Arte Público P, 2000) ed and trans. by José Angel Gutiérrez. The religious aspect of Tijerina's political ideas is the subject of Rudy V. Busto, *King Tiger: The Religious Vision of Reies López Tijerina* (Albuquerque: UNM P, 2005).

[5] The Crusade for Justice was a civil rights organization founded by Rodolfo "Corky" Gonzales in 1966. Made up of families, the Crusade hosted the Denver Youth Conferences and also developed a school that promoted culture and education.

We women must learn to function again like full humans, as did our ancestors. We are the ones that feel the deep AMOR Y DOLOR for our people. I know many women who would give their lives for their Raza. Let's look around and see where we can give the most and where we are needed. And then let's plunge right into action. Let's hold our heads high and proud and walk in beauty.

July 26, 1969

Chicana Resolution

The Chicano Youth Conference in Denver was not only the rebirth of a nation—Aztlán—but with it the birth of hope and inspiration for Raza wherever we may be.

La Raza is opening its eyes. Little by little we see it happening to us and we do something about it. As our eyes open, our mind grows and we see more and more. We see ourselves as a people. We feel as a people. And with this feeling, with this awakening, the woman of La Raza stirs to join hands in the molding of our people, in the cultivating of our culture.

With this in mind, the resolution from the Chicana Workshop can be seen as a source of strength to continue in the struggle for the building and strengthening of our familia de la Raza. La familia de Aztlán.

The resolution from the Chicana Workshop is a combination of many ideas, opinions and expressions voiced by the women in attendance, women working in all levels, varying in ages and experience, and from many different parts of the country.

Resolution from Chicana Workshop

THE CHICANA WOMEN RESOLVE NOT TO SEPARATE BUT TO STRENGTHEN AZTLÁN, THE FAMILY OF LA RAZA!

With the grave responsibility of the rebirth and forming of our nation of Aztlán, the women have come to realize that they must begin to develop and function as complete human beings. We have reached a point in our struggle for the liberation of La Raza where the growth of our women and their participation has become of utmost necessity. The woman is repressed as a great potential of strength and knowledge. We must, through education, develop a full consciousness and, awareness of the woman to the revolution and of the revolution to the woman. This is the beginning of women to free themselves as inferior beings, and to educate themselves so that they too can implement the Plan de Aztlán. In order to implement the Plan we must understand all of the things that it calls for.

With the preceding things kept in mind, we resolve the following:

1. All women must participate according to their capability in all levels of the struggle.

2. We encourage all Chicanas to meet in their own groups for the purpose of education and discussion.

3. *Self-determination* of the women in terms of how they will implement their goal of becoming full human beings and of participating totally in the struggle for la Raza must be respected.

4. We must change the concept of the alienated family where the woman assumes total responsibility for the care of the home and the raising of the children to the concept of la Raza as the united family.

With the basis being brotherhood, la Raza, both men and women, young and old, all must assume the responsibility for the love, care, education and orientation of all the children of Aztlán.

When we speak of community control we are speaking of self-determination of la Raza to decide how it wants to live. The changing concept of the family must run through all our actions in the area of community control.

5. All of the preceding ideas must be included in the ideology of the La Raza Independent Political Party so that everyone, men and women, will work consciously towards the goal of a total liberation of our people. For the purpose of unity and direction, the women of la Raza have set up communication in the form of a newsletter to be shared by all women active in the struggle for the liberation of our people.

We resolve not to separate but to strengthen and free our nation of Aztlán, men, women, and children.

April 29, 1970

¡Soy Chicana Primero!

The Chicana today is becoming very serious and observant. On one hand, she watches and evaluates the white women's liberation movement and, on the other hand, she hears echoes of "Chicano" Movement, "Viva la Raza," the radical raps and rhetoric. For some it becomes fashionable—while, for many of us, it becomes survival itself. Some of our own Chicanas may be attracted to the white woman's liberation movement, but we really don't feel comfortable there. We want to be a Chicana primero. We want to walk hand-in-hand with the Chicano brothers, with our children, viejitos, our familia de la Raza.

Then, too, we hear the whisper that if you are a radical Chicana, you lose some of your femininity as a woman. And we question this as we look at the world struggles and that show this accusation as to femininity doesn't make sense. After all, we have seen the Vietnamese women fight for survival with a gun in one hand and a child sucking on her breast on the other arm. She is certainly feminine. Our own people that fought in the revolution were brave and beautiful, even more human because of the struggles we fought for.[1]

So we begin to see what our people are up against as we take very seriously our responsibility to our people—and to our children—as we sense the waging battle for cultural survival. We know that this means we have hardships to endure and we wish to strengthen our endurance in order that we may further strengthen the endurance of our coming generations: Nuestros hijos that are here and those that are yet to come. Our people would often say when they saw a strong spirited woman: viene de buen barro (She comes from a good clay). Thus

---

[1] Vasquez is referring here to the Mexican Revolution, 1910-1917.

we now must make our children strong with the realization that they, too, "vienen de buen barro."

When we discuss the Chicana, we have to be informed and show how we relate to the white women's liberation movement in order to come up with some of our own answers. This requires a basic analysis, not just a lot of static. Looking at the issues of the women's lib movement, it is easy to relate to the struggle itself as a struggle. We understand this because the Raza people are no newcomers to struggles: We can sympathize with many basic struggles. However, it is not our business as Chicanas to identify with the white women's liberation movement as the homebase for working for our people. We couldn't lead our people there, could we? Remember, Raza is our home ground and family—and we have strong basic issues and grievances *as a people*.

In looking at women's lib we see issues that are relevant to that materialistic, competitive society of the Gringo. This society is only able to function through the sharpening of wits and development of the human instinct of rivalry. For this same dominant society and mentality to arrive at a point where there is now a white women's liberation movement is *dangerous* and *cruel* in that the social structure has reached the point of fracture and competition of the male and female. This competitive thought pattern can lead to the conclusion that the man is the enemy and thus create conflict of the sexes.

Now we, Raza, are a colonized people, (we have been a colony of New Spain, we have been Mexico, and have only a veneer of U. S. of A. rule since 1848, just 100 years) and an oppressed people. We must have a clearer vision of our plight and certainly we cannot blame our men for oppression of the women. Our men are not the power structure that oppresses us as a whole. We know who stole our lands. We know who discriminates against us. We know who came in (our parents still remember), threw out our Spanish books and brought in new, fresh-written history books. And we know who wrote those books for us to read. In other words, we know where we hurt and why. And even more important, we cannot afford to fight within and among ourselves anymore, much less male pitted against female.

When our man is beaten down by society, in employment, housing or whatever, he should no longer come home and beat his wife and family. And when the woman doesn't have all she needs at home or she perhaps has a family to raise alone, she should not turn around and hate her husband or men for it. Both the man and the woman have to realize where we hurt, we have to figure out why we hurt, and why these things are happening to us. And more important, through all of these sufferings and tests, we have to receive and share strength from each other and together fight the social system that is destroying us and our families, that is eating away at us, little by little. And we have to build a social system of our own.

One of the greatest strengths of Raza is that of our understanding and obedience to nature and its balance and creation. This same awareness makes us realize that it takes a male and a female to make a whole. One sex cannot have total fulfillment without the other. Life requires both in order for it to go on, to reproduce. This same basic need of each other is the total fulfillment of beauty in its most creative form. Now the reason that we discuss this is that we must think of life generally, without the BAD and TABOO connotation that has been placed on our most basic functions. We cannot allow negative attitudes in regard to our physical capacities, because when we allow this kind of control on ourselves, we are allowing ourselves to be castrated, controlled and destroyed at our very basic essential level. This can affect generations to come.

In working for our people, a woman becomes more and more capable. This Raza woman gains confidence, pride and strength—and this strength is both personal and as a people. She gains independence, security, and more human strength because she is working in a familiar area, one in which she puts her corazón and love. When a man sees this kind of spirit and strength, the Chicana may be understood as having lost her femininity. A man may misinterpret this and feel it as a threat. But he, too, must stop and evaluate this. He should not react against her because this is a great source of strength for him, for her, for our children, for the familia de la Raza. This kind of spirit and strength that builds and holds firm la familia de la Raza. This is love, my Raza. We cannot compete with "el barro" that has held us firm for so long. This is total *respect* and *equality* of humanity, equality of humans that have love for ourselves, love for our men, love for our elders, love for our children. It is this love that is the spirit that cannot be broken and destroyed. It is this force that has allowed us to endure through the centuries and it is the strength that carries on the struggle of our people—the demand for justice.

With this kind of strength, how can we possibly question the femininity of the Chicana? Femininity is something more than the outer shell. What the Chicana has within makes the exterior seem so limiting. When we consider the physical and psychological make-up of the women, the exterior stereotyping of the woman seems like such a materialistic attitude. That kind of judgment should not be placed on the woman; it can lead her to become commercial and competitive.

Let us remember that many of the Raza women can and do relate to the earth. La Tierra. After all, many of us have worked in the fields. Many of us come from migrant and campesino workers. We are not afraid of the sweet smell of sweat from our bodies. How many of us who have seen our mothers wearing coveralls with knee patches, thinning beets and working in the fields, would dare to say that this woman is not feminine? This woman is a big part of our people. When we are the sons and daughters of a strong peasant people of the earth, surely we have the strength not to be so materialistic as to judge each other by our exterior and possessions.

No, mi gente, what we have going for us as a people is much stronger than that which we can see. It is that "barro" of which we are made of. It is that which is our spirit within us. Our Indio roots that live. The Church did not give us a spirit or humanity. We have always had it. The Church taught us Christianity and the beauty of Jesus Christ, but the world corporation, the BUSINESS built upon the spiritual concept, is quite another thing. That we have let this corporation control us, is something else that we must question because we can no longer let anything drain our spiritual strength—and we are realizing more and more where our strength is. We must give it to each other.

If the Chicana chooses to go white women's liberation, she has chosen to alienate herself from her people and has chosen to make it on her own, by herself. Her strength is lost to her people. If the Chicana chooses to become a Chicana PRIMERO, to stand by and for her people, then she has become stronger by joining the struggle for her people. And we do need her very, very much. All of this means that today we face a time of commitment and the Chicana, too, must make a choice. Her people wait for her, la familia de la Raza needs her for the building of our nación de Aztlán. Our own society needs everyone. YOU MUST BE A CHICANA FIRST—for when you are a Chicana primero, you can wander all over, you can relate to many struggles, for they must all someday come together. BUT you will be home, in Aztlán, working with your own familia, to build for your own people, within the spirit that comes from "el barro." PORQUE SÍ VENIMOS DE BUEN BARRO . . .

April 26, 1971

National Chicana Conference, Houston

Viva La Raza, viva la Chicana y viva el Machismo, for I am machismo too. The machismo that protects its people without self-interest.[1] Those are some of the cries heard and passions felt by Chicanas as we were caught up in the ecstasy of sisterhood at the National Chicana Conference in Houston, Texas, last May.[2]

The best result of the conference is that we all learned. You see, Comadres, that's how Raza lives—by living, by learning, by being vibrant, con gusto; by laughing, suffering, crying and learning more everywhere we go, in everything we do. That's our secret of endurance, to live, whether we're getting our teeth kicked in a housing project of the barrio or on the farm. We know we are part of a people, part of a life that throbs for us everyday, within the artery of "El Corazón de La Raza."

The Conference was also good in that it brought together many who had never been involved. Chicanas from all parts of the country met and discussed many important issues, while others renewed friendships within La Causa.

An exciting moment in the conference came Saturday evening, after the mariachi Mass. We were all in the patio waiting to eat and, while we waited, the mariachi group played for us. It was then, that our Chicanismo tore down the curtain of inhibitions and we let out

---

[1] In a U.S. context, machismo has come to mean Latino male dominance over, and beliefs of male superiority to, women. In a Mexican context, machismo generally refers to culturally specific values and meanings about how men should behave and what values they should hold. In both contexts, the implied outcome is unequal relations of power between men and women with men as the dominant figure, protector of home, and guardian. As viewed in these two sentences, Vasquez was applying the term machismo to ideas about protection of one's own.

[2] The First National Conference of Chicanas Por La Raza (often referred to as the "First National Chicana Conference" or "The Houston Conference") was held Memorial Day Weekend, May 28–30, 1971, at the Magnolia Branch of the Houston YWCA.

screams of "ay, ay, ay y ¡aajúaa!" We began dancing all over the place. It was exciting and beautiful to see women together gozando de la vida in each other's company. Women danced to the mariachi sounds, out of pure joy. It was a fountain of sisterhood flowing with childlike innocence and delight.

Our dancing was not that of exhibition but the pure expression and partaking of a musical, rhythmic physical pleasure. All was interwoven with enjoyment of our culture, our music, our dancing, our sisters' company in living. Some of the sisters even began dunking each other in a pool in the patio. We went wild.

Perhaps this spark of sharing in joy is the clue to the spirit of our Chicano Movement, our people as a whole. For another thing we learned at the conference is that the Chicana has a lot of soul searching to do. This, in addition to understanding what the Raza movement is all about. Also, that we need a lot of self-development, to learn about ourselves and our culture—and then relate and function *to* and *for* us, as a people.

That we had a walkout the last day of the conference seemed inevitable. There was much expounding about La Chicana, but it didn't tie in with our movement issues. The conference had the aura of being self-centered with a competitive attitude toward the Chicano Movement.

Another thing we seemed to lack was control of our own Conference. The Y.W.C.A. in Houston is smack in the center of a Chicano neighborhood, yet there were few barrio people participating in the conference. We expected Houston participation—particularly after the insane shooting of the Rodriguez family in Dallas and other police killings in Texas.[3] Some Chicanas found it hard to be alienated from

---

[3] In February 1971, police stormed a family home in the middle of the night, shooting Thomas Rodriguez and his wife in front of their eight children. Based on erroneous information, the police thought the family was harboring fugitives who, earlier in the month, had kidnapped five deputy sheriffs and killed three. Both Rodriguezes survived and were completely cleared of charges. Their case came to symbolize for many Mexican Americans in Dallas their vulnerability to a violent and prejudiced police force. See Shirley Achor, *Mexican Americans in a Dallas Barrio,* (Tucson, Arizona: U of Arizona P, 1978), 106-8.

the people. Perhaps we must face the fact that an institution of the system isn't going to be an instrument of unity for us.

Let's hope, too, that when there is a conference held under the banner of Chicanismo, there will be a large panel of Chicanas exposed to the news media. Those of us who have long been involved will not be used by any one spokesman (or spokeswoman). We have in our Chicanas a lot of good hard workers that know and live Raza.

After the walkout, many of us marched to Salazar Park, where we broke up into workshops. As we met there, we saw the people come out from their homes and gradually join us. By the time we prepared, collected, and read our workshop resolutions, we had all ages of neighborhood people sitting [and] listening. It was inspiring to see children's faces glow as they related to our "Viva La Raza" slogans. From the Chicana conference "En el Parque," we drew up resolutions that related to the Raza movement as a whole as well as the Chicanas.

We know that the era of the stoic Chicana is becoming a thing of the past. The Chicana is saying "hasta aquí no más," in joining hands with our people on the move. We know too, that we have many issues to resolve. At the conference, for example, there was petty gossip about our own sisters. We better begin by knowing who and what we are angry with. Who is the enemy? Not each other. Let's not fall into the trap of being competitive with each other. One way to test ourselves is by deciding who we are going to be dedicated to—just to Chicanas or to our people as a whole? For it is this decision that will tell us whether we speak only of equal work, equal pay (for men and women), or also about *equal opportunity* minorities.

Let's clarify issues. Shall we worry, for example, about the fact that Jesus Christ was a man and the Bible is written by men, or do we get down to business and face the Catholic Church (90 per cent of us are Catholic) for putting guilt chains on us, instead of letting us know how truly spiritual we are? Maybe we better begin ministering love and Christianity to each other by practicing it.

And what of our culture as to sex? We seem afraid to talk of sex and womanly functions. So, instead, we find ourselves blaming our mother and viejitas. Baloney, we need our viejitas, because *they* have many answers. The Chicana cannot afford the luxury of a so-called "generation gap." Let's remember we bear the children, we raise them, and we better start figuring out what to teach them.

And on top of all this we have that political monster to contend with. We can't avoid it. We have to learn how he works. Otherwise, we will only be bearing our children to feed into it. The Democratic and Republican animal is a big monster. That's why we need our Raza Unida under the banner of our Nation of Aztlán. We must dedicate ourselves to build what is ours.

The Chicana cannot hold back anymore. We must overcome the fear of giving ourselves to the Raza movement. This will be hard for some of us, mostly because we have been kicked around time and again by the system and by our own. But we must overcome those fears or find ourselves alone again without our people, without our roots, to wander in a dying system that has planned our genocide, to watch our children lose themselves in the hypocrisy of a money-mind.

The legacy of La Chicana is our children, the entire Raza people. We cannot fail now. We must become strong, for that is how we will build our own society. "Chicana: Our children are the spiritual conscience of Raza and the moment of Raza begins with the movement of a child in its mother's womb."

August 20, 1971

Corporate Institutions and Industrial Society

Introduction
Lorena Oropeza

During the post-World War II era, the United States enjoyed a period of unprecedented economic prosperity and technological progress. Determined to wage a global struggle against communism by 1947, the U.S. government invested unprecedented sums in military-related research. Federal money invested in such new industries as aeronautics and electronics positively affected the economy. Also spurring economic growth was unleashed consumer demand. Following nearly two decades of depression and war, many Americans were eager to buy new cars, refrigerators, houses, and clothes. Happily for them, purchasing power more than matched consumer desire. Between 1947 and 1961, national income rose more than 60 percent.[1]

By the early 1960s, Enriqueta Vasquez had overcome many obstacles to share in this prosperity, yet ultimately she rejected it. Her participation in the Chicano Movement prompted her to question mainstream values, including the value placed on material possessions. Indeed, in 1968, despite the loss of income to her and to her family, Vasquez decided to embrace a life of full-time political activism. As a columnist for *El Grito del Norte*, she constantly urged her readers to cultivate human relationships instead of trying to maximize their personal wealth, offered meaningful alternatives to the endless drive for profit, and surveyed the technological accomplishments of industrial society with a critical eye.

The root of the problem for American individuals and corporations alike, Vasquez argued, was the overwhelming desire for "MONEY." Eager for money to buy more things, Americans constantly marched to the drumbeat of acquisition. Consequently, they had less time for each other or for making the world a better, more equitable place. Meanwhile, businesses sought bigger and bigger profits even if securing those profits caused worker exploitation and environmental degradation. To Vasquez, such an overriding emphasis on accruing wealth directly contributed to a modern society that was emotionally barren and often literally toxic.

Despite such grave warnings, Vasquez was not opposed to money altogether any more than she was opposed to all technology. As she explained in "Money, Money, Money," "We are not saying that being a technical-industrial society is all bad . . . [or] that money is all bad either." Only when making

---

[1] Jaqueline Jones, et al. *Created Equal: A Social and Political History of the United States*, Volume II, from 1865, Brief ed. (New York: Pearson Longham, 2005) 575.

money became an exclusive priority at the expense of caring for other people did money become a "monster," she explained in "Values Lost."

Her take on technology was likewise nuanced. On the one hand, she viewed the use of atomic weaponry as a monstrous example of technology in action. On the other hand, sharing a popular suggestion of the era, Vasquez believed that the problem of unemployment might be solved if workers kept their wages but worked only half as many hours. In this case, technology had a positive role to play to lighten the labor load of most Americans.

At other times, Vasquez's critique of modern industrial society sounded stunningly contemporary. In a column entitled "Smog and Money Politics," for example, she blasted American dependence on foreign oil. Writing well before the energy crisis of the early 1970s, Vasquez promoted the use of public mass transportation systems and the manufacture of fuel-efficient automobiles to protect the environment. Lamenting widespread resistance to these suggested changes, she pointed a finger of blame at "rich oil people" who were also "powerful politicos."

Unafraid of controversy, Vasquez also pointedly included the Roman Catholic Church on her list of corporate evildoers. "The Church Has Made Us Slaves," blared her second column. To a readership that was largely Catholic, Vasquez maintained that instead of helping the poor, the Church had historically retained control over "the little man" by instilling fear and guilt. Although Vasquez had the utmost respect for some individual priests and nuns, she viewed with great suspicion the wealth of the institutional Church. The desire to keep and increase these financial holdings, she argued, explained the conservative politics of the church hierarchy.

Vasquez did more than criticize; she suggested that an alternative way of life could be found in what she called in an article about the Apollo IX space mission the "cultural base of the Southwest." Specifically, Vasquez asserted that Mexican Americans instinctively lived in closer harmony with nature and with their fellow human beings than did their Anglo American counterparts. Certainly, inherent in this comparison was an idealized and essentialized Chicano culture. Nonetheless, Vasquez, who had succeeded in removing herself from the rat race and dedicating herself to the advancement of social justice, held out the hope that others could do so too.

The Church Has Made Us Slaves

The other day in a discussion, I came upon some interesting ideas about the religious beliefs of our Raza. Many religious persons are dear friends of mine, and we have often discussed the issues of the day—the problems of the country and how people relate to them in their every-day lives. Religion is a very dear thing to all of us. However, the Church as an institution has certainly made first-class slaves of us.

I wonder if the time has come when we must learn to live our religion? When we must learn to practice Christianity. When we must learn to walk alone and no longer use the Church as a crutch that makes us slaves. Has the time come when we must make worship a thing that is lived with our feelings and emotions, and not just saying and listening to empty words?

In speaking of sin, for example, it seems to me that the little man is given a deep sense of guilt and sin when truthfully he should be made to feel like the rich, free human being that he really is. So many of us can be obsessed with sin and this is a heavy burden to bear. We tend to look down upon a person who is leading a free, open life. Many times, this is mostly because that other person may be doing the things which we would like to do but without feeling guilty. Therefore we point to the "sinner" and continue to sacrifice our pleasures in order to be a martyr.

What are the things that are really harmful to man? What are some of the things that a businessman can get away with and not be punished by law? I have seen a man lose his land because of a grocery debt to feed his family. Why can the rich man practice injustice and do it legally—plus not have a guilty conscience? Why can law enforcement agencies force morals on the people and punish the little man for trivial deeds, but the biggest thieves of all and the biggest sin-

143

ners of all can go free to do as they please? Why are ordinary people held in line and enslaved with a conscience, while the big money bags can feel free and just cry "law and order"—with the armies backing them up 100%?

Many wars have been fought and much blood shed in the name of religion. I wonder if it wasn't just in the name of oppression. Even our own Catholic Church is the biggest and richest corporation in the world.[1] It is a business, you know, and it owns so many businesses that you can never imagine. They are the masters. They control our very souls and are making money at the same time. (And they don't have to pay taxes either.) Not once in the history of the Church have they stood by the little man. All they say is "sea por Dios." They have always stood by the big power. Why? Could it be an investment on their part?

In Texas, we had two good priests who were helping the cantaloupe workers asking for higher wages. The two priests were immediately moved to another state. Why do we lose good men who fight for justice? Some of these men know what is right, and I notice that we have a few who are finally speaking out even if they get criticized. I hope that more and more of these good men stand up. I hope they stand up and make themselves heard.

Let's listen carefully, let's evaluate the Church and our lives. Times are changing and we can see by what is happening every day that there are many things which are not well. When you read about riots, beatings, and police killings, there is a lot more to it than just being able to say any one person or one thing is to blame. The pressure of what is happening everywhere has been mounting and believe

---

[1] Vasquez was hardly alone in objecting to the wealth of the Roman Catholic Church. In 1968, one critic noted that "[t]he only sovereign state that never publishes a budget, the Vatican is the one organized church that keeps its money affairs strictly to itself," a situation which, as he also noted, clearly complicated attempts to identify the Catholic Church's relative wealth and financial power with any precision. See Nino Lo Bello, *The Vatican Empire* (New York: Trident P, 1968), 12. In 1984, another scholar suggested that the Vatican's vast holdings of land and gold, and its position as "the largest single stockholder in the world," were important indicators of its enormous wealth. See Malachi Martin, *Rich Church, Poor Church* (New York: G.P. Putnam's Sons, 1984), 14.

me, it is going to get worse and worse before it gets better. The time has come for us to take our heads out of the sand and evaluate the problems of the nation, the state, the community and our own family living. The time is here in which we must take a look at ourselves and our families. Let's begin to think more and more about it. Let's talk to our friends, let's face the issues. Let's examine our spiritual lives and let's learn to walk like proud people who have found themselves and can walk alone.

¡Despierten, mis hermanos! Entre la raza somos gente humilde y honesta. Nunca nos podemos imaginar las injusticias del hombre rico y poderoso. Esos son los verdaderos pecadores. Vamos a vivir vidas cristianas, pero no nos permitamos ser esclavos de pecados que no existen. Las iglesias son negocios y el verdadero poder humano está en nosotros, no en las instituciones. Defendamos a nuestra raza, eso no se vende ni se compra. Es nuestro.[2]

September 15, 1968

---

[2] Wake up, my brothers and sisters! Among our people, La Raza, we are humble and honest. We can never imagine the injustices of the rich and powerful. *They* are the true sinners. We are going to live Christian lives; however, we will not allow ourselves to be slaves of sins that do not exist. Churches are businesses and the true human power is within us, not in the institutions. Let's defend our Raza, it is neither bought nor sold. It is ours.
Translated by Herminia S. Reyes.

Values Lost

Some time back I was talking with a Raza who is now working on a government program funded to help the people in job training, etc. He was talking about the problems of the PEOPLE and explaining just what he was doing. I didn't say too much, I only listened, and finally he said, "You know, I don't know what has happened to me, I used to be militant. I used to love my people and I had pride. I know now that I had a different way of life. Now I am earning over $9,000 a year, I bought a beautiful home in a nice neighborhood, I have a nice car and my wife has good furniture. I can say that I never had it so good. But, somehow I feel that I have had a great loss. I don't know why, but I have never been so unhappy. I talk about the problems of the people and they seem to be such empty words. I catch myself talking down to my old friends. I seem to have a lot of time to do nothing. I feel trapped."

I can have nothing but compassion for this man. What can one tell him? How could I tell him that as Raza he had been alive with a full sense of values? How could I explain to him that he had moved into the so-called MAINSTREAM of the Gringo society? How could I explain to him that he had been bought out? He bought that other set of values, lock, stock, and barrel. He was now hooked, BUT GOOD. This opening of OPPORTUNITIES was given to him and it worked beautifully, it shut him up and brought him into the MAINSTREAM. Here is an example of a man who was taken from the ranks of my Raza, fitted into a business suit, white shirt and tie, given a briefcase plus the pep talk and a pat on the back and with a smile and a handshake, he was placed on the market of humanity.

Why would a Raza have such a hard time adjusting to this way of life? The real reason is that we know another way of life. We know

146

what brotherly love is. We know how it feels to be alive. Our way of life has been based on humanity, not MONEY and MACHINES. Let's face it, the Gringo way of life is based on a strictly dog-eat-dog concept with a total goal and commitment named MONEY. To a Gringo this is a very acceptable way of life. It is the system that he set up for the people. But the Raza is feeling the pressure, we are feeling the squeeze and more and more we know that something is very wrong and WE DON'T LIKE IT.

More and more you will see the Raza rebel against this monster. We are stopping to figure things out and in the people that I speak to, I see that more and more we are saying to each other and to the Gringo, "No, we will not have that sick way of life imposed on us. We want you to come out of that white ivory tower of yours and see human reality. We want you to come out and face yourself as you are. We want you to come out and be yourself. We want you to quit being phonies, quit playing roles, just be plain HUMAN. There's nothing wrong with being PEOPLE. When you discover yourself as a person instead of a robot, you may even find yourself enjoying other people. You might even like visiting neighbors more than watching TV."

This, Hermanos is what we have to realize that we have in ourselves. This is why we have to realize how much we have to live for. This is why we have to find ourselves and know exactly what we have. This is why we have to keep ourselves aware of what is going on in the world, we have to keep informed of what is going on in the nation and then in our own communities. Because it looks to me as if the U.S. way of life is hated throughout the world. That sick society needs help badly. I say we better begin to show them where they are wrong. We better give them something worthwhile in life. Let's help them find something: THEMSELVES.

So some of our people have to work on these so-called programs. Well, work there if you must, but don't for one minute quit hollering. Raise your voices, that's WHY you are there. If you were militant before, get even more militant now. Live your own way of life, change those rules, change those people that you work for. Don't let them tell you how you have to change, YOU tell them how THEY better change.

Don't just sit there and get fat, GET BUSY. Your people need YOU to represent them as YOU are.

¡Despierten, hermanos! El modo de vivir de la raza es un modo con orgullo e historia humana. Más y más, vemos nuestros modos cambiándose y nuestros valores empezando a paracerse a los del anglo, en materialismo y dinero. Tenemos que expresar nuestra cultura humanitaria de raza y darnos a ver en nuestro modo de vivir. Tenemos que enseñarle al anglo cómo vivir. Tenemos que darle de nuestra cultura y enseñarle nuestras ideas. Nuestras costumbres no se venden ni se compran. Las compartimos porque son nuestras.[1]

March 10, 1969

---

[1]Wake up, my brothers and sisters! Our people's way of life is a life filled with pride and human history. More and more we see our style of life changing and our values beginning to mirror those of the Anglo, in terms of materialism and money-making. We need to practice our humanitarian Raza culture and to showcase our way of life. We need to show the Anglo how to live; we need to share our culture and teach him our ideas. Our customs are neither sold nor bought. We share them because they are ours.
Translated by Herminia S. Reyes.

Apollo IX

Hip, hip hooray, we now have the Apollo IX up in orbit looking for new worlds to conquer.[1] Time and again many people plant themselves in front of the TV set and watch the progress of science. Since I talk so very much about MACHINES I thought maybe I could see what machines could do for man. We have to find a place for them; let's face it, they are here to stay. And I don't think there is anything wrong with them. Matter of fact this COULD be the best thing that ever happened to us.

BUT, I hope that we learn to use those machines to serve man and not to DISPLACE man. With the coming of machines I see where if we had a government truly interested in HUMANITY and PEOPLE, we could develop a very advanced new man. What would happen, for instance, if people were only required to work 4 hours a day or 3 days a week and had to find something to do with their time? It would solve our employment problems and everyone could have something to do and earn their keep. Right now the object seems to be that of keeping people running in all directions, doing nothing constructive. This prevents them from even thinking and with this feeling they gradually become machines without emotions or feelings.

You have but to visit some of the cities in this country to see this over and over again. People can witness a crime and it doesn't move them to do a thing about it. What makes a human this way? Why can they witness even the police beating up people and they will not speak

---

[1] The *Apollo 9* mission of March 1969 put the spacecraft in orbit around the Earth for ten days. The *Apollo 11* mission of July 1969 famously landed a man on the moon for the first time. See Courtney G. Brooks, James M. Grimwood, and Loyd S. Swenson, Jr., *Chariots for Apollo: A History of Manned Lunar Spacecraft,* The NASA History Series (Washington, D.C.: Scientific and Technical Information Branch, National Aeronautics and Space Administration, 1979), 290-300, 337-52.

149

up against it? What is making people lose their sense of emotion? What is making people alienate themselves from each other? What is making people scared to death to the point where they would rather remain in a shell and not look at the bloodshed?

I don't know what the answers are but maybe it is the definition of what man is and what the heck man is supposed to be doing. I have a tendency to believe that the base of the Gringo society is so materialistic and commercial that it has totally destroyed the human man. This is why I believe that in the Southwest, where there is a human cultural base that can be saved, maybe there is a chance for this country to be saved. Could it be that the Gringo looks at the Indian as primitive and uncivilized but in fact the Gringo has not been able to measure up to the natural freedom of the Indian? Does the conqueror have to come and impose their cultural values (MONEY) on the conquered or is it time that we, the conquered, teach the conqueror a thing or two? Maybe it is time we stand up and say, "STOP, let's take a close look at you, you machine monster."

Then we get back to this thing of what should the new man be like. Here we could say that a new man could be a *successful* (by whose standards?), wealthy, well-dressed, educated, (or rather, with a degree) two cars, color TV, etc., etc. In other words SORT OF like a machine that works with precise clockwork. Then, on the other hand, the new man could be a person that is totally aware of what is happening to his fellowman. One that relates totally to his neighbors, to the welfare of his community, to the welfare of his state and his country and is so conscientious that he is aware of his fellowman in other countries.

I think that more and more we are seeing all over the world where man is becoming aware of what is happening in powerful governments and people don't like it. Is this why they riot? There is more and more oppression, more conflict. We see this exists in this country. This is going to continue, it will become more intense rather than less. Some people are taking a stand on the issues and they are waking up. They are demanding changes. The Raza is beginning to stir and they demand to be heard. It will be in listening to these echoes that they will find the guidelines for what is to come. Here will lie the answer as to what is to be done and how we should change our social values. We must make changes to benefit MAN. Science and MACHINES must be used also in helping Man throughout the world. We must do something about what ails man. We must make ourselves heard.

¡Despierten, hermanos! Figúrense ya, los gringos echaron otro cuete a la luna. Ya no nos acabamos con gobernar a este mundo pero buscamos otros mundos para conquistar. ¿Y qué culpa tiene la luna de los lunáticos aquí? Pues ya verán qué tanto dinero que gastamos en estos proyectos y siempre se quejan de ayudarle a la gente. Entre más y más vemos injusticias y la raza es víctima de muchas de éstas. Vamos a examinar nuestro modo de vivir, y aunque nos quieren hacer blancos en nuestros modo de vivir, vamos a estudiar este monstruo de gobierno sin corazón ni cultura humana. Veamos a nuestros hermanos en el mundo como hermanos y vamos a fijarnos y luchar por nuestra hermandad y cultura. ¡Despierten, hermanos![2]

March 28, 1969

---

[2]Wake up, my brothers and sisters! Just imagine, the Gringos launched another rocket to the moon! It is not enough to rule this world, but we now look toward conquering new worlds. And what fault is it of the moon for the lunatics here? Well, now you see how much money is spent on these projects and still they complain about helping people. We see more and more injustices, and our people, La Raza, are the victims of many of these injustices. We are going to look at our way of life, and even though they want to make us white in our way of life, we will study this monster of a government that has no heart or human culture. Let's look at our brothers in the world as brothers and let's take notice and fight for our brotherhood and culture. Awaken, my brothers and sisters!
Translated by Herminia S. Reyes.

Smog and Money Politics

Lots of the time we talk about the Raza knowing a way of life that is part of our culture and is humanitarian and then too we talk about the Americano society being a DOLLAR culture. We can see this time and time again where Tío Sam is so busy playing in the world of money he forgets the people that live here. Because he gives the people new cars, new TVs, houses, this and that, that is supposed to make everybody happy. Oh, yes, and when the people have all of these things, they are supposed to feel *good* and *better* than the other guy. Of course, most of this stuff is on *credit* and not really yours; you better be sure you make those monthly payments.

You know just the other day I was looking at a picture in the paper where they have designed a new mask that can be worn over your head for SMOG and they say that soon we will all have to wear these when we go outside. Also in California, some of the doctors are now putting on the death certificates, cause of death: SMOG. We hear so very much about pollution of the waters, air, etc. I guess, in other words, we are killing ourselves.[1]

---

[1] During the late 1960s and early 1970s, scientists studied the connection between Los Angeles smog and respiratory conditions such as emphysema; some doctors even recommended that their patients leave the Los Angeles area, and approximately 2500 patients did so. In October 1967, the Los Angeles County Medical Association testified that "[a] 'major catastrophe' may be imminent," and that "[a]ir pollution . . . may cause a 'great' number of deaths in the Los Angeles community." Doctors also blamed air pollution for causing 168 deaths in New York City during a few particularly smoggy days in late November 1966. See "Smog: A Catastrophe Imminent for L.A.?" *Los Angeles Times*, Oct. 8, 1967. section G, pg. 5; Philip M. Boffey, "Smog: Los Angeles Running Hard, Standing Still," *Science,* New Series, vol. 161, no. 3845, Sept. 6, 1968, 161; and "Medical Study Shows 168 N.Y. Smog Deaths" *Los Angeles Times*, Oct. 28, 1967, 5. Regarding New York City and smog, see "Emphysema Study to Focus on Smog," by Nancy J. Adler, special to the *New York Times,* Sept. 1, 1968. The article was accessed via ProQuest Historical Newspapers, *The New York Times*, 1857-Current file.

Let's see what could be done about SMOG *if* the U.S. of A. was really interested in HUMAN BEINGS. First of all about 50% of the smog in the cities (and it is now floating to the mountains and plains) is caused by cars.[2] In this highly developed and civilized country, we have been able to build transportation to the moon, why haven't we built big metro systems in the cities? They could be electric and for free or so cheap that people would not *want* to drive. Right now, people drive because the buses give poor service in certain areas and they are too expensive. If we had cheap bus service people would be glad to give up driving cars.

Then on the highways, if *families* could ride the buses and trains as cheaply as they drive, they wouldn't bother driving, I know I wouldn't. Then how about our good old railroad. They have been pushed more and more out of the picture of transportation. Here is a perfectly safe, enjoyable way to travel. We could be using the railroads more and get some of these big trucks off the highways. Rail travel could be made cheap, particularly to family travel and shipping of goods through this system could become very practical? ¿Qué no?

Now let's see why Uncle Sam will *not* do these things. First of all the U.S. already has and has had for some time fuels that can be used in cars that will not give off the carbon. However, these cannot be put on the market because what would happen to all of the usage of petroleum products? Our oil men would not be able to make the millions they make now. These rich oil people are powerful politicos.

Next, we have been real suckers for buying new cars every year. (They tell us, to be a good soul and as good as the next guy we need

---

[2] In an October 1969 article detailing nation-wide efforts to curb air pollution, the *New York Times* estimated that "roughly half of all air pollution appears to come from automobiles." Among contemporary innovations aimed to reduce gasoline vehicle emissions of nitric oxides, unburned hydrocarbons, and carbon monoxide were exhaust controls on new cars, as well as exploratory use of natural gas and liquefied petroleum gas (propane) as alternative fuels. See "Air Pollution Grows Despite Rising Public Alarm," *New York Times,* October 19, 1969, accessed via ProQuest Historical Newspapers, *The New York Times,* 1857-Current file. See also Philip M. Boffey, "Smog: Los Angeles Running Hard, Standing Still," *Science,* New Series, vol. 161, no. 3845, Sept. 6, 1968, 990-92; and Lester Lees et. al, Environmental Quality Laboratory, California Institute of Technology, *Smog: A Report to the People* (Los Angeles: Anderson, Ritchie & Simon, 1972), 52-53.

a *newer, better* car). Sooooo, who is getting rich? Rich by selling us cars? When we talk about cars and smog, you don't think for one minute that Chrysler and General Motors is going to sit back and say, "Ok, for the good of the people, we really shouldn't have this many cars." You bet your boots they aren't. And they now have MONEY AND POWER so you can't get those cars off the streets, even if it means us and our kids are going to die from smog.

Now when we look at the smog situation, and then at part of the cause, (industry is something else), it looks to me like humans are beginning to die because of POLITICS and MONEY. See why we say Tío Sam is a DOLLAR culture?

I guess if HUMANS want to live they have to fight politics and money. Then the interesting thing is too, those people that say, "We shouldn't have people speak up and march." I guess people are supposed to be submissive and robot-like and take all of this crap. I think we have to stop and figure these things out. Tío Sam no longer cares for the needs of the people. Certainly things like the smog have been building up for many years now and they know exactly how much longer this can go on. But I do believe that the only thing that Tío Sam will listen to anymore is violence and demonstration, if you don't have power and money to be heard. That is why more people are standing up and saying BASTA YA. If the only thing that Tío Sam will listen to is POWER and MONEY, then I guess all we can do is raise holy hell, LOUD and STRONG on all issues and in every way. ¿Qué no?

January 17, 1970

The Church and the People

St Luke: Chapter 19, Verses 45 and 46

"And he went into the temple, and began to cast out them that sold therein, and them that bought.

"Saying unto them, it is written, my house is the house of prayer; but ye have made it a den of thieves."

It seems that people are taking a good close look at their Church. They now question the real meaning of Christianity. Why are the Blacks DEMANDING reparation from the Church? Why have the Young Lords in Harlem taken over a church for a community center?[1] Why did Raza in Los Angeles enter a church on Christmas Eve?[2] Why is UMAS (United Mexican American Students) in Denver picketing the Church? Why are groups seen picketing various churches of our country today?

People have come to the point where they know the difference between CHURCH, CHRISTIANITY, and a real SPIRITUAL LIFE. Where a church was said to be a house of God people now realize that that house is built brick by brick on human exploitation, huge land holdings throughout the world, major stockholders in business wars, bloodshed, political maneuvering and out and out hypocrisy. People have come to realize that one church is a CORPORATION FOR PROFIT, and one of the world's richest corporations.

---

[1] The Young Lords were a Puerto Rican activist youth group similar to the Chicano Brown Berets.

[2] In Los Angeles, Católicos Por La Raza interrupted a 1969 Christmas Eve Mass at St. Basil's Roman Catholic Church to protest the Catholic hierarchy's inattentiveness to Chicano needs. The protest received coverage in the group's own newsletter of the same name, which can be found on microfilm at the Ethnic Studies Library at the University of California, Berkeley. A fictionalized account of this protest also opens Oscar Zeta Acosta's *Revolt of the Cockroach People* (San Francisco: Straight Arrow Books, 1972; New York: Vintage Books, 1989).

So now the house of God, the rock of Peter, is a house of commerce and people know the difference between this business and love of God. People now know the temple of God is within each and every one of us.

Christianity is being looked at in a different light. Jesus Christ is being seen as the radical he really is. He is seen as a revolutionist through the eyes of the revolutionaries, for it is from him that we draw strength. When we see the teachings of Jesus Christ we see what he fought, we see him become angry with money merchants and again we see where after his lifetime of teaching those in power turned around and built bigger and stronger the very same type organizations he fought. The church institutions are the biggest BLASPHEMISTS of all.

Spiritual life is what we know we have. This is what guides us in our day-to-day living. The Church has too often played the role of a powerful patron who is not interested in ministering to all of the needs of the people. The Church has remained uninvolved and uninterested in the social conditions of the world. It has preached with deaf ears. It seems to serve as a pacifier. It talks of a way of life completely contrary to the society we live in. Yet it does nothing about our human needs; it only rakes in the gold to add to its bricks of the impenetrable tower.

It is common knowledge that the Catholic Church is a block of power in society and that the property and purchases of the Church rate second only to the government. True Christianity demands that this institutional power and wealth of the Church be brought to bear in solving the current Chicano urban and rural crisis . . . This religious dollar must be invested, without return expected, in the barrios . . .

The Church must come to realize that her commitment to serve the poor today means the investment of land and seed money for La Raza's self-help projects such as housing development corporations, management development corporations, small business corporations, credit unions and co-ops, the profit from which will be used to further our own barrios . . .

Spanish-surnamed clergy and laity should determine the priorities of goals and objectives in a given barrio. Financial assistance must be provided without stringent controls and bureaucratic attachments.

Because of the incredibly high dropout rate among Mexican American students, tutorial services, study halls, bilingual programs, programs for dropouts, etc., must be initiated and funded.

In conclusion, to build power among Mexican-Americans presents a threat to the Church; to demand reform of Anglo-controlled institutions stirs up dissension . . . However, if representatives of the Church are immobilized and compromised into silence, the Church will not only remain irrelevant to the real needs and efforts of La Raza in the barrios, but our young leaders of today will continue to scorn the Church and view it as an obstacle to their struggle for social, political and economic independence.

February 11, 1970

Money, Money, Money

A little while ago, they announced over TV that in New Mexico some farmers association of some kind had met and were going to spray for caterpillars in the southern New Mexico area. (By the way, this is a particularly bad year for caterpillars. Traveling from Pueblo to La Junta in Colorado, you can see the caterpillars streaming across the highway.) According to this group that met, it seems that in New Mexico there are two kinds of insecticides available for use against the caterpillars.

It seems that these two insecticides are equally effective against caterpillars. However, one of these sprays—toxaphene—will kill the fish in the streams and the other wildlife in the area that gets sprayed.[1] In other words, you get rid of the caterpillars and *BY CHOICE* you will have made a barren piece of land. It would be like one year you would look out into the fields and see acres and acres of beautiful green corn to feed the people and cattle, and the next year you would look out upon the same fields and see a desert.

---

[1] Throughout the 1960s, researchers became increasingly critical of the use of pesticides like toxaphene and DDT. Among other alarming incidents, the deaths of many thousands of fish in the Missouri River in May of 1968 (with as many as 660 dead fish floating past one point in an hour) seemed to have been linked to the spraying of toxaphene and dieldrin to combat army worms in wheat fields. On June 17, 1970, the Interior Department banned the use of toxaphene and most other pesticides on 500 million acres of Federal lands, and three years later the Environmental Protection Agency included toxaphene in a list of toxic pollutants "that cause death, disease, cancer or genetic malfunctions in any organism with which they come in contact." See articles accessed via ProQuest Historical Newspapers, *The New York Times*, (1857-Current file): "New Ruling on Pesticides," November 16, 1969, D45; Donald Janson, special to the *New York Times*, "Fish Deaths End in Missouri River," May 29, 1964, 58; and Richard D. Lyons, special to the *New York Times*, "E.P.A. Acts to Curb Water Pollutants," July 6, 1973, 28.

Now the other insecticide will kill the caterpillar and not harm the wildlife in the area. AND which of the two insecticides did these responsible citizens pick to use? It is hard to believe, but they picked the dangerous insecticide that would kill the wildlife as well as the caterpillars. WHY? On the sole basis of MONEY. The insecticide that kills wildlife along with the caterpillars is cheaper than the one that is safe for wildlife and kills the caterpillars. These responsible citizens (?) decided to use the cheaper insecticide despite all other facts in the matter. This decision was made solely on the basis of MONEY, not nature or people.

It is a bit creepy and scary to think of a decision of this kind coming from humans. The fact is that an insecticide so dangerous as toxaphene shouldn't even be manufactured—it's as bad as napalm. But actually, Raza, this is just an example of one of the cultural differences that we have to deal with when we study the mentality of the Anglo and his society. The Anglo values have him so obsessed with money that his is ruled by it in almost every decision that he has to make. His society is built upon MONEY, MONEY tells him how to live and he lives that way.

The only value that is truly built into the Anglo social mentality is that of possession and material goods. The Anglo treats land in the manner of possession and values it in the manner of money. One has but to look at the trespassing laws in the State of Texas where people can be shot just for stepping on someone's land.[2] The Gringo came

---

[2] Article 1142 of the Texas Penal Code made it lawful to use violence against a person "in preventing or interrupting an intrusion upon the lawful possession of property," or "in self defense, or in defense of another against unlawful violence offered to his person or property" although Article 1142 also stipulated that only the minimum of violence required to defend person or property was legal. However, in the 1942 case *Redmon v. Caplei,* Texas courts found in favor of the defendant, who was accused of assault for having shot at a home intruder, thus upholding the right, in some cases, to shoot trespassers. Article 1142 remained part of the Texas Penal Code until 1974, when Texas repealed and restructured the penal code. *Vernon's Annotated Penal Code of the State of Texas* vol. 2A, Penal Code Articles 979-1268, Trade and Commerce Offenses Against the Person (Kansas City, MO: Vernon Law Book Company, 1961), 191, 196; and *Vernon's Texas Codes Annotated*, Penal Code Sections 36.01 to End, Appendix (Repealed Articles of Former Penal Code) (St. Paul, Minn.: West Publishing Co., 1974), III-IV, 622-3.

here with the concept of possession and built this into his laws. We have all heard of the fact that possession is 9/10 of the law. The only question in our minds now, particularly coming out in the Southwest is, WHOSE LAW??

The Indian and Raza (los que no quieren hacerse Gringos) still respect nature, we can still look at the land, the air and nature and know in reality that it belongs to no one, for it belongs to everyone. It is here to be used to survive by, to exist, and to live by. Man can live in harmony with nature and this is as it should be, for, after all, nature rules. But the Anglo has never understood this, he has never understood nature, he refuses to accept it, he refuses to obey anything, he refuses to live by anyone's rules but his own. He has placed himself in the role of the creator.

And this superior attitude is the Anglo mind, the mind of the white ruling class in this country. As a young lady in San Jose City College was telling me, "What is patriotism in this country now? The choice is money worship—you love, worship and live materialism, which leads to insanity—or you go the opposite. If you think different and your values are different, then you are called unpatriotic. These crazy Gringos think it is unpatriotic to fight this thing called money, to fight for humanity, and yet that is the only sane thing to do."

I guess, when you think about it, that is what the awakening of Raza is all about. That's what our nation of Aztlán is all about. A basic human nature concept: people against a big technical, money-crazy culture and people. It's a tough fight, but it's our only chance for survival as a people. A HUMAN PEOPLE.

We have to take into consideration also that we are not saying that being a technical-industrial society is all bad and that money is all bad either, but what we are saying is that these things should be used for the benefit of humanity. And they can only be used for the benefit of humanity if they are totally controlled by humanity and used for humanity. But when money becomes a way of life, when money becomes a daily obsession, when money becomes a form of slavery, it becomes a ruler.

And with all of this we find the Anglo slowly building his destruction by this thing called MONEY. In everything that these uncultured people do, we see them build in destruction for man. This happens because they are the ruling class because of their money. Now as he builds this destruction against nature and people, this includes us too, Raza. Just a small example like the insecticide matter in this state shows us how little concern they have for humanity. This shows us also how these supposedly responsible citizens are running around in some kind of death sleep that makes them concerned over MONEY, not people. And this very thing is built into our laws as well as all of the mentality of the Gringo.

This is why Raza has lost faith in the Gringo society, because we know that we have values that are more sensible for mankind. We know that Raza is capable of a more human concept to live by. This is why Aztlán as a nation is coming about for Raza. This is why we are now thinking in terms of our own society, our own nation, of AZTLÁN. We have now seen the values of the Gringo Society and we don't want to commit that kind of suicide, either for ourselves or for our kids and so we build AZTLÁN.

July 5, 1970

The Atomic Age

On August 6, twenty-five years ago, the first atomic bomb was dropped on the people of Hiroshima, Japan, and the world finally found out what had been going on at Los Alamos, N.M., "the secret city."

In a few seconds, that single bomb blew to pieces or burned to death some 100,000 men, women, children, babies and unborn human beings of this earth. How many were crippled for life, we do not know.

The politicos of that time told us that this incredible murder was necessary, "to save American lives." But we soon found out that Japan had shown itself ready to surrender even before the bomb was dropped.[1]

Today, Los Alamos and newspapers like *The New Mexican* are celebrating August 6. They call it "The 25th Anniversary of the Atomic City", or the birth of "The Atomic Age," but those are just fine words for a Day of Murder—for the single most horrible slaughter in human history.

We cannot celebrate Murder with them. We will celebrate instead the awakening of ourselves and all the Sleeping Giants, rising up everywhere in the world to cry BASTA YA. Let the Manufacturers of Death celebrate the birth of their Atomic Age. We will celebrate the dawn of the People's Age.

Power, at last, to the People!

July 26, 1970

---

[1] Scholars have long debated the reasons behind the decision to drop atomic bombs on Japan. A summary of the scholarly debate and an overview of the war's end in the Pacific and can be found in J. Samuel Walker in *Prompt and Utter Destruction: President Truman and the Use of Atomic Bombs Against Japan* (Chapel Hill: U of North Carolina P, rev. ed., 2005). Historians who share Vasquez's skepticism concerning the necessity of the bomb's use include Martin Sherwin, *A World Destroyed: Hiroshima and its Legacies* (Stanford: Stanford UP, 2003) Gar Alperovitz, *The Decision to Use the Atomic Bomb and the Architecture of an American Myth* (New York: Knopf, 1995); and Ronald Takaki, *Hiroshima: Why America Dropped the Atomic Bomb* (Boston: Little, Brown, and Co. 1995).

Railroads and Land

A while back a young man was talking to me and saying that things are really very good in New Mexico. Life is good, life is beautiful. And just two days later, I talked with a man who just made me explode. Que desgracia. You know, it seems that the more we open our eyes, the more we see. There is no turning back, no denying the facts of life. I saw a very clear case of the poor people being used by the rich again. This was in a matter that involved Southern Colorado and Northern New Mexico.

In the article "Railroad in Chama" (*El Grito del Norte*, Aug. 29), it tells how they were calling for volunteers to help build up a narrow-gauge railroad tourist attraction. This was very interesting indeed. And about this time I met and talked to a very wealthy man in Denver who is involved in promoting this railroad. He is writing radio tapes and speaking on the radio about New Mexico and La Raza. What is his interest in this matter? YEP, you guessed right, it's money. Money for himself, and he is using the poor people to promote it.

How? Here is his plan according to his manuscript for one of the radio tapes. This is how he is going to solve the problems of the poor people of the area:

First he quotes figures and talks about how "poor" the people in Southern Colorado and Northern New Mexico are. He talks about our being on welfare and our not having skills. Then, he comes up with the solution to all of *our* problems. (Realistically, I get a stinking suspicion *he* is one of our biggest problems.)

According to him, in order to have the "true atmosphere" of the Southwest for this tourist trap railroad, it will be "quaint" to have Raza working on this railroad project. The planners will come into the area (where they already bought 76 acres) and recruit people for training.

Men can be trained to run the railroad. Women and men can learn to be waitresses and waiters. They will be able to get jobs working, as well as lending to the atmosphere, at the restaurants and other businesses that will serve the rail line. Not only that, but when these Raza have skills, they can move into the cities and make a better living.

Sounds nice, huh? But let's look at this a little closer. As I asked the man, *first* where did you get the 76 acres of land in Chama? That's land grant land, disputed territory so to speak. *Secondly*, who is going to own these businesses of which you speak, the ones that will have a Raza atmosphere? *Thirdly*, how much of the profits will go to Raza? *Lastly*, what is you *true* interest? How much of the business are you going to control?

¡Despierten Hermanos! Una cosa es ser pobre, otra ser ignorante. And we are poor in money only, not in brains. We're not stupid. We see in this case that in the name of poverty this rich man, who, I might add already owns a Raza-atmosphere, fancy restaurant, this man is now promoting business ideas for HIM. This is called promoting and speculating. He is using the poor people of the area, FOR WHO AND FOR WHAT? I figure it seems to be for himself. That's the trick to the whole thing.

Now, I am not against the railroad, just like I am not against money or technology, *but* I would like to see the people be benefactors instead of always being on the BEING USED and losing end of things. The Chama railroad and all business enterprises connected with it should be decided, owned and run by the people they affect.

I have enough faith in my Raza to know that they could take this and really make it work for them. It could give Raza pride and a feeling of contribution to work at this railroad. Those who do the work and contribute could really enjoy what they are doing. They wouldn't be working just for money and skills, but for what is theirs. They wouldn't be thinking of moving into the city and leaving their land with skills but building for their children right where they are.

This developing of skills to go into the city stinks. It's OK to go to the city of our own free will, but to be forced and programmed into it is something else. And when the Raza goes into the city the Gringo is always willing and ready to take over the land we leave.

Remember that in New Mexico and Southern Colorado our people are losing their land everyday. And even now Texas corporations are buying supposedly second and third class land in New Mexico like crazy. WHY? (And who is this R. K. Reneger, an engineer from Amarillo, Texas? He's supposed to be helping to run the railroad—but WHY?) Could it be that they are again speculating? Could it be that these companies are getting in the position to benefit from the poor again? Our politicos are speculators, too, and work closely with these corporations when the time is ripe to make some money. We don't have to look far to see the politicos that get rich overnight.

Quién sabe, hermanos, let's watch everything they do FOR Raza, and if the ideas are good, let's get in there and speak up and question all of the decisions. ¡Ya basta! Somos pobres de dinero, pero no ignorantes . . . . .

No, some things are not bad in New Mexico. The people are good, my Raza is beautiful, Raza is a happy people by nature. The only thing now is, let's not let ourselves be used, anymore. Let's look at the things that are happening around us, in our families, our communities, in our state and country and for that matter in the whole world. Let's see what is happening to people all over. We can be poor in money, pero no somos ignorantes.

Editor's Note:

Last month the narrow-gauge railroad train that is supposed to help the poor made its first run with 50 businessmen from Antonito, Colo. and some newsmen on board. The train got stuck, and there were all those bigshots stuck on a mesa without water or food for hours. They were in an open car, out in the sun, too. Pobrecitos! The train was supposed to go all the way from Antonito to Chama, N.M., but it made only 10 miles—and then had to turn back. It seems as though the Anglo exploiters can't even be efficient sometimes.

On October 4, the train finally made it all the way to Chama.

October 8, 1970

International Politics

Introduction
Lorena Oropeza

Anti-war, anti-imperialist, and pro-Cuba, Enriqueta Vasquez's critical per-spective of U.S. foreign policy manifested the strong connection between her personal experiences and leftist convictions. During the 1960s and 1970s, many political activists shared Vasquez's commitment to radical change at home and around the globe. Her advocacy of Third World unity, for example, contributed to, and was influenced by, larger political currents of the time. Yet Vasquez's opposition viewpoint was also impossible to divorce from the insights that she gained and indignities that she endured as a Chicana living in the American Southwest. Local history and homegrown injustice, as much as socialist sympathies, informed her understanding of international affairs.

Objecting to American troops in Vietnam, for example, Vasquez under-stood that her anti-war views clashed with an ethnic group tradition of proven loyalty during wartime. Noting that Mexican American soldiers had served with distinction and pride in previous American conflicts, Vasquez nonetheless insisted that the war in Vietnam was a pointless endeavor that was taking too many Chicano lives. In her columns, she repeated a popular grievance of the era lamenting that working-class and minority youth, includ-ing Chicanos, were suffering disproportionate casualties. Virtually shouting through the use of capital letters in "El Soldado Raso Today," she demanded to know "For what?" To Vasquez, neither defending national honor nor halt-ing the spread of communism justified the loss of Chicano lives or, for that matter, Vietnamese ones. Redefining courage to mean taking a stand against the war, she urged young men to refuse to serve in Southeast Asia and also endorsed a series of Chicano movement anti-war demonstrations called Chi-cano Moratoriums.

Much of Vasquez's anti-war sentiment stemmed from her identification with the Vietnamese. As she mentioned in "Draft and Our Youth," just as Chi-canos were "little people" at the mercy of draft boards and beset by a lack of economic opportunities the Vietnamese were also "little people" facing a "big power," namely the American war machine. In addition, Vasquez often drew parallels between U.S. territorial expansion during the 1840s and U.S. military intervention and economic imperialism more than a century later. Despite the guarantees of the 1848 Treaty of Guadalupe Hidalgo that had ended the war between the United States and Mexico, Mexicans in the new American Southwest had lost both their lands and their status. This history of colonization, Vasquez maintained, united Chicanos and Chicanas with their Third World brothers and sisters in Vietnam and elsewhere.

Indeed, as Vasquez explained the term in her column "Third World Women Meet," the Third World included the "nations and peoples of Asia, Africa, Latin America, and Aztlán." All had "been oppressed by colonialist European powers and the U.S." Yet to Vasquez, to be part of the Third World was more than a political designation, it was an agenda. In 1972, she argued that central task before the people of the Third World was to come together and stop American "economic and political expansion." Toward that end, she assigned a special role to Chicanas whose daily struggle for survival in the United States, she suggested, made them sympathetic ambassadors to their counterparts battling exploitation in other regions in the world.

Charging that U.S. policy was exploitative and shortsighted, Vasquez herself spoke vigorously in defense of Latin Americans. A full decade before the United States confronted guerrilla warfare in El Salvador and revolution in Nicaragua, Vasquez warned that another Vietnam was brewing in the hemisphere. In her article, "Tio Sam Says, 'Gimme!'" she dismissed U.S. economic aid to the region as self-serving and denounced U.S. corporate profits in Latin America as larcenous. In short, the United States, which also consumed more than its fair share of the world's resources, was an international bully. Having personally endured great poverty, Vasquez insisted that the root of the problem, evident at home as well as abroad, was that, among Americans, the worship of the "almighty dollar" trumped treating all human beings with respect. Identifying with poor of the hemisphere just as she had identified with the suffering of Vietnam, Vasquez urged the United States to rethink its Latin American policy, including its trade embargo against Cuba.

After visiting the island in 1969, Vasquez was exuberant in her praise of a revolution that served as a potential model for Chicanos and Chicanas. Whereas U.S. policy-makers objected to the repression of political dissidents and the nationalization of private property, Vasquez extolled the redistribution of economic wealth and the improved education and social welfare system. To Vasquez, the revolution in Cuba had created the conditions for experiencing real freedom. Liberated from capitalism's endless search for profit and granted the basic necessities for survival, she wrote, the island's inhabitants were ambassadors of compassion and creativity. Less convincingly, Vasquez also defended the Castro government as protective of individual civil liberties. Written a generation before the collapse of the Soviet Union and communist governments in Eastern Europe, her support of the Cuban Revolution reflected the enthusiasm of many early observers who saw positive changes occurring on the island. Most important to Vasquez was the extraordinary possibility that here, finally, was a society no longer divided between the haves and have-nots.

Draft and Our Youth

In looking at our young people I realize what decisions they have to make in life and what little choice they have. A while back, I saw a young boy that was faced with the draft and was drinking every day. He didn't want to go to the Army and couldn't understand what it was all about. To him it wasn't a matter of patriotism or a matter of conscience. It was only a matter of custom.

One young man I know is very much opposed to the war in Vietnam. He thinks it is immoral and unjust. However, what can he do about it? He says his friends are going because it is something to do, and it is not a thing of patriotism or honor.

Another young man really gave me the shivers. He had been in Vietnam, liked the fighting and had been injured and was ready to go back and fight some more. When asked what he was fighting for, he only said, "Who cares, I like it and have nothing better to do here. I travel and have my fun."

What does war do to our young men? I have seen men scarred for life, in that it seems to make animals of them. What it does to the minds of our sons can never be repaired and what it is doing to the little people of Vietnam can never be undone. It doesn't seem right that some of the leaders of this country can actually make a decision, without even declaring war, and order thousands of our young men to FORWARD, MARCH. It looks to me like we are really fighting China in Vietnam. Why can't we come out and do it openly if this is so? But instead we are tearing up a little country.

Another thing I notice is that the casualties of the minorities in this war are far larger than the population of the minorities.[1] And I see that many rich Gringos seem to find all kinds of loopholes to get out of going to war.[2] When are we going to realize that we are raising kids to fight the wars for big power? And when are we going to put a stop to this madness? When are we going to stop and take a look at ourselves and say, "That's it, we have had enough"? The leaders keep their hands clean of bloodshed, they don't kill directly, they just order the little people to do the killing for them. Your sons and mine. You and I.

And let's take a look at Guatemala and other countries. Are we going to raise our kids to go kill our brothers there too? I believe that the time has come when we must learn to stand up and say "No." The time has come for us to silence the guns throughout the world. The time has come for us to teach our young people that they have something else to do in the world and another purpose for living besides WAR.

---

[1] In a 1968 report, Rafael Guzman, a political scientist, concluded that, "American servicemen of Mexican descent have a higher death rate in Vietnam than all other G.I.s." As part of his work with the Ford Foundation's Mexican-American Study Project, Guzman had examined the names of Vietnam war dead from January 1, 1961, to February 28, 1967, as compared to U.S. census data from 1960. Estimating that Spanish-surnamed "males of military age" made up 13.8 percent of the total population in the Southwestern states of Texas, New Mexico, Arizona, California and Colorado in 1960, Guzman found that "Spanish-surnamed individuals" accounted for 19.4 percent of the war dead from these states during the period studied. Additional casualty information from December 1967 to March 1969 echoed Guzman's original findings. His findings were first published in *La Raza Yearbook 1968* (Los Angeles), 33, but they had been circulated among ethnic group activists before then. His supplemental report was printed in *La Raza* (Los Angeles) 1969, 12-16. During the 1960s, African American activists likewise expressed concern that blacks were dying in disproportional numbers. Department of Defense statistics show that African American casualties as a percent of total casualties peaked in 1966 at 16% but by 1968 had declined to 13% in part, scholars have suggested, because of the Army was responding to complaints lodged by civil rights activists. According to the 1970 Census, African Americans accounted for 11% of the U.S. population overall. See Brady Foust and Howard Botts, "Age, Ethnicity, and Class in the Vietnam War: Evidence from the Casualties File," unpublished 1989 conference paper, in the author's possession.

[2] For more information about the class biases of the draft during the Vietnam war era, see Christine G. Appy's *Working-Class War: American Combat Soldiers and Vietnam* (Chapel Hill: U of North Carolina P, 1993), especially pages 28-37.

Sure, some of us are veterans, etc. but remember that there may have been some just wars where the world was behind the U.S. But those times are long gone and now we see the riots throughout the world and we see where we have become the most hated country on the face of the earth. We see the forming of superiority, evil and hate.

What I can't understand is, why do we sit back and permit this? Why are mothers satisfied in getting medals and $10,000 for their sons' lives? Why aren't we enraged? Some people say we need an honorable solution to get out. Well, in my mind this country doesn't have that much honor in the eyes of the world and I can't be convinced that honor is worth one drop of blood of my fellowman. Honor or money is not worth our sons' lives and blood.

Then some people say we are fighting Communism. Well, I need more than just one word to justify a war. It reminds me of when I was little, all of our families taught us that being Catholic was the only thing that would get you to heaven, and we were to stay away from Protestants. It was a sin to even go into a Protestant Church. But as time has gone on, I have known a lot of Protestants and you know what I found out? Well, they are people like myself. They are humans and they love the same God. So I just wonder and guess about the Vietnamese. I'll bet they are people like you and I.

Vamos a fijarnos en estas guerras y en lo que le hacen a la juventud. Nuestros hijos mueren, ¿por qué? ¿Es justa esta guerra? Estamos matando mujeres y niños, ¿por qué?¿Quién toma beneficio sobre esta guerra? ¿Quién dice bueno o malo? ¿Quién sabe quién es justo en el gobierno y quién es el que sufre? NOSOTROS. Nuestros hijos mueren y sufren mentalmente al matar a sus hermanos y ¡nosotros lo permitimos! Despierten y piénsenlo bien.[3]

November 27, 1968

---

[3] Let's pay attention to these wars and to what they are doing to the youth. Our sons die—why? Is this war just? We are killing women and children—why? Who is benefiting from this war? Who decides what is right or wrong? Who knows who in government is a just person? And who is it that suffers? WE DO. Our children kill and they endure mental anguish whenever they kill their brothers and we let this happen! Wake up and think hard about all this.
Translated by Herminia S. Reyes.

Tío Sam Says: "Gimme!"

¡Ay caray y újule! What did you think of Rockefeller's visit to Latin America?[1] What a blow to find out our neighbors to the south don't love the red, white, and blue, huh? Let's look a little closer and see why. How come some of those people are beginning to throw rocks and say "Yankee go home"? They have been saying that some time, you know.

First of all, I believe, we have to realize this country thrives and is built on the worship of the almighty DOLLAR. Everything is business and money and the Americano is going to get this regardless of who they have to walk over. We have but to look at TV advertising and commercialism to realize that half of what people spend money on is plain JUNK. But then this keeps the economy going, so that they keep pushing this crap down our throats as well as that of our children. Nowadays you are not even supposed to be happy with a car that runs—you are supposed to buy a new one every year.

Now, it isn't bad enough that we are enslaved to all of this useless stuff, but people are so wasteful that we are presently using up 60% of the WORLD'S raw materials in order for the rich to get richer in this country.[2] Comparing this country with other countries, one could say

---

[1] In 1969, Nelson A. Rockfeller, governor of New York and the grandson of John D. Rockfeller, the founder of the Standard Oil Company, made four fact-finding trips to Latin America during which he experienced many anti-American demonstrations. Having been asked by the Nixon administration to review U.S. policy toward the region, Rockfeller's final report that August recommended strong U.S. support for military rulers in the area. Standard Oil had invested heavily in Latin America since the 1880s.

[2] The 60% figure is certainly an overestimate. Among environmental activists in 2005, estimates were that the United States, with less than five percent of the world's population, accounts for roughly 25% of the globe's consumption. The estimate, for example, appeared on the Sierra Club website, http://www.sierraclub.org/population/consumption/, accessed October 10, 2005.

that it is sort of like a PIG. It eats constantly and is getting fatter and fatter and sloppier and sloppier and places like Latin America have just about had enough and are wishing they could now come in for the slaughter.

Knowing these things, let's see why Latin America would not LOVE us. In 1967, U.S. investors brought home PROFITS of over $1,000,000,000.00.[3] You know what this means? Let's say that you were struggling with a little farm and trying to make it produce and along comes your GOOD NEIGHBOR, sets up an oil well ON YOUR LAND and takes all this oil money home with him. He lives in a fancy castle on the hill, and waves to you now and then, and comes over to shake your hand in GOOD WILL. That is just ONE of the realities that is facing Latin America today. We are over in their countries making money off of those people. That is EXPLOITATION!

Then some people say here, "Tough luck, why do they let this happen to them?" This is what is also very interesting. You see, many of the governments are under the control of the U.S. The people in power are paid off and have become so powerful with U.S. backing that they too help the exploiter rob the land. Rockefeller says, "We can't impose democracy," but just look at the U.S. troops in the Latin countries, do you think they are there developing good will? I just really think they are there protecting U.S. PRIVATE INVESTORS. Our NOT RICH boys are there protecting the investments of people like Rockefeller.

Another thing we hear are the good guys that say, "We give them U.S. loans." Yep, we sure do. We give them loans with all kinds of conditions. For example, this money has to be spent on high-priced U.S. goods, shipped in U.S. ships, at high rates. Every dollar of U.S. aid is

---

[3] Here Vasquez's estimate was right on target. From 1965 to 1967, profits from direct private U.S. investments in Latin America totaled $3.634 billion, $769 million of which was reinvested. Therefore, for those three years, total annual profits averaged approximately $1.211 billion. General Secretariat of the Organization of American States, *External Financing for Latin American Development* (Baltimore: Johns Hopkins UP, 1971), 69.

reduced to 60 cents after all the strings are, attached to it.[4] So actually we are not GIVING any aid. We are not LOANING with good will. We are INVESTING in a sure thing and getting a BIG RETURN on our GOOD WILL loans.

Now, another point. Everywhere this country's money goes, our flag goes too—with its ARMS. Like Rockefeller said, "to help control international disorder." We do not respect other countries, but we want everyone to worship this one. The dispute between the International Petroleum Company and Peru is a good example. Peru claims 200 miles of territorial waters which are the most productive fishing areas in the world. Peru is backed by Ecuador and Chile. They want to license the U.S. fishing fleets which have been long exploiting these grounds and the U.S. fails to understand why Peru would want to do this. But on the other hand, the U.S. feels that it is alright to have up to 250 miles of oil-producing grounds in Latin America. We can certainly see this is how we mistreat our neighbors. In this case it is like saying, "It is alright to pull oil out of your country, but I certainly can't understand why you fellows won't let me fish in your nice waters all I want."[5]

The biggest blunder of all comes when we say it's up to the Latin American nations "to work out their own problems. We believe in NON INTERVENTION." We say this when we use military force and have troops all over the place. WHAT FOR? I am sure that the people

---

[4] Aid experts contended that little had changed at the start of the new century. The report, *The Reality of Aid 2000* wrote about the United States, "71.6% of its bilateral aid commitments were tied to the purchase of goods and services from the US." (London: Earthscan Publications, 2000) 81. Other sources echoed or exceeded the 70 percent figure. See Thalif Dean, "Tied Aid Strangling Nations, Says U.N.", *Inter Press News Agency*, July 6, 2004, online at http://www.ipsnews.net/interna. asp?idnews=24509, accessed October 13, 2005; and, contending that the United States had the "worst record for spending its aid budget on itself," Julian Borger and Charlotte Denny, "War of pledges gives hope to world's poor," *The Guardian* (United Kingdom) March 21, 2002, online at http://www.guardian.co.uk/debt/Story/0,2763,671171,00.html#article_continue, accessed October 13, 2005.

[5] Peru underwent a military coup in October 1968 after which leftist military officers nationalized the holdings of International Petroleum Company, a subsidiary of Standard Oil. In February 1969, a Peruvian gunboat fired upon two American fishing vessels that it claimed were poaching in Peruvian coastal waters. Both incidents strained U.S.-Peruvian relations.

here in the U.S. would not for one minute put up with foreign troops in this country guarding foreign interests. But when American interests are expropriated it is called "AN UNWARRANTED INTRUSION." Here again it shows how this country thinks in terms of GIMME, GIMME, GIMME, and they couldn't care less about giving. All they want is to give GOOD WILL and a HANDSHAKE and a visit from Rockefeller, who incidentally owns big chunks of our Latin countries.

What is the answer to this Latin American Problem? Looking at the situation from the Latin side of it, I guess that I too would be out there throwing rocks at Rockefeller and yelling "go home." Will this country ever learn that it cannot exploit other countries forever? Will if ever learn to mind it's own business? Will it ever learn that there are other good people on this earth? That there are other countries on the map? That there are PEOPLE that are EQUAL HUMANS everywhere? That because the rich worship money every day, the masses, the poor, do not cease to exist.

I would say that the days are numbered for the U.S. and if we want peace in this continent, we better become humble, bring ourselves AND THE TROOPS out of these countries and hope for friendship and forgiveness from these people. Otherwise, I would predict that a Vietnam is fermenting in Latin America, and with our domestic problems here, we know what may happen and why.

Despierten, hermanos, miren lo que le estamos haciendo a otros países y lo que les sucede a nuestros hermanos en América Latina. Nuestros hijos también tienen que ir a América Latina a pelear para cuidar intereses americanos. Esto no está bien, esto no debe ser, esto tiene que acabar porque ya se ve que no se van a dejar de nosotros para siempre. Se fomenta otro Vietnam. ¿Esto es lo que le queremos dar a nuestros hijos? ¿A nuestra juventud?[6]

December 6, 1969

---

[6] Wake up, brothers and sisters, look at what we are doing to other countries and look at what is happening to our brothers and sisters in Latin America. Our sons also have to go to Latin America to fight to protect American interests. This is not right, it should not be. This has to end because we know now that they will fight back; they cannot leave us alone forever. Another Vietnam is brewing. Is this what we want to give to our children? To our youth?
Translated by Herminia S. Reyes.

¡Qué Linda Es Cuba!: Part I

The Chicano Press Association, including *El Grito del Norte*, was invited to send representatives to the January 2, 1969 celebration of the 10th anniversary of the Cuban Revolution. There were many North American magazines and newspapers represented; for example, *Seventeen Magazine, Monthly Review, Wall Street Journal, Look,* and many foreign news services. This is the first of a series of articles on Cuba that will be published in *El Grito.*

Looking at the Cuban people, one can say, "What hard-working people! Not only do they have a cause, but the rewards are meaningful. The soul of man is being fed and there is a reason for living." For ten years now, the most powerful nation in the world has looked upon this little island and said, "Die! How dare you make fools of us?" "Beg and admit you are wrong, you are wiped out." But you see these people struggle, work hard and continue to survive. WHY???

In exchange for hard work the people have freedom. Not only freedom from want but freedom to develop themselves as individuals. They have shelter, no mortgages, sufficient food for survival and sufficient clothing. There are few cars, as this is really a luxury item, and what cars there are, are for the use of the people. There are many buses. These buses are all made in France or England. In Havana, transportation is only 5 cents. If you have it, you pay it *consciously,* if not you can ride anyway. I used to watch the people get on and everyone seemed to pay. Public telephones are free. Medical care is completely free to everyone. Even sports events are free.

Food is rationed, not because there is not enough but because it is necessary to have control of [the] surplus in order to be able to ship more of it out of the country in exchange for needed goods and farm machinery. Children and elders have priority on milk and juices. Chil-

dren are fed in schools and eat very well. People are *not* starving. I
believe that this is one of the reasons that Cuba is such a threat to
Latin America. The Cubans are becoming more and more independent and are able to feed their people.

Clothing is rationed so that all may share equally. There are not a
few people with too much and others with too little; instead, everyone
has enough. In traveling all over the island it is interesting to note that
in the country and in the city one sees linens, towels, underwear and
sufficient clothing hanging on the clothes-lines. I was particularly
aware of this, as it is not common in Latin countries. All homes are
furnished with the necessities. They are clean and simple. All have
good mattresses and plumbing and showers. Electricity and water are
available and personal hygiene has been taught to all, even in the
remotest of areas.

January 6 is El Día de Los Reyes, the Day of the Kings. Some
people call it El Día de Los Niños. At this time every child in Cuba
received a toy, those in the campo as well as those in the city. In a village we visited, we talked to the children that were playing with their
toys and riding their bicycles.

The lives of the people of Cuba have changed completely from
what they were during the Batista Regime.[1] One woman in the hotel
where I stayed had been there 15 years ago and spoke to us of life
there at that time. Havana was called the "Paris of the Caribbean." It
had a night life, gambling, and was completely foreign-owned.

For the Cubans this meant prostitution, beggars, and thievery. This
is no more. There has been complete social change. The students were
sent out to teach everyone how to read and write and now literacy is
96%. This is a great accomplishment when compared with the 65% to
80% *illiteracy* of Latin America.[2]

Education is free to all. At one time education was only for the
wealthy but now is available to all. Scholarships are for everyone. You
can chose your profession and attend any university. It is interesting

---

[1] Ousted by the Cuban revolution, General Fulgencio Batista had ruled Cuba since
1934.

[2] Cuba's literacy rates, estimated between 96 and 97 percent, were considered one of
the great successes of the revolution.

to see the enthusiasm among the students for education. I asked what the motivation for education would be, since money and "status" are not part of the social system. The answer came to me from a student, fast and simple. Education is necessary in order to serve society and our fellow humans. We are all responsible for each other.

These are some of the results of the revolution. What has happened to the rich? They are the ones that have suffered. No longer can they make money from the work of others. They have to work also. And this is very difficult for many of them, since they are not accustomed to work. It is for this reason that many leave the country. They are free to do so. The very wealthy homes in Cuba have all been turned over for the use of the people. They are now used for Círculos Infantiles, nurseries and nursery schools and dormitories for the scholarship students that attend the universities. All are being used for the people's needs. None are used for private bourgeois homes. The gambling casinos are closed and the big hotels are now used by the people. Everyone is entitled to a 20-day vacation once a year and they can stay in any hotel with meals and everything paid in full.

The battle of survival of the Cuban people can be seen as a very brave stand on what humanity can do when thrown upon its own resources. The U.S. has a blockade which will not allow many countries receiving U.S. foreign aid to trade with Cuba, and for this reason there are shortages in Cuba.[3] The Cubans are not able to trade on the open market and they are forced to sell their products to very few countries and not at the best price. However, they continue to survive miraculously.

The freedom of the Cuban people is unbelievable. One can hear people talk against the revolution and everyone respects these opinions and freedoms. They are allowed to talk all they wish as long as they do not take counter-revolutionary action. I talked to some of these people also. Basically, one of the problems for them was adjusting to the equality of people. Losing the class system was a hard blow to those who liked being a little better off than their fellow man.

[3] The U.S. trade embargo against Cuba began in 1960. It continued in 2006.

The churches are still there and many are functioning. Those who wish to go are free to support and believe, and they are not harassed in any way. The matter of religion is up to the individual. The churches are not persecuted; they are powerless and in their place. We visited a cathedral in old Havana where there are 60 seminarians studying for the priesthood.

Cuba has what is called a people's army. Anyone who wants to can help in guarding against sabotage. This is used to raise the consciousness of the people. I might mention that the people have arms and guns, so if the masses were against Fidel Castro, I doubt that he would have lived so long. When one sees the guns and guards, one thinks of the military in other countries. But in talking to the people and guards, it is clear that they have not forgotten that they were invaded and bombed by the U.S. a few years ago. They have not forgotten that and I doubt they ever will. The Cuban people do not intend to let their revolution be destroyed by anybody. As one Cuban friend said, "The Cuban people will sink with the island before they give it up."

May 19, 1969

Raza, Nos Están Matando. They Are Killing Us, Did You Know?

One of the most important things to Raza now is that of a rounded-out education. This means Raza studies in the schools. For only by teaching our young people what we have in our beautiful culture will we be able to conserve it. Only by having good social studies can we understand ourselves and build to strengthen our own people. This is very important in this day and age.

It is important that our young people know our history, not just as history but as the history that our ancestors made and our people are making today. It is important that our people know such things as the fact that the first colony in the United States was not at Plymouth Rock and that the first settlers of this country were not the pilgrims but, in fact, the first colony was in 1609 in Santa Fe, Nuevo Méjico, 11 years before the pilgrims arrived at Plymouth Rock. This colony was the first in the United States as known today and the first in Aztlán.

Even more important are the facts of what is happening to Raza and who is making our history for Raza today. Who is this César Chávez, and how did his grape boycott begin and how does it affect us today? He may be in California, and we know that wherever he is, he has a struggle for the campesino and he is Raza and we will support him. He says BOYCOTT GRAPES, and we intend to support him and BOYCOTT GRAPES.

What was it that Reies López Tijerina did to the history of Raza? And let's look at the man fairly, sin envidia, sin criticar. Let's see what the man really had to say to us, the history that he uncovered for us to see. Let's quit burying it away; it is not just history in the past. It is history we are living now. It is that of a treaty that should apply and be alive today.[1] And it affects everybody, you and me.

Corky Gonzales is a strong leader. What is he saying? What is he doing, and more important, why? He has to deal with the problems of many of our people that go into the city. How can he have a building where they give FREE services to the people? If you are in trouble, if you need housing, if you need food, if you need clothes, legal aid, all of these things combined, you can get them through the Crusade for Justice. How many of us would be that committed to our people?[2]

It was an education for me to meet with our young Raza on the campuses in the Oakland, California, area. I traveled and talked to the young people at the colleges and universities of Haywood, Merritt, Berkeley, Stanford, and Foothills.[3] It was beautiful to see our young people and know that they are thinking about the issues and what stand they will take. The young people all over are talking about the issues of Vietnam and the wars in general. Our young people are really concerned about these issues. At Merritt, the young people decided that since there was no school they would go into the Raza Community to work with the people. They are going to work on the Chicano Moratorium for May 30, in San Francisco. César Chávez will speak there.

One can ask, why should Raza take a stand on Vietnam and Cambodia? Well, I would say the following:

Raza is 3% of the population of this country and 19% of the casualties. That is 19% of RAZA.[4] One of the young men that spoke in California spoke of the fact that in Vietnam we are EQUAL and WELL QUALIFIED. There are minorities all over the front lines. WHY? The

---

[1] Vasquez was referring to the 1848 Treaty of Guadalupe Hidalgo that ended the war between the United States and Mexico. The treaty, which granted the United States roughly half of Mexico's national territory in exchange for $15 million dollars, also included provisions guaranteeing Mexicans living in the conquered territory property rights and other privileges of American citizenship. These provisions were largely ignored. As a result, many Chicano movement participants, most notably New Mexico's Reies López Tijerina, argued that people of Mexican-origin still held legal claim to the Southwest.

[2] Rodolfo "Corky" Gonzales was the founder of a Denver-based civil rights organization called the Crusade for Justice. Comprised of families, the organization served as an informal welfare agency, hosted a series of youth conferences, and developed a school that promoted culture and education.

[3] The schools that Vasquez visited in 1970 were Hayward (not Haywood) College, now California State University East Bay, Merritt College in Oakland, the University of California, Berkeley, Stanford University, and Foothill College in Los Altos, California.

Anglo is the majority here, why is he not the majority in Vietnam? Despierte, mi Raza. Why do we have to raise our beautiful children to feed them into that war machine? Can't we give our hijos a better future? I think we can and should. That is why I, too, take a stand on the Vietnam War. I would prefer to see our young men here doing nothing than que vayan a poner su cuerpo y sangre por nada.

A young man returned from Vietnam said that he was really shocked by the experience of having to go to Vietnam and having to kill these brown people. He said, "I felt like I was killing my brothers, I have nothing against these little villagers. With this feeling, you either want to cry or you overcome it and become a KILLER." It hurts me to think that this is the kind of situation we send our young men into.

Another situation taken into deep consideration by the Raza college students was that of Latin America. The young people know that Latin America is fermenting into a Vietnam and they don't like it one bit. The young people feel that we have no business in other countries and when it comes to going into Latin America to kill our brothers, they feel it must stop *SOMEWHERE*.

As Benito Juárez, the father of the Mexican constitution, stated: El respeto al derecho ajeno es la conservación de la paz.[5] This Benito Juárez always practiced, and this applies from the individual who wants to be heard and respected for what he believes, all the way to the national level, where Benito Juárez was wise in teaching the respect of other nations to live and believe as they wished.

---

[4] Vasquez was referring to studies done by Rafael Guzmán, a political scientist working with the Ford Foundation's Mexican-American Study Project. Guzmán had examined the names of Vietnam war dead from January 1, 1961, to February 28, 1967, as compared to U.S. census data from 1960. Estimating that Spanish-surnamed "males of military age" made up 13.8 percent (not three percent) of the total population in the Southwestern states of Texas, New Mexico, Arizona, California and Colorado in 1960, Guzman found that "Spanish-surnamed individuals" accounted for 19.4 percent of the war dead from these states during the period studied. His findings were first published in *La Raza Yearbook 1968* (Los Angeles), 33, but they had been circulated among ethnic group activists before then.

[5] A president of Mexico and one of the nation's most admired figures, Benito Juárez was among the drafters of Mexico's 1857 constitution. He defeated Conservative forces that opposed the document during Mexico's Guerra de la Reforma from 1858 to 1861 and later led resistance against the French-imposed reign of the Archduke Maximilian von Hapsburg from 1864 to 1867. The maxim translates to "Respect for the rights of others is the conservation of peace."

This respect should be practiced by this country, and by the people NOW. And when we say "the people," it is not just you and I, but the rich controlling investors in this country . . . . Why the Rich? Because they are making money in the materials squeezed from foreign countries. The fact remains that the U.S. is 8% of the WORLD POPULATION AND IT USES 74% OF THE WORLD'S RAW MATERIALS.[6]

Despierten, hermanos. Cuando anduve en los colegios y en las universidades en California sentí mucho por los problemas por los que se ocupa la juventud. Visité y hablé con mucha de nuestra joven, raza. Se ven algo preocupados por la posición de este país en guerras lejanas. Hay que oír a esta juventud porque ellos son los cuerpos que pelean las guerras, por eso deben tener algo qué decir tocante a la política de este país. Según la decisión de los jóvenes, nosotros, los padres, podemos comprender y darles fuerza [valor] a sus ideas. Si no se pueden comunicar con nosotros, ¿pues a quién le pueden hablar? Vamos a oír lo que nos dicen y a examinar nuestra conciencia.[7]

May 19, 1970

---

[6] The 74 percent figure is certainly an exaggeration. In 2005, environmental activists estimated that the United States, with roughly five percent of the world's population, probably used between 25 and 30 percent of the world's resources. The estimate, for example, appeared on the Sierra Club website, http://www.sierraclub.org/population/consumption/, accessed October 10, 2005.

[7] Wake up, brothers and sisters. When I was visiting the colleges and universities in California, I felt deeply the problems that concern young people. I visited and spoke with many of our Raza young people. They are worried about the participation of this country in faraway wars. These young people must be listened to because it is they who risk their lives to fight the wars, and so they should have a say regarding the politics of this country. According to these young people, we, the parents, can understand and support their ideas. If they cannot communicate with us, well with whom can they speak? Let us listen to what they tell us and examine our conscience. Translated by Herminia S. Reyes.

¡Qué Linda Es Cuba!: Part II

In visiting Cuba and viewing the Cuban revolution, one wonders what is being done for the education of the youth and what they are striving for. Knowing what the conditions of many Latin countries are, one sees and senses in Cuba a totally different society. You don't know where to begin to find answers to many questions. I had heard of the "new man" and I had heard of the education for today's Cuban youth and children who are going to be the men and women of the future.[1] And I had heard that Cuba views those children as the caretakers of the development of the revolution. Also I had heard that the revolution lives everyday and that it must continue to change and live everyday if it is to be truly of and for the people.

With all of this feeling and puzzlement to mind we visited the Isla de Piños, (Isle of Pines) also called La Isla de La Juventud (The Island of Youth). It was here that I learned of the "new man." The history of this island as well as what is being done now is very inspirational and interesting.

Travel to the island is by plane or car and ferry; the ferry trip takes about six hours. Before the revolution this island was privately owned by big ranchers who spent very little time there. The main things going on in the island at that time were the tourist trade and smuggling. There were 12 schools, total, and 13 whorehouses. The Hotel Colony was built to be a gambling casino and was completed and

---

[1] Vasquez was referring to an attempt by the Cuban revolution to remake society by encouraging the development of a "new man," a person guided by socialist principles.

opened two days before the revolution.[2] Also there was a big prison that held 5,000 men.

It is interesting to hear what happened to this playground for the wealthy at the time of the revolution against Batista.[3] Here the movement was very weak. The landowners used the prisoners to work for them for nothing and therefore this was the ideal place for them. At the time of the revolution, places like the Colony did not drive out the wealthy; they just opened their doors to everyone and the poor and working-class people came here to join the rich in enjoyment. Then the rich left rather than associate with the common people.

In 1966, Hurricane Alma hit and practically destroyed this island. After the hurricane, many of the young people volunteered to come and clean up the island. 1,000 youth came and out of this came the idea for making the island into a garden. As they studied and worked together, there came from them many of the ideas for the development of a "new man."

As one drives through the countryside here, one sees much of the work that has been done and much more that is yet to be done. The clearing of the land alone has been a big accomplishment. With the clearing of the land came the building of four large dams to be completed this year. By 1970 there will be 600 other small dams throughout the island. These will insure success of the agricultural plan of the island. Even now we saw much of the island being irrigated with a sprinkler system. The island produces high quality citrus fruits and cattle. In two years they have planted ten times the amount of land ever planted in the whole history of the country.

---

[2] From 1977 to 1997, Isla de la Juventud was a center of education, hosting thousands of students from throughout Latin America and Africa. Throughout the 1990s, however, the island suffered economically after the fall of the Soviet Union. See Jane McManus, *Cuba's Island of Dreams: Voices from the Isle of Pines and Youth* (Gainesville: UP of Florida, 2000), 129, 153, 161-5. More recently, hurricanes also have exacted a toll. In 2004, the growing tourist industry on the Isla de la Juventud relied on dollars brought by cruise ship passengers and scuba divers, and environmentalists were attempting to hold off destruction of the island's indigenous species and natural beauty. The Hotel Colony meanwhile had become a major international destination for surfers.

[3] Fulgencio Batista was the former dictator of Cuba.

We visited the youth camps as well as the villages. People can sign up to work on the island for two years. Married couples sign up to work on the island and are provided with complete child care, either during the day or, if they wish, from Monday until Friday. With the providing of child care, the parents have sufficient time to work and attend school as well. The island is presently underpopulated and the people are encouraged to live and make their homes here permanently. Completely furnished homes are available for about $5.00 month.

The youth also sign up for two years. They all work on the farms but are also bussed into the schools daily. During the day they always allot time to study. They attend school five days a week.

It was interesting to observe the young people here and see the idea of the "new man" put into practice. The youth coming to the island arrive as very young people in a playful eager mood. Then, in talking with some of the youth who have been on the island for a while, one finds the awareness and aliveness of a thinking adult. It seems that a spiritual growth has taken place.

This is where we learned of the "new man" and the purpose behind the whole idea. The new man is a person of the future. The idea of the new man (and new woman) is the realization that human beings have no limit for development. They have great capacity. They can be unselfish, and with[out] *envidia*. They can all work together for the common good. They can be freed from the pressure of getting money, and become real humans instead of work-machines.

The Revolution is preparing the youth for the fact that machines will take over the work of people in the future. The population is preparing for mechanization. Because of mechanization, Cuba is planning to incorporate people into another kind of work. The Cubans know that they must develop a highly cultural and technical man. A thinking man. A man who knows how to make use of the resources available. A man who can fulfill people's material needs but also, and more important, fulfill the need to create and help—to be human.

In this new society, money must disappear completely. "We want an abundant society with a different kind of man," the Cubans said. In other words, people will not work for money—they will not have to sell their hard work to somebody else. They will work for the good of the land, for the good of all the people.

I asked some of the people there, "Why do you stress the building of what you call consciousness?" It was explained to me by a young girl that with the building of consciousness, one rids oneself of individual selfishness and material goals. Also, by working in the area of agriculture the low value that was once placed on common labor has been completely broken down. By doing this work the people have become accustomed to doing without and have learned to respect their fellow humans everywhere. By being productive in agriculture, they feel that they are giving of themselves toward creating a new world and new thoughts. They thus have become human-oriented rather than material-oriented.

I gazed with amazement upon this beautiful, proud Cuba and asked "How old are you?" She smiled and answered "19." As we boarded the bus, I could only look and think that this is why Cubans walk with such pride on their island. This is why they touch the heart of people all over the world. This is why they live so victoriously and bravely exist. This is why they say "VENCEREMOS."

June 14, 1969

Kent State

Fue para mí un placer y una gran oportunidad cuando me convidaron en dos ocasiones a visitar colegios y universidades en California el mes pasado. Es muy importante hablar y comunicarnos con nuestros estudiantes "chicanos" en el sistema educativo. ¡Qué linda es mi raza! Qué preciosas sus caras jóvenes de bronce en las clases y con sus libros estudiando para determinar su destino.

En la juventud chicana hay mucha esperanza para la raza. En nuestros hijos se va formando el conocimiento de nuestra raza.

Durante el tiempo que estuve en el área de Oakland, se presentó la crisis de los cuatro estudiantes que fueron asesinados en Kent University en Ohio.[1] Esto fue [durante] una demostración en contra de las tropas Americanas que extendieron a la nación de Cambodia. Al suceder este asunto se levantaron los estudiantes anglos y tuvieron una huelga, "Strike", en las universidades y colegios por todos los Estados Unidos. Por esta razón de "huelga", el presidente y los gobernadores ordenaron que se cerraran todos los colegios y las universidades.[2]

¿Qué fue la posición de los estudiantes chicanos? ¿Y cuáles fueron sus problemas?

En el asunto de Kent University se presentó una crisis dirigida directamente a los anglos.

En los colegios, los anglos hablaban en contra de la guerra en Vietnam y en contra de las tropas que entraron a Cambodia. Se oía

---

[1] On May 4, 1970, Ohio National Guardsmen killed four students and wounded nine when they fired into a crowd of anti-war protestors at Kent State University. The killings further divided national opinion concerning the Vietnam War and the right of students to protest. See William A. Gordon, *The Fourth of May: Killings and Coverups at Kent State* (Buffalo: Prometheus Books, 1990), 15-18.

[2] In the wake of the Kent State violence, an estimated 1.5 million students across the country participated in hundreds of student strikes. In California, Governor Ronald Reagan's response was to shut down the entire University of California system for five days.

hablar del racismo, del negro, del chicano y del asiático. Se oía hablar de explotación. Se oía hablar de opresión y de fascismo. Todo esto dicho por estudiantes blancos.

La cuestión es que, con tanto que nosotros los de la raza sabemos y hemos sufrido y hemos dicho y gritado, al fin se oía que el anglo lo estaba diciendo. Al fin de los cuatro muertos, el blanco está comprendiendo de lo que es capaz su gobierno. Ahora comprende el blanco, ahora que ha corrido sangre de piel blanca.

En esta crisis en los colegios, se decidió cerrar los colegios e inmediatamente los estudiantes chicanos tuvieron una junta para decidir qué posición tomar.

Los chicanos en este asunto decidieron tomar la posición de que el asunto de Kent era asunto de los blancos. Así es que los estudiantes de la raza también iban a tomar parte en la "huelga" pero por razones chicanas.

Durante el tiempo de la "huelga" iban a trabajar en la comunidad de raza para apoyar la demostración del 30 de mayo en San Francisco.

Esta demostración es parte del "Chicano Moratorium" nacional que tendrá lugar en Los Ángeles el 29 de agosto de 1970. La razón por la cual la raza está demostrando contra de la guerra en Vietnam es que en la lista de muertos en el suroeste, la raza representa 19% de los muertos, mientras que nosotros somos nada mas que como 5% entera del país. Así es que por esta razón la raza se empieza a mover en contra de esta guerra injusta.[3]

---

[3] Vasquez was correct in that nationwide the "Spanish-surnamed population" accounted to roughly 5% of the total U.S. population, according to the 1970 U.S. census. However, she was referring to a series of studies done by Rafael Guzmán, a political scientist, who suggested that Chicanos suffered disproportionate casualties by comparing casualty rates in the five southwestern states of Texas, New Mexico, Arizona, California and Colorado to the percentage of the Spanish-surnamed population of military age in just these states (and not nationwide). Examining the names of Vietnam war dead from January 1, 1961, to February 28, 1967, Guzman estimated that "Spanish-surnamed individuals" accounted for 19.4 percent of the war dead during this time period although Spanish-surnamed "males of military age" made up only 13.8 percent of the total population in these five states. Additional casualty information from December 1967 to March 1969 echoed Guzman's original findings. His report was first published in *La Raza Yearbook 1968* (Los Angeles), 33. The supplemental report was printed in *La Raza* (Los Angeles) 1969, 12-16.

Nosotros de la raza tenemos que comunicarnos unos con los otros. Y los estudiantes son muy importantes. Importantes en que ellos están jóvenes pero necesitan el apoyo de la comunidad en comprenderlos.

Al mismo tiempo es muy importante que los estudiantes regresen a la comunidad, que se comuniquen con el pueblo, con la raza. Que no se equivoquen al pensar que con una educación no necesitan de su gente.

Nos necesitamos los unos a los otros.[4]

5 de junio de 1970

---

[4] It was a pleasure as well as a great opportunity for me to visit colleges and universities during two separate occasions to last month. It is very important to speak and communicate with our "Chicano" students who are participating in the educational system. How beautiful my Raza is! How precious to see their young, bronze faces in the classrooms and with their books studying to determine their destiny.

In our youth, we can see much hope for la Raza. In our youth, the consciousness of our Raza is emerging.

During the time I was in Oakland, the crisis of the four students who were killed on the campus of Kent State in Ohio occurred.[2] This was [during] a demonstration against the incursion of American troops in Cambodia. Afterwards, Anglo students rose up and went on strike in universities and colleges throughout the United States. Because of the "huelga," the president and the [state] governors ordered that the colleges and universities be shut down.[3]

What was the response of Chicano students? And what were their grievances? The Kent State affair was a crisis directed specifically at Anglos.

On college campuses, Anglos spoke against the war in Vietnam and against the troops that entered Cambodia. Talk was heard against racism, and about [the situation of] the Black, the Chicano, and the Asian. Talk was heard about exploitation. Talk was heard about oppression and fascism. White students spoke about all of this.

The thing is, just as we Raza know [about injustice] and have suffered and have spoken and shouted, finally we hear that the Anglo is talking about it. After the death of four people, whites are finally realizing what their government is capable of. Now the white person understands, now that blood has poured from white skin.

At this moment of crisis, it was decided to shut down the colleges, and immediately Chicanos had a meeting to decide what their response should be. Chicanos took the position that Kent State was a white matter. Accordingly, Chicanos are going to participate in the school strikes but for their own Chicano reasons.

During the strike, they are going to work in their communities to build support for the May 30 demonstration in San Francisco.

This demonstration is part of the national "Chicano Moratorium" that will take place in Los Angeles on August 29, 1970. The reason that Raza is demonstrating against the war is because casualty lists from the Southwest show that Chicanos represent 19 percent of the dead while we are no more than 5 percent of the population of the whole country. For this reason, Raza is starting to move against this unjust war.[4]

We who are Raza need to communicate one with the other. And the students are very important. Important because they are young; but they need the support and understanding of the community. At the same time, it is very important that the students return to the community, that they speak with the people, with Raza. It is important that they do not make the mistake of thinking that once they are educated they do not need their people.

We all need each other.

Translated by Herminia S. Reyes.

El Soldado Raso de Hoy

"El Soldado Raso" es una de nuestras viejas canciones que la raza ha cantado mientras sangran nuestros corazones por el soldado joven que se va a la guerra. Muchas veces mi mamá se sintió conmovida por la canción durante la Segunda Guerra Mundial al estar sentada silenciosamente por horas, su cabello volviéndose canoso con la idea de la sangre derramada por nuestros jóvenes y sus hijos. Y con Vietnam llevándose a nuestros jóvenes, la canción "El Soldado Raso" otra vez arde y suena en nuestros oídos y el dolor nos hiere el corazón al ahogarnos en lágrimas por el chicano joven, "El Soldado Raso," regando su sangre en la tierra extraña de Vietnam.

Y con las multitudes que se mueven por todo el país contra la guerra de Vietnam, nosotros observamos, pesamos y escuchamos todos los lados del conflicto de Vietnam. Mientras nuestros jóvenes pelean, nosotros preguntamos, "¿Por qué están muriendo? ¿Para qué?" ¿Quién sabe? Dicen que por patriotismo, eso es lo que dice el anglo pero, nosotros no somos anglos, en el pasado no nos han visto como ciudadanos de primera clase, no tenemos voz entre la clase que manda en este país, y hemos sufrido el robo de nuestras tierras, hemos visto al Tratado de Guadalupe Hidalgo, una farsa en sí mismo, violado sin compasión, sin respeto. La palabra del gringo se ha comprobado que es pura mentira.

Nosotros, la raza, no podemos poner fe y lealtad en una estructura que en toda nuestra historia nos ha mentido. Después de todo, al mirar al suroeste, al mirar a Aztlán vemos lo que una vez fue de México y de que parte de nuestra herencia es india, y con esta historia vemos en México un país que luchó muy duro por su soberanía e independencia. Vemos la agitación en este país. Y mientras luchaba México en sus momentos más débiles, vemos sobre su tierra tropas francesas, tropas inglesas, tropas españolas y tropas de los Estados Unidos. Todas estas tropas de mojados trataron de robar la tierra mexicana y declararla suya. Todos trataron de conquistar a la débil nación, como buitres que esperan hasta que el animal no se puede defender para atacarlo.

Oímos la primera estrofa del himno de la marina, que se atreve a hablar de esta conquista, "de los salones de Moctezuma," y nos da una idea de cómo agredió este país a una nación soberana. Y nos ponemos a pensar, "¿Qué demonios estaban haciendo los infantes de la marina en los salones de Moctezuma?"

Con esto, que es parte de la historia de nuestro mero suroeste, vemos a Vietnam teniendo en su historia a la misma gente tratando de vencerlos. Siempre hay alguien tratando de gobernarlos y colonizarlos. Ellos también han tenido tropas francesas, inglesas, españolas y de Estados Unidos en su suelo. En Vietnam vemos a los colonizadores haciendo guerra política, religiosa, económica (el 67% de nuestros impuestos van hacia la guerra) y de todas clases contra esta pobre gente. Escuchamos de nuestros jóvenes que regresan, las atrocidades que se cometen, y vemos las enfermedades con que regresan de haber ido a hacer ese sucio trabajo. Los vemos ir con mucha incertidumbre, obedeciendo las órdenes de este país. Muchos agachan la cabeza y van como borregos al rastro.

Y también los vemos, al regresar, abrir los ojos y ver la enfermedad aquí. Algunos quieren culpar a Vietnam y poner su atención en esa pequeña gente y pueden hasta regresar allá para no tener que enfrentar la realidad en casa. Nada más para no tener que enfrentar el punto de origen del conflicto de Vietnam. Nada más para no tener que enfrentar el foco volcánico de la enfermedad de Vietnam. Pueden ellos hasta decir que ponen su fe en la administración y en el liderato. Pero en realidad no quieren discutirlo porque tienen temor de las respuestas. Temen descubrir que la guerra de Vietnam no es ni siquiera una guerra declarada y que los jóvenes que murieron, ¿PARA QUÉ?

Y con la raza, vemos una aurora, vemos al verdadero SOLDADO RASO hablar. Vemos a Rosalío U. Muñoz de Los Ángeles, a Ernie Vigil de Denver, Manuel Gómez de Oakland, Fred Aviles de Chicago,

Steven Trujillo de Nuevo México, Montenegro de Arizona, Francisco Chávez (hijo de César), Juan Flores de Texas, Louie Lucero de California y muchos, muchos más. Y vemos al verdadero SOLDADO RASO levantarse con toda su hombría, con su machismo para decirle a la mayoría, "No, no pueden calmar su conciencia y culpabilidad matando a gente inocente en Vietnam, no pueden cambiar mi enfoque haciéndome asesino para matar a mis hermanos. Yo sé donde está en realidad el problema de Vietnam, yo sé quién es el opresor y el agresor. Mi historia es muy parecida a la historia de Vietnam, y rehúso creerte cuando me dices que esa gente es mi enemigo. Ahora yo sé donde está y quién es mi verdadero enemigo".

Estos jóvenes se levantan y hablan, hablan con cariño para su gente, y nos vemos forzados a escoger, forzados a tomar una posición.

Nuestros jóvenes dicen, "El gringo me tenía creyendo que mi machismo era de él. Lo usaba para conquistarme". Y ahora nuestro SOLDADO RASO sabe que su machismo le pertenece a su pueblo, para el uso de su gente y no contra ellos, para usarse aquí en el corazón de la raza, en Aztlán.

Y las palabras de la canción, EL SOLDADO RASO resuenan, "Madre Querida", nosotras las madres nos animamos y al ver a nuestros jóvenes Soldados Rasos, al ver a ellos a quienes parimos, nuestros hijos, les decimos, "Si debes morir, hijo mío, que sea por nuestra gente, en nuestra tierra donde vivieron nuestros antepasados hace 25,000 años.

Y marchamos.

26 julio de 1970

El Soldado Raso Today

"El Soldado Raso" is one of our old songs that has been sung by Raza as our hearts bleed for the young soldier that goes to war. My mother was often moved by it during the Second World War as she sat quietly and her hair turned grey with the thought of the bloodshed of our young men, and that of her sons. And with Vietnam taking our young men, the song, "El Soldado Raso" again rages and rings in our ears and the pain strikes our hearts as we choke in tears because the young Chicano, "El Soldado Raso," sheds his blood in the foreign land of Vietnam.[1]

With the masses that move throughout the country against the war in Vietnam, we sit and weigh and observe and listen to all sides of the Vietnam conflict. As our young men fight, we ask, "Why are they dying? What for? Quién sabe." They say patriotism, that's what the Anglo says, but then we are not the Anglo. We have in the past not been looked upon as first class citizens, we have no say-so among the ruling class of this country and we have seen our lands stolen, we have seen our Treaty of Guadalupe Hidalgo, a farce in itself, but even that has been pitifully violated, without respect. The word of the Gringo has proven itself to be but a pack of lies.

We, the Raza, certainly cannot put our good faith and loyalty into a structure that has lied to us throughout our entire history. After all, as we look upon the Southwest, upon Aztlán, we see what was once Mexico's and of which part of our heritage is Indian, and with this history we see in Mexico a country that fought so hard for sovereignty

---

[1] The song, "El Soldado Raso" became popular among Mexican Americans during the Second World War. It spoke of a plain foot soldier, a "soldado raso" from the verb "rasar" meaning to level, saying goodbye to his mother and his sweetheart. In the original articles the phrase was spelled "soldado razo" perhaps an unintentional allusion to "la raza" although in Spanish, the "s" and the "z" sound alike.

and independence. We see the turmoil upon this land. *During Mexico's struggle, during its weak moments, we see upon its land French troops, English troops, Spanish troops and the troops of the U.S. of A.*[2] All of these wetback troops from Europe tried to claim and steal, at one time or another, Mexican land for their own. They made a bid for conquest of the weak nation. Like vultures that wait to move in on a weak animal as it lies helpless.

We hear the first line of the Marine hymn, that dares to speak of the conquest, "from the halls of Moctezuma," and this gives us a hint of how this country was aggressive against a sovereign nation. And we stop to wonder, "What the hell were the Marines doing in the Halls of Moctezuma?"

With this, which is part of the history of our very Southwest, we see Vietnam having in its history with the very same people trying to defeat another nation. Someone else is always there to rule them and attempt to colonize them. *They, too, have had French, English, Spanish and U.S. troops on their soil.*[3] In Vietnam we see the colonizers fighting a political, religious, economic, (67% of your tax dollar goes to this war) and every other kind of war crimes against these poor people.[4] We hear from our returning young men of the atrocities and we see the sicknesses of our young men as they return from doing a dirty job. We see them go, with much hesitancy, in obedience to the orders of this country. Many lower their heads and leave like sheep going to slaughter.

[2] English troops joined the French in occupying Veracruz in 1864 because of Mexico's non-payment of loans. The French went on to establish a government under Emperor Maximillian.

[3] During the mid-nineteenth century, English and Spanish troops landed on Vietnamese soil to protect their nationals who were missionaries. Indochina was a French colony until 1954. Massive U.S. troop involvement in Southeast Asia began in 1965.

[4] According to U.S. Census data, between 1967 and 1970 national defense accounted for approximately 43% of the national budget, roughly equal to the amount of money brought in by individual income taxes. At 26%, the next largest category of federal spending was health and income security; commerce and transportation, education, and agriculture combined made up 12% of federal outlays. U.S. Bureau of the Census, *Statistical Abstract of the United States: 1970*, 91st ed., (Washington, D.C., 1970), 376.

And as the young men return, they open their eyes and see the sickness here. Some want to blame Vietnam and focus their vision upon these people and may even return there just not to have to face the reality of home. Just not to face the source of the Vietnam conflict, the volcanic core of the sickness of Vietnam. Just not to face the volcanic core of the sickness of Vietnam. They may even say that they place their faith in the administration and leadership, in reality, they do not want to question that, they fear the answers. They fear learning that Vietnam is not even a *declared* war and all the young men died. FOR WHAT?

And with la Raza we see an awakening, we see the real SOLDA-DO RASO speak, we see Rosalío U. Muñoz from Los Angeles; Ernie Vigil de Denver, Manuel Gómez, de Oakland area; Fred Aviles de Chicago; Steven Trujillo de Nuevo Mexico; Montenegro de Arizona[5]; Francisco Chávez (hijo de César), Juan Flores de Texas; Louie Lucero de California and many, many more. We see the real "Soldado Raso" arise with all his manhood, in his machismo to say to the majority, "No, you cannot ease your conscience and guilt by killing innocent people in Vietnam, you cannot change my focus and turn me into a killer to kill my brothers. I know where the Vietnam trouble really is, I know who the oppressor and aggressor really is. My history is much like that of Vietnam history, I refuse to let you make me believe that is my enemy. I know now where and who my real enemy is."

These young men arise and speak, they speak with love of their people and we all see ourselves having to choose, having to take our stand. Our young men say. "The Gringo had me believing my machismo was his. He used it to conquer me." And our Soldado Raso knows his Machismo belongs to his people, to be used for his people not against them, to be used right here in the heartland of mi Raza, in Aztlán.

And the words of the song "El Soldado Raso" ring out, "Madre, Querida," we mothers stir and we look upon the young Soldados Rasos, upon those whom we bore, our sons, and we say, if you must

---

[5]The draft resister from Arizona was Salomón Baldenegro from Tucson.

die, my son, let it be here, let it be here for our children, for our people, on our land where our ancestors lived over 25, 000 years ago.

And so we march with our heads held high, las madres, los padres, los hijos, las hijas, los niños, la familia de la raza we cling together in support of the Chicano "Soldado Raso."

August 29, 1970

Third World Women Meet

There was the strong feeling of human insight in attending the Third World Women's Conference held in San Anselmo, California in November 1972. The conference was sponsored by the Division of Church and Race of the United Presbyterian Church and was a first in the history of the Church.

The purpose of the conference was to develop communication between Third World women as well as increase participation in the struggles of our people here and throughout the world. Also to include women at decision-making levels as well as to heighten and explore third world concerns and build solidarity between third world women and men.

The Presbyterian Church is a Chicano resource that has a La Raza Churchman group in Los Angeles [that] fortunately has a dedicated Raza Churchwoman, Josephine Granados Aleman. Josephine is not only concerned with the welfare of La Raza community but is very much aware of the extreme importance of a strong Chicana as being a need that affects the whole community. Any of us who have lived in projects, barrios and ghettos and have had to raise families alone know the urgency of "la Chicana." With this well in mind, seven of us made up the Chicana caucus. We presented our mestizo history as to the Chicano nation of Aztlán and we learned of other views and struggles. To learn of other struggles and peoples was no threat to our Chicanismo but rather a reaffirmation of our struggle and what is yet to come. We came together aware of our differences but with the realization of what brought us together; *a deep concern for the necessity of unity within the issues of humanity on a long term world basis.* There was a welding and respect to recognize dedication and concern for the struggles within the U.S. to be meted with world struggles.

Probably one of the lessons we felt in blending with other peoples is to live a humanity under the skin. How stirring to feel the strength of a Japanese who lived in a concentration camp; the endurance of Chinese and Filipino whose cheap labors were imported to the U.S.; the stoic quiet of a Korean whose land and genetic family has been torn by politics; and the consistent spirit of the Native American and the vitality of the blacks, the cradle of humanity.

To meet with people from other struggles makes one aware of the meaning and the affects of systemic genocide, personally as well as within our descendant family trees. It makes one further aware of the meaning of the sufferings and turmoil of Vietnam, Angola, Puerto Rico, Latin America and the whole of Asia. Also to take a stand against genocide is to refuse and repudiate one's share of the guilt of bloodshed.

It was a living experience of Jose Vasconcelos' Raza Cósmica, La Raza de Colores, which tells us of Raza being elements of the whole of humanity and its colors-white, black, yellow, red, brown.

To see and speak with these women of the third world was to see oneself.

There were blacks who looked like me,

There were Indians who looked like me,

There were Asians with traces of me.

    All were pieces of struggles;

        pieces of reality;

        pieces of flesh

        All were pieces of me . . . .

What Is the Third World?

An important purpose of the third world conference was to adopt a definition of "third world," and to heighten and explore third world consciousness and concerns, and to strengthen the work of individual caucuses by building solidarity between third world women and men. Also, to develop communication between third world women and to encourage women to participate in the overall struggles of peoples and be included at decision-making levels.

Third world means the colonized and formerly colonized countries of the world. It includes nations and peoples of Asia, Africa, Latin America and Aztlán. All have been oppressed by colonial European powers and the U.S.

The first world is—United States, the weakened European nations built on 'free enterprise' (England, France, Germany, Belgium, Portugal) and most recently Israel and South Africa.

The second world is—Socialist nations, led by the Soviet Union, who have broken the bondage of capitalism and are creating socialist societies.

Historically, third world peoples have suffered severe oppression. Through slavery, Africans found themselves scattered throughout the world, Asians found their labor exploited and imported to the U.S. and their lands invaded and pillaged while their cultures and religions were trampled and repressed. Native Americans and Chicanos became foreigners in their own lands, left with only broken treaties.

Within the United States, the third world consists of colonized peoples from Las Américas, the Caribbean, Africa, and Asia. The third world idea can not be used to adopt an attitude [of "neutrality;"] the fact remains that there is no middle road. We know that to combat international enemies (expansionism in the name of God and "free enterprise"), international cooperation is needed. There is a need for world unity of all peoples suffering exploitation and colonial oppression here in the United States as well as with our brothers and sisters in homelands outside the U.S. There is a need for those of us who live within the U.S., the most wealthy, powerful and expansionist country in the world, to identify ourselves as third world peoples in order to end this economic and political expansion.

We must realize that nations and people can be part of the third world and still be oppressors and exploiters. (Japan is an example of this, together with other nations run by puppets of neo-colonization such a Chiang Kai Shek, Mobutu, Governor Ferre, etc.).[1] Third world is not an ideology unto itself. It describes oppressed and exploited lands

---

[1] Chiang Kai Shek (Jiang Jieshi) was the leader of the Nationalist armies of China. In 1949, defeated by the Communists, the Nationalists fled to Taiwan. Mobotu Sese Seko was the anti-communist dictator of Zaire (now the Democratic Republic of the Congo) from 1965 to 1972. Both were strongly supported by the United States. Luis Ferre served one-term as governor of Puerto Rico from 1969 to 1973. He favored statehood for the island.

and peoples who suffer internal and external colonialism. Through imperialist expansion and oppression of peoples of the third world, the international nature of the oppressor has been exposed.

Commitment to liberation is wherever struggles may be, and struggles must interlock to obtain effective results. The third world has suffered under the yoke of white racism and economic pillage by expansionist powers. We are concerned with the long-range results of our struggles; we have a common oppressor, we hope to achieve [a] society free of racism, exploitation of human by human, nation by nation, and woman by man.

In spite of cultural differences, historical oppression unites us in the struggle to eradicate these evils. We occupy a unique place, located within the most expansionist country in the world at a critical time in the history of humanity. Many third world nations have spoken against U.S. power policies (Latin America, Indochina, Africa) to no avail. Third world people in the United States must identify our exploitative history in order to end this economic and political expansionism.

November 19, 1972

Rethinking Cultural Nationalism and La Familia through Women's Communities: Enriqueta Vasquez and Chicana Feminist Thought

At the First Denver Youth Conference held in March 1969, the Chicana workshop, after an intense discussion about women's role in the Chicano movement, announced to the rest of the assembled group: "It was the consensus of the group that the Chicana woman does not want to be liberated!"[1] Enriqueta Longeaux y Vasquez, a conference participant, responded to the statement made by the Chicana Caucus in her groundbreaking article, "The Woman of La Raza I." She wrote, "As a woman who has been faced with having to live as a member of the 'Mexican-American' minority as a breadwinner and a mother raising children, living in the housing projects and having much concern for other humans, leading to much community involvement, this was quite a blow. I could have cried."[2] "The Woman of La Raza I" then went on to detail the lived experiences of working-class and poor Chicanas in the urban environment. Resonating for women in the movement, "The Woman of La Raza I " served as a *testimonio*, which, while heavily based on Vasquez's personal experiences of divorce, single parenthood, life in the city, and struggles with unemployment, also served as an urgent communication that gave voice to the material conditions and social construction of racialization, poverty and gender for many urban Chicanas.[3]

Printed in her regular column ¡Despierten Hermanos! for *El Grito Del Norte* newspaper (1968-1973), the "Woman of La Raza I" circulated within the print media cultures of at least three social movements—the Chicano movement, the women's movement, and the socialist left.[4] It was available to the readerships of, for example, *Magazín* (a Texas-based Chicano movement periodical), *Sisterhood is Powerful* (a landmark anthology of the women's movement), and *The Militant* (a socialist newspaper). Such circulation of her ideas—apparent also in the reprinting of another essay, "¡Soy Chicana Primero!"— gave Vasquez a prominent place as an activist woman participating in the debates about women's roles in the Chicano movement, particularly as it became increasingly evident that the cultural nationalist concept of *la familia* authorized gender inequality. The dialogue among women activists throughout the Southwest was part of a dynamic and growing Chicana feminist movement composed of grassroots, student, and professional women from diverse generations, regions, political histories, and movement sectors.

A fundamental context influential in Vasquez's Chicana feminist thought is her involvement with *El Grito del Norte* newspaper. *El Grito del Norte* was the product of a circle of progressive political activists in Northern New Mexico who worked in collaboration with local community members. The majority of the activists involved with the paper were women including editor-in-chief Elizabeth "Betita" Martínez, a seasoned activist in the Black Civil Rights and Women's movements; activist/writer Valentina Valdez (who had just completed high school when she joined the staff); and nationally-known lawyer Beverly Axelrod, who had represented activists in the Black Panthers Party, AIM, and the land grant movement. As a primarily woman-staffed entity, *El Grito Del Norte*'s collective represented a kind of women's organization (although there were several men who contributed to the paper) that provided working-class and poor women with opportunities to publish their perspectives on a variety of issues. Such work garnered commendation from individuals such as Texas-based feminist Marta Cotera, who referred to the important work of *El Grito Del Norte*—and especially Martínez and Vasquez—in her survey of Chicana history, *Diosa y Hembra* (1976). She praised their progressive writings about women, as well as their "sophisticated and comprehensive" attention to Chicanos, Third World people, and the war in Vietnam.[5]

Vasquez's writing emerged from and helped to forge, the vision of the Northern New Mexican circle, a specific local and regional formation with its particular struggles, approaches, and demographics. The activists of *El Grito del Norte* were embedded within local struggles of the region and were initially affiliated with Northern New Mexico's *Alianza Federal de Mercede*s, while Vasquez also claimed an alliance with Denver's Crusade for Justice. These regional and local events were placed, in the pages of *El Grito del Norte*, in the national context of the Chicano, Black Power, and Native American movements and in the global context of anti-imperialist movements. *El Grito del Norte*'s approach to gender was similarly local and global in perspective—the knowledge of community women, activities of women in the *Alianza*, historical retellings of *las soldaderas* and *las soldadas* in the Mexican Revolution, and the courage of Vietnamese women guerillas—all were represented within its pages.

In six installments of her column interspersed across five years, Vasquez engaged in a conversation with the movement about the topics of women's roles, feminism, gender equality, the family, nationalism, women's communities, coalition politics, and movement priorities. She published six essays on the "woman question" (as it was often deemed in movement parlance) in *El Grito Del Norte*: "The Woman of La Raza-Part One,"(July 6, 1969), "The Woman of La Raza– Part Two," (July 26, 1969), "La Chicana: Let's Build a New Life," (November 15, 1969), "Soy Chicana Primero" (April 26, 1971), "National Chicana Conference-Houston," (August 20, 1971), and "Third World Women Meet" (Jan-Feb, 1973). In these pieces, *El Grito Del Norte*'s characteristic layering of the local, regional, national and global in its news reporting informed Vasquez's perspectives on feminism and cultural nationalism. Personal experience, generation, and broader movement dynamics also played a role in her understanding of major issues regarding women and gender in the movement. These factors culminated in her particular mode of synthesis and interpretation—her contribution to what has come to be known as the debate on cultural nationalism and feminism.[6]

Among the early feminists, Vasquez is particularly significant because she fundamentally accepted Chicano nationalism as a strategy of struggle for *raza* liberation and self-determination. She was convinced that cultural nationalism did not have to be a restrictive and constraining ideology for women. Rather, she criticized how the male construction of cultural nationalism equated tradition with women's subordination. Vasquez' columns on women ultimately sought to reconcile some of the ideals of cultural nationalism with the promotion of women's advancement and flourishing as activists in the movement. As a result, her columns on Chicanas explored how to join the competitive identities attached to the categories "nation" and "woman" in a complex maneuvering between cultural nationalism's gendering process and an emergent Chicana feminism.

At times, Vasquez found herself confronting the limitations of movement discourses of cultural nationalism and *la familia*. These limitations required a rethinking of cultural nationalism—an approach that, from a Chicana perspective, implied a cultural nationalism that was more flexible—as well as more woman-friendly and, internationalist in scope. While she did not advocate separatism through autonomous feminist organizations, her writings did seek a framework that would be able to respond to the complexity of oppressions. She understood the significant role of women's communities as a means of developing women's leadership and potential. She eventually extended the scope of women's circles toward international solidarity and developed a layered conception of how multiple social movements could intersect in order to achieve their vision of comprehensive social change.

This essay is a critical appreciation of Vasquez's contribution to the debate on cultural nationalism and feminism. The aim here is to provide a consideration of the complexity of her thought as she attempted to identify a coherence between women's self-determination and cultural nationalism—and therefore carve out a "safe space" for Chicana activists within the *movimiento*. Three major themes in her writings chart the ways in which she grappled with these issues: the role of the Chicana within la familia as movement activists; the negotiation of separate spaces for Chicanas (which requires envisioning women's communities); and, the relationship between Chicana activism, women's liberation, and anti-imperialist movements.

Chicanas within La Familia de La Raza

While Vasquez' earliest work articulated a concern for unity and described a form of peoplehood as "La Raza Unida" that was not based exclusively on the family, the adoption of la familia and nationalism as official movement ideology via *El Plan Espiritual de Aztlán* during the Denver Youth Conference of 1969 had an effect upon Vasquez' subsequent writings.[7] Vasquez's willingness to commit to the ideology of cultural nationalism as la familia was not different from that of other activists. Her goal was to support the struggle for social justice and to make a contribution through her writings. Additional factors included her collegial ties to movement leader Rodolfo "Corky" Gonzales and her participation in an *El Grito del Norte*-sponsored trip to Cuba in the tenth year of the revolution.

Vasquez attended the Denver Youth Conferences not only as a movement supporter but also as a veteran activist who had organized with Rodolfo "Corky" Gonzales during her earlier days in Denver, Colorado, as a volunteer for Project SER (Service, Employment and Redevelopment Project). Vasquez had witnessed Gonzales' rise to leadership and the founding of the Crusade for Justice, a civil rights organization that had sponsored the Denver Youth Conferences. When he—along with the student activists—became a proponent of Chicano nationalism and defined it in terms of "la familia," Vasquez saw a need for Chicanas to participate in the elaboration of this conceptual framework for *raza* mobilization.

Additionally, Vasquez's trip to Cuba in 1969 had convinced her that revolution was possible. In Cuba, she saw the application of Marxist ideas of classless society through processes of communal ownership and work. She also witnessed how the challenge to anti-imperialism, articulated in nationalist concepts of self-determination, motivated the ongoing commitment to the revolution. She documented her visit to Cuba in her two-part column entitled, "¡Qué Linda es

Cuba!" Among her observations, she sensed that women had made gains as a result of the revolution. What she saw in Cuba reinforced her sense that the revolution had fostered the "human" potential of individuals:[8]

> For ten years now, the most powerful nation in the world has looked upon this little island and said, "Die!" "How dare you make fools of us? "Beg and admit you are wrong, you are wiped out." But you see these people struggle, work hard, and continue to survive. WHY??? In exchange for hard work the people have freedom. Not only freedom from want but freedom to develop themselves as individuals.[9]

Cuba represented the possibility of developing a social order in which human development was valued and in which people's basic needs would be met based on Marxist and nationalist concepts of revolutionary social change.

The ideology of Chicano cultural nationalism as "La Familia de la Raza" therefore appeared as a first step toward building the unity needed to bring about revolutionary social change for Chicanos in the United States. Following its inauguration as the "key to unity" with the unveiling of *El Plan Espiritual de Aztlán* at the Denver Youth Conference, Vasquez joined the heightened effort to promote nationalism and la familia de la raza as the primary unifying ideology of the Chicano movement. Indeed, the majority of her columns refer in some way to "la familia de la Raza" as a unifying concept and goal. For example, Vasquez joined the chorus of voices sounding *la familia* in "The Woman of La Raza I":

> The Mexican-American movement is not that of just adults fighting the social system, but it is a total commitment of a family unit living what it believes to be a better way of life in demanding social change for the benefit of mankind.[10]

Vasquez refers in this passage to the family as a "unit" which evoked the ideal of a nuclear family with a father, mother, and children.

Although she represented the family, in "The Woman of La Raza, I" as a unit, Vasquez sketched a portrait of the paradigmatic Chicana community activist as a single mother, apparently contrasting with the dominant emphasis of the movement on the traditional family as patriarchal.[11] Vasquez also sidestepped any criticism of single motherhood by framing that reality as a product of social fragmentation. To counter the mentality of the dominant society which "blamed the victims" of broken families and to counter Chicano cultural taboos on divorced women, she suggested that the break up of families was due to a faltering economy in which male breadwinners brought their oppression by dominant society into the home where their "failed" capacity to provide was part of a cycle that perpetuated patriarchal dominance and domestic violence. Given this context, the traditional family for Vasquez represented an image of wholeness and community where men, women, and their children ideally lived in harmony.

But the terrain of Chicano cultural nationalism as *la familia* was not easy to negotiate, especially given the increasing ways in which tradition was being defined as male-dominant in movement rhetoric, visual representation, and organizational ideologies.[12] The patriarchal underpinnings of nationalism's familial metaphors have been exposed by feminist scholars of nationalism and gender. Anne McClintock, a scholar of gender, nationalism, and imperialism, argued that, beginning in the mid-nineteenth century in the European West, "the family offers a 'natural' figure for sanctioning social *hierarchy* within a putative *organic unity* of interests."[13] Although it was a grassroots movement that was contesting domination and "internal" colonialism, the Chicano Movement ideology of the family presumed a unity of interests among its members and presumed to inform women that their interests were to maintain a traditional—read "subordinate"—role to men, even as many women had already challenged that role through their work, college attendance, and other life experiences.

Vasquez challenged the reinscription of women's subordination under the sign of a male-dominant family within cultural nationalism. She made the case for redefining *la familia* as a more inclusive and more egalitarian—albeit generally, heterosexual—formation available for *raza* mobilization. To accomplish this redefinition, she adopted three kinds of rhetorical arguments to make the case for an expanded role for women within the familia of the Chicano movement: an "equal rights" approach, the "precolonial matriarchy" thesis, and, the "women's superior values" argument.

An equal rights argument generally claims that women are no different from men—we are all humans. Implicitly referring to this kind of claim, Vasquez offered a harsh critique of any movement in which women's equality with men was not understood as fundamental. For Vasquez, "total liberation" would only be "total" when the liberation of woman was seen as intrinsic to the liberation of a people:

> When a family is involved in a human rights movement, as is the Mexican-American, there should not have to be a Woman's liberation movement within it. There should not have to be a definition of a woman's role. We should get down to the business at hand. Do we want a liberation for the Raza? Is this supposed to be a total liberation? (11)

Vasquez, as did many Chicanas of the time, identified "Woman's liberation" as a white women's movement and discouraged its influence. But this complex passage actually offers a critique of the Chicano movement's politics of gender. When she stated, "there should not have to be a Woman's liberation movement," she was not undermining women's claims to equality. Rather, she argued that defining women's roles within a movement for "total" liberation was redundant. In other words, if the movement really had made as its goal "total liberation" for a people, then it would have already taken into account women's liberation. Passages such as this demonstrated Vasquez's rhetorical negotiations as she walked a line between cultural nationalism and the increasing attractiveness of feminist organizing to Chicanas who were beginning to call out their unequal treatment in the movement.

Vasquez represented the family as a unit founded upon a relationship between two groups generally recognized as different: a man and a woman. How can difference also allow for equality? For Vasquez, men and women were complementary parts of a whole in a family unit.[14] This complementarity allowed Vasquez to acknowledge that that were differences between women and men, but then to subsume those differences into a "natural" relation within the family. This left women very little room, when taken literally, to participate in the movement outside of the role of wife in a family based formation, which, given the existing division of labor, assumed men's greater value and dominance over women. For example, Vasquez challenged the model's male dominance in the following passage, which refigured the terms of women's participation in a family formation:

> The woman must help liberate the man and the man must look upon this liberation with the woman at his side, not behind him, following, but alongside of him leading. The family must come up together.[15]

The above statement is reminiscent of the popular movement slogan, "I want to walk alongside my man," which voiced a concern for inclusion of women as wives and girlfriends within the *marchas* of the movement toward social justice. While Vasquez argued vehemently for equal partnership, the family model positioned women as partners modeled on the marriage relationship within a family, which limited the options for men and women as political partners in a larger collective struggle.

In her article, "Political Familism: Toward Sex Role Equality," sociologist Maxine Baca Zinn argued the case for *la familia* as a productive mobilizing principle of the movement drawing examples from the Crusade for Justice and the United Farm Worker's Movement. Her examples were convincing, particularly as the *familia* drew upon concepts which had a strong resonance among Chicanos. Nevertheless she also admitted, "Political familism itself does not transcend sex role subordination." Enriqueta Vasquez struggled with the contradictions of the family model and her own goal of mapping out equality for women within the movement's *familia*. In fact, her increasing awareness of how the contradictions of *la familia* were playing out for women in the movement prompted a considerable revision in her analysis.

The revision was evident in "Woman of La Raza II," published in *El Grito* two months later. The subtitle of the piece, "¡Despierten, Hermanas! (Wake up, Sisters!)" played on the presumed universality of her column, ¡Despierten, Hermanos! By marking Chicanas as gender-specific, Vasquez suggested that Chicanas could not be subsumed into a melting pot of a male-dominant familia. Instead, Vasquez now made the case for equality by referencing women's distinct roles in precolonial societies where they were centrally involved in governance, political economy, and cultural life. This argument challenged the stereotype of the family as inherently requiring women's subservience:

> It seems that before the Europeans came to the Americas, our highly cultured Indian woman usually held an honored position in the "primitive" society in which she lived. She was mistress of the home and took full part in tribal elections. The position of the woman was not only free, but honorable. She was a strong laborer, a good mechanic, a good craftsman, a trapper, a doctor, a preacher and, if need be, a leader. It seems that among the so-called SAVAGE people of this continent, women held a degree of political influence never equaled in any CIVILIZED nation. The woman of the Aztecs was far superior to that of Spain, then and now. And in Oaxaca, Mexico, the Mayan woman to this day is equal to her men.[16]

These claims drew upon the tendencies of cultural nationalism—the recovery of an ancient, glorious precolonial past—and redirected them to a woman-based agenda. For Chicanas in the Chicano movement, observations of women's ancient power offered alternative scenarios of women's lives and contributions to society. As a result, Chicanas were now more than equal partners who could be absorbed into the familia: The recovery of Chicana history created the possibility for a different understanding of the role of women within the family and, by extension, within Chicano culture.

As she developed the implications of this perspective, Vasquez framed Chicanas as ideal nation-builders who could realize the dream of an alternative society. "La Chicana: Let's Build a New Life" (November 15, 1969) drew upon languages of revolutionary social change ("new society"), the cooperative movement, motherist movements, and the romanticism of the country as an escape from the city. Identifying the difficulties of the city housing projects for single parents (many of whom were, she observed, women), Vasquez proposed that Chicanas initiate the creation of a co-operative community in the countryside. Addressing these Chicanas directly in the beginning of the piece ("Bueno, Comadres, here we go again on the woman thing."), she described a model of women's community as the "key" to this "new society":

> . . . I really think that the Chicana woman can come back and rebuild the society and homeland that the Chicanos need to relate to. This would be a community that would be giving itself to the people. It would be a community of children that belong to everyone, and the mothers would form the solid foundation of the strong spirit needed from which to draw strength for all Chicanos. This could be the rebirth of a truly tribal community and an example from which would come expansion and more communities like these. (11)

There are certainly precedents for her claim that Mexican women had the capacity for building: The *enjarradoras* were New Mexican women who had traditionally maintained the physical structure of the adobes prior to the 20th century.[17] Additionally, as Vasquez penned these words, movimiento discourses of *indigenismo* began to surface more explicitly as a model of communal life.

In a 1970 interview with Froben Lozada of *The Militant* on "Women and Chicano Liberation," Vasquez insisted upon the need for Chicana perspectives in the movimiento. She also qualified her understanding of "La Familia de la Raza" as more than a literal, nuclear family unit by describing it as a "workable" ideology that enabled a challenge to the given social system. When asked by Lozada to comment on "La Familia de la Raza," she claimed that the concept was more than a nuclear family unit:

La familia de la Raza is something that Raza can really live because we understand the concept of living as human beings— as an extended family. For instance, many us were raised in colonias, barrios, or villages, and old people used to treat the children as their children—regardless of whose children they were, as we see this now. [. . .]. It is a heritage of our Indian way of life. La familia de la Raza is a big family. If we are really going to challenge this system on a human level this is going to be the level that we should really emphasize. Some of the young girls were asking me about la familia de la Raza—they were looking at it as a unit. We have to remember that this is the gringo way, that is as an alienated family, as a single unit. Raza is not that way.

By referencing an indigenous concept of the family, one based in extended family relations and fictive kin, Vasquez began to unravel the ties between a nuclear family and Chicano nationalism to explore other kinds of ties and connections that could ground a community seeking to implement egalitarian principles and to build a sustainable existence.

In fact, "La Chicana: Let's Build a New Life" argued that Chicanas possessed the cultural identity, values, and knowledge that provided a more substantive grounding for a new society. Vasquez' representation of women as cultural bearers, nation builders, and visionaries was reminiscent of a trend in nineteenth-century socialist thought which constructed women as morally advanced in comparison to men or as spiritual placeholders for the vision of a more evolved future: "the very durability of this imaginative projection of a time for and of 'women' bears witness to its power. Indeed it echoes through feminisms today: the Future can still be Female. In this returning and visionary narrative, that new space which fully realized women will come to occupy will be transformed by them to the good."[18]

At this point in her thought, Vasquez' s ideas also resonated with a growing trend within the women's movement known as "cultural feminism." Cultural feminism argued that women's inherent values— often seen as completely opposite and inferior to men—were, in fact, superior to those of men. Vasquez's centering of a society based on Chicana values and knowledges resonated with these ideas, although within a culturally specific context and strategy. Feminist social movement theorists have argued that a cultural feminist approach operates effectively as a strategy at the level of validating identity and putting into practice a system of alternative values.[19] Culture as a basis of resistance offers a means of challenging dominant values and preserving the integrity of identity under oppression.[20] The recovery of ancient indigenous women's cultural knowledge had an important place in encouraging an appreciation of oral narratives and elder's history that had been lost or ignored.[21] Through these explorations, Vasquez continued to see how far cultural nationalist themes of group unity could stretch to include Chicanas.

Negotiating "Separatism as Strategy"[22]: Toward Women's Communities

At the Second Denver Chicano Youth Conference, held in 1970, the Chicana workshop presented the following resolution, "The Chicana women resolve not to separate but to strengthen Aztlán, the family of la Raza!" The specific points of the resolution revolved around three major ideas that implied various levels of critique of then existing gender relations in the movement. First, the resolution emphasized the importance of women's inclusion and self-determination in the movement "according to their capability in all levels of the struggle." Second, the resolution encouraged women to "meet in their own groups for the purpose of education and discussion" as well as the creation of a women's newsletter to share ideas. Finally, several observations that the "alienated" family—in which the woman stays home and takes care of the children—needed to be changed so that both men and women were responsible for the care of children in "the united family." These themes in the resolution touched upon the possibilities of women's communities as well as more egalitarian family structures. At the same time, they reasserted the priority for Chicanas to remain within the fold of the movement's *familia* rather than to create an autonomous feminist movement.

Adopted at the height of debates regarding cultural nationalism's *familia* and feminism in the Chicano movement, the resolution was printed and prefaced on April 29, 1970 with a few words of commentary by Vasquez in her column ¡Despierten, Hermanos! Her presentation of the resolution indicated support for its sentiments and one response to the dialogue taking place among women across the Southwest and beyond regarding gender inequality, male dominance, the "woman" question, and sexism in the Chicano movement. The ambivalent messages of the resolution's key points, in contrast to the definitive statement "We Resolve Not to Separate but to Strengthen Aztlán," perhaps reflected what Vasquez described as the "combination of many ideas, opinions and expressions voiced by the women in attendance, women working in all levels, varying in ages and experience, and from many different parts of the country." A fragile sense of unity persisted among Chicanas as the debate continued.

One of the messages communicated in the resolution, the encouragement of Chicana group discussions and meetings, sanctioned the growing number of symposia and conferences focused on women activists in the Chicano movement, the most significant of which was the Conferencia de Mujeres Para La Raza, held at the Magnolia Branch YWCA in Houston on Memorial Day weekend, May 28-30, 1971. Opening the door to the potential of a Chicana collective voice, this landmark conference gathered over 600 Chicanas to develop a women's agenda for the movement. In her account of the conference, published in *El Grito* two months later, Vasquez, who was a participant, provided the following description of the feeling among conference attendees:

> Viva La Raza, viva la Chicana y viva el Machismo, for I am machismo too. The machismo that protects its people without self-interest. Those are some of the cries heard and passions felt by Chicanas as we were caught up in the ecstasy of sisterhood at the National Chicana Conference in Houston, Tex., last May.[23]

The reference to machismo here was curious, although it was qualified as "the machismo that protects its people without self-interest."

Vasquez's desire to stretch machismo to signify a depth of feeling—
cries, passions, ecstasy—reflected the lack of a public language for
women's cultural and political connections to each other.[24] Unhinging
machismo's articulation with men, male bodies, and assertions of
male dominance, Vasquez placed it in the context of the "ecstasy of
sisterhood" where it became associated with expressions of women's
solidarity.

The transposition of nationalist bonding from macho self-interest
and power over another (generally women) to some other kind of formation also appeared in a carnivalesque scenario describing women's
enjoyment of cultural space:

> An exciting moment in the conference came Saturday evening,
> after the Mariachi Mass. We were all in the patio waiting to eat
> and, while we waited, the mariachi group played for us. It was
> then that our Chicanismo tore down the curtain of inhibitions and
> we let out screams of ay, ay, ay y aajúaa! We began dancing all
> over the place. It was exciting and beautiful to see women togeth-
> er "gozando la vida" in each other's company. Women danced to
> the mariachi sounds, out of pure joy. It was a fountain of sister-
> hood flowing with childlike innocence and delight.
>
> Our dancing was not that of exhibition but the pure expression
> and partaking of a musical, rhythmic pleasure. All was interwov-
> en with enjoyment of our culture, our music, our dancing, our sis-
> ter's company in living. Some of the sisters even began dunking
> each other in a pool in the patio. We went wild. (18)

Vasquez' distinction between "exhibition" and "expression" implies
that when Chicanas share space outside of the gaze of others—non
Chicanos or men they are able to experience joy. Indulging in
"musical, rhythmic pleasure," carried away by cultural enjoyment,
Chicana sisterhood and nationalism does not require a voyeur to witness or to authorize women's connection to each other.[25]

This wild scene of "pure expression" and "pleasure" might be
viewed as the Chicana feminist corollary to Chicano lawyer and writer
Oscar Acosta's description, in his semi-fictional novel *Revolt of the*

Cockroach People, of an "orgy of nationalism" at a movement rally at which he is the center of attention. For Acosta, cultural nationalism's feeling of group identity led to the loss of the self as he merged into community, and, according to critic Carlos Gutiérrez-Jones, bordered on homophobic panic.[26] Expressing a concern for the projection of voyeurism onto women's community, the description of Chicana nationalist unity in Vasquez' account sidestepped the loss of self and homophobic panic because it flows with "childlike innocence and delight," which can be read as a negotiation of the perceived threat that women gathering together might pose to some or as a desire for a moment before a fall from innocence into the reality of sexism in the Chicano movement.[27]

Vasquez's report on the First National Chicana Conference both affirmed women's enjoyment of a separate space and negotiated the threat of separate spaces. However, by the end of the piece, Chicana communities were subsumed once again within the sphere of the Chicano movement familia:

> The Chicana cannot hold back anymore. We must overcome the fear of giving ourselves to the Raza movement. This may be hard for some of us, mostly because we have been kicked around time and again by the system and by our own. But we must overcome those fears or find ourselves alone again— without our people, without our roots, to wander in a decaying system that has planned our genocide, to watch our brown children lose themselves in the hypocrisy of a money mind.

The language of submission used here—"giving ourselves"—coded the struggle for Chicanas as a decision to merge into a community as opposed to "wandering" alone. Vasquez's call for Chicanas to "give themselves" to the movement admitted that the positions from which one joined the movement were unequal, that for Chicanas, this entrance required a leap of faith in the face of one's oppression by "the system" and "one's own," and that the survival of the self had everything to do with the survival of the group. Her construction of Chicana communities in this passage once again seems to absorb Chicanas into the movement rather. At this point, Vasquez reached a place in her thought where prevailing movement ideology and attitudes towards feminism did not allow for a wholesale endorsement of autonomous Chicana feminism.[28]

In reality, the broad based "collective consciousness" of women's issues broke down at the Houston conference along lines of regional feminist and women oriented groups with divergent priorities and perspectives on the Chicano movement agenda and feminism.[29] As a result of miscommunication, criticism, possible infiltrators and different ideas about the goals of the conference, approximately 300 women walked out of the YWCA to hold their own meeting at a local park.[30] In her report, Vasquez stated that her reasons for walking out included the group's concerns about the racism and classism of the YWCA. Nevertheless, her observations on the walkout also reflected a concern about feminist autonomy: "That we had a walkout on the last day of the conference seemed inevitable. There was much expounding about La Chicana, but it didn't tie in with our movement issues. The conference had the aura of being self-centered, with a competitive attitude toward the Chicano movement."

A survey of the historical accounts suggests rifts at the Chicana Conference stemming from the complex relationship between feminism and cultural nationalism. It seemed impossible to build a consensus on how to incorporate women's gender interests into the agenda of the movimiento. What Anna Nieto-Gómez referred to as "feministas" in her insightful essay, "La Feminista" (1974) were Chicana activists who supported a women's agenda that directly challenged the sexist and patriarchal underpinnings of Chicano cultural views on womanhood, sexuality, and the family, views which undermined women activists' full inclusion and recognition as leaders and organizers (despite abundant evidence of their hard, committed, and effective work in organizations). Such an agenda, ideally, would be incorporated into the movement's issues and speak to women's interests. In contrast, the "loyalists" according to Nicto-Gomez's analysis, did not support the development or discussion of a distinct women's agenda as they were in agreement with cultural nationalism's emphasis on la familia.[31]

What Nieto-Gomez does not delve into—and here is where hindsight enables another layer of analysis—was that the "loyalists" in her construction (those who walked out) were composed of women representing a spectrum of positions regarding the movement's existing agenda including, for example: antifeminists who wanted to follow and reinforce the male defined agenda of the movement and opposed the development of a women's agenda; those who sought to work within the terms of cultural nationalism as women, who would transform it by virtue of their inclusion; and, those who felt that class or anti-imperialist struggles were as compelling as—or even more significant than—gender struggles.

An article in *El Grito Del Norte* entitled, "Chicanas of Today Say What They Want" listed both the Chicana feminist resolutions as well as those adopted by the women who met in the park.[32] While the resolutions of the "feministas" touched upon the topics of sex, institutionalized religion, the raising of sons, birth control, day care, and equal pay for equal work, the resolutions from "El Parque" focused on the concept of Aztlán, Chicanos in the midwest, the Vietnam War, the prison system, and farmworkers. In her account of the Chicana Conference "En el Parque," she explained, "we drew up resolutions that related to the Raza movement as a whole as well as the Chicanas."[33]

Vasquez saw the resolutions as overlapping raza issues and Chicana issues, but the final sentences of the resolutions from "El Parque" inadvertently retrenched traditionalism and even justified the "double job" of the Chicana to maintain the "family unit" while also becoming an activist within a family based structure. Vasquez's report on the Houston Conference described a glimpse of women's communities and strongly endorsed the power of Chicana sisterhood, but the relationship between gender, the family, nationalism, and feminism continued to prove a tense intersection of interests and ideas about the role of women within—and outside of—la familia.

Coalition Politics and Third World Solidarity

As the debate among Chicana activists regarding nationalism and feminism reached a fever pitch, Vasquez continued to seek a way of reconciling what were increasingly viewed as antithetical positions for Chicanas to occupy. Her most productive foray into the realm of intersecting and overlapping interests appeared with the publication of "Soy Chicana Primero," shortly before the Houston Conference.[34] Often read as an inflexible statement of loyalty to the Chicano Movement because of its insistence that Chicana's belong "at home" with the *movimiento*, "Soy Chicana Primero" went beyond the debate between cultural nationalism and feminism and moved toward coalition politics.

"Soy Chicana Primero," was published at the height of internal conflict between and among Marxisms, feminisms, and cultural nationalism. Resonating strongly with the movement slogan "Mi Raza Primero" which meant that one's community was the first priority, "soy Chicana primero," affirmed that a Chicana's first priority should be on her people.[35] Vasquez' insistence upon accountability to community was certainly adamant: "YOU MUST BE A CHICANA FIRST." Such vehemence derived from a critique of the white women's movement—where gender was singled out separate from race and culture. Although she felt that white women's liberation was not an appropriate starting point, she did not dismiss the validity of the struggles upon which the white women's movement was based. She declared, "we can sympathize with many basic struggles," while insisting upon a Chicana "homebase" in Aztlán: "Remember *Raza* is our home ground and family and we have strong basic issues and grievances as a people."

An argument could be made for nationalism's strategic uses in specific instances. Coalition theorist Bernice Reagon, an African American civil rights activist, argued that nationalism functioned as a "safe-house"—those in the house are presumed to be of the same identity group confronting the same enemy.[36] While the "safe-house" concept represents an ideal state, it breaks down if home represents a space of confinement or requires a double life, silence, and/or is unsafe (as is often the case for women, gays, and lesbians). Additionally, the reality is that individuals are members of multiple identity groups with different—and potentially conflicting—interests or perspectives. Intersections of identity, in fact, make virtually every presumed "nationalist" identity group a coalition of multiple and heterogeneous individuals.

"Soy Chicana Primero" might be interpreted as circumscribing Chicana activism within the movement to one aspect of identity—a Chicana's cultural/national identity. Alma M. García, a historian and theorist of Chicana feminism, noted the nuanced implication of Vasquez's essay in "The Development of Chicana Feminist Discourse, 1970-1980": "When Vasquez (1971) states that she was 'Chicana *primero*,' she was stressing the saliency of race over gender in explaining the oppression experienced by Chicanas. The word *Chicana* however, simultaneously expresses a woman's race and gender."[37] García's suggestion is that Vasquez was not fully aware of the implications of her statement. Yet Vasquez must have been conscious of the strands of possibility communicated in the following:

> Our own society needs everyone, YOU MUST BE A CHICANA FIRST for when you are a Chicana Primero, you can wander all over, you can relate to many struggles for they must all someday come together, BUT you will be home in Aztlán, working with your own familia, to build for your own people within the spirit that comes from *el barro*.

"Soy Chicana Primero"—an example of theory made in the actual undertaking of a struggle—gestured toward a compromise between the "home" and other spaces and struggles with which Chicanas might find common cause. Vasquez may have insisted upon the necessity of starting with the homebase, but she also claimed that Chicanas with roots in Aztlán could also "wander all over" and "relate to many struggles."

"Relating to many struggles," was the project of the *El Grito Del Norte* newspaper, which covered local, national, and global social justice movements. In fact, as a Chicana, Vasquez often found herself identifying with the people of Latin America and Vietnam, in opposition to U.S. foreign policies in these regions.[38] Her position on U.S. foreign policy and her participation in conferences of Vietnamese, African, and other third world women shaped her embrace of a Third World women's perspective—a key evolution in her thought.[39] Commenting on her participation at a Third World Women's Conference in November 1972, she wrote, in "Third World Women Meet" (1973), "To learn of other struggles and people's was no threat to our Chicanisma." According to Vasquez,

> Commitment to liberation is wherever struggles may be, and struggles must interlock to obtain effective results. The third world has suffered under the yoke of white racism and economic pillage by expansionist powers.[40]

While Vasquez recognized the difference between one's location within the U.S. and one's location among the "third world nations," and acknowledged the specific histories of oppression of several racial-ethnic groups, she also saw the need for a collective struggle by third world women. This struggle would be waged against various forms of inequality worldwide in order "to achieve a society free from racism, exploitation of human by human, nation by nation, and woman by man."[41] For Vasquez, third world women's solidarity—no longer framed in terms of *la familia* or cultural nationalism—provided the basis for embarking upon comprehensive social change.

Conclusion

The concept of an early feminist implies the first glimmers of a particular kind of consciousness that undergoes further development and elaboration a historical unfolding from a past moment to a later one. Vasquez's writings provide a glimpse of the process through which she produced theory—a perspective on Chicana activism, nationalism, internationalism, and feminism that reflected her particular embedded and situated location, experience, and interpretation. Her essays provided affirmations of women's cultural integrity, explorations of the possibility of women's spaces and communities, a retooling of "traditional" Chicano cultural values in woman-friendly terms, and, finally, an extending out of women's circles towards international solidarity with third world women.

Scholars Beatriz M. Pesquera and Denise A. Segura argued, in their discussion of what has come to be known as the "cultural nationalism versus feminism" debate in the Chicano movement, that individual women activists may have sought to resolve the tension between cultural nationalism and feminism, but that these were largely "philosophical" resolutions, given the difficulties of transforming masculinist and sexist practices. According to Segura and Pesquera, rather than actually transforming sexist organizations, Chicanas "fashioned a discourse" in which they "gave formal recognition to patriarchal contours while eroding its base through underground subversive separatism."[42] "Underground subversive separatism" can be glimpsed in Vasquez' rhetorical arguments for Chicanas as nation-builders and superior bearers of cultural knowledge, her reports on the possibilities of women's communities, and her sense of the productive relationship between Chicanas and third world feminism.

While Vasquez grappled with how to map out this place, she did not outwardly advocate separatism or autonomous feminist groupings. Her explorations of cultural nationalism, gender, women, feminism, and internationalism represented a significant attempt to widen the scope of cultural nationalism to be more inclusive of women and more expansive in its conception of gender roles, tradition, and women's self-determination. Her work also underscores the importance, for many Chicanas, of maintaining their ties to a Chicano community that had been subject to racialization and class oppression. The dilemma becomes, how does a Chicana combine her multiple interests in challenging race, class, and gender domination?

Thirty years after the emergence of Chicano, women's and gay/lesbian movements, Enriqueta Vasquez' discursive engagement with the nationalist versus feminist debate reverberates in ongoing conversations within Chicana/o and other communities regarding oppression, strategies for social change, group identity, coalition, solidarity, and separate spaces. As an individual woman who sought to mediate the debate by calling for a transformation of la familia, a revisiting of her work reminds us to continue the conversation about how to build a truly inclusive, egalitarian society—with the hope of a future that does not require Chicana to compartmentalize her identity or to decide how important familia is to her, or which familia would most capture her loyalty.

Dionne Espinoza

---

[1] Vasquez authored her columns as "Longeaux y Vasquez" which was a combination of her name and that of her second husband Bill Longeaux. I will refer to her as "Enriqueta Vasquez" in the paper because that has been her preferred self-reference.

[2] Nevertheless, she also related: "I understood why the statement had been made and I realized that going along with the feelings of the men at the convention was perhaps the best thing to do at the time." One reason why it may have been important is hinted at in Ernesto Vigil's *The Crusade for Justice*, who refers to the more traditional orientation of women in the Crusade at the First Denver Youth Conference (97). These tensions suggest the influence of local political cultures on the surfacing of feminist ideology and the negotiations taking place among women (Madison: U of Wisconsin P, 1999). For more on the dynamics of cultural nationalism and gender among Chicano organizations, see Dionne Espinoza, *Revolutionary Sisters: Chicana Activism and the Cultural Politics of Chicano Power, 1968-1978* (Forthcoming, UT P).

[3] On *testimonio*, the best sources come from the Latin American context, e.g. John Beverly, *Testimonio: On the Politics of Truth* (Minneapolis: U of Minnesota P, 2004).

[4] Maylei Blackwell has asserted in her work on the role of print media in the development of Chicana feminisms, the circulation of Chicana writings operates as a mode of activism. See Blackwell, "Contested Histories: Las Hijas de Cuauhtemoc, Chicana Feminisms, and Print Culture in the Chicano Movement, 1968-1972," *Chicana Feminisms: A Critical Reader*. Eds. Gabriela F. Arredondo et. Al. Durham: Duke UP, 2003, 58-89. The Woman of La Raza, Part I" appeared in *El Grito Del Norte*, July 2, 1969, p. 8-9. It was then reprinted as "The Mexican American Woman" in Robin Morgan's anthology of women's liberation, *Sisterhood is Powerful* (New York: Random House, 1970) 370-384; and as "La Chicana" in *Magazin* 1.4 (April 1972): 66-68. A representation of other reprintings included Luis Omar Salinas and Lillian Faderman *From the Barrio: A Chicano Anthology* (San Francisco: Canfield, 1973) 20-24; and *Regeneración*, special issue on La mujer, 2.4 (1975): 34-36.

[5] *Diosa y Hembra* (Austin, Texas: Statehouse Printing, 1976) especially pp. 164-167 for a list of Chicana edited newsletters and magazines.

[6] The argument that feminist strategies must be examined within their local contexts, rather than simply subsumed within a broad, national narrative has led to important

new studies of women's organizing. A recent example is Stephanie Gilmore, "The Dynamics of Second-Wave Feminist Activism in Memphis, 1971-1982: Rethinking the Liberal/Radical Divide," *NWSA Journal* 15.1 (Spring) 94-117.

[7] *El Grito Del Norte*, Oct. 5, 1968, p. 6.

[8] *El Grito Del Norte*, May 19, 1969, p. 8-9; June 14, 1969, p. 12.

[9] *El Grito Del Norte*, May 19, 1969, p. 8.

[10] *El Grito Del Norte*, "The Woman of La Raza, Part I," July 6, 1969, p. 11.

[11] For an excellent discussion of the representation of the family in the print media, see Richard T. Rodriguez, "Serial Kinship: Representing La Familia in Early Chicano Publications." *Aztlán* 27.1 (Spring 2002) 123-138.

[12] Maxine Baca Zinn developed the concept of "political familism" to describe the strategic use of Chicano cultural values in the context of a decolonization movement. Written shortly after the height of movement activity, Baca Zinn situates herself within debates around modernization and acculturation theories. These theories view changes in traditional sex roles as the products of assimilation into mainstream American society and of the urbanization of Chicano families. As a result of these changes, Chicano patriarchy and familism appear to be "lost in urban space." But Baca Zinn counters that "political familism" demands family loyalty and persists as a defense against internal colonialism and becomes a viable mobilization strategy for urban social movements. She defines "political familism" as "a phenomenon in which the continuity of family groups and adherence to family ideology provide the basis for struggle" (16). "Political Familism: Toward Sex Role Equality in Chicano Families," *Aztlán* 6.1 (Spring 1975): 13-26. See "Chicano Men and Masculinity" *The Journal of Ethnic Studies* 10.2 (1982): 29-44 for an argument that clarifies and subtly contradicts "Political Familism."

[13] For a useful feminist discussion of nationalist tropes of the family in the context of the nation-state in general, and South Africa in particular, see Mc Clintock "Family Feuds: Gender, Nationalism, and the Family" *Feminist Review* 44 (Summer 1993): 61-80 esp. 63-64. This observation further refines Baca Zinn's critique of modernization theory's promise to equalize gender roles in urban spaces, by underscoring the replication of inequality within the family as a project of mid-nineteenth century European thought in its highest period of colonialist and capitalist development (78).

[14] Elsewhere she stated, "one sex cannot have total fulfillment without the other," a statement that assumes heterosexuality as norm, but must also be understood in a context where the gay and lesbian rights movement was in its beginning stages.

[15] *El Grito Del Norte*, "The Woman of La Raza, Part I," p. 11.

[16] July 26, 1969. The indigenous groups that populate the area around and including Oaxaca are the Zapotec and Mixtec. Scholars who have studied this area have shown that women did have a central role in social organization as merchants.

[17] I first learned of the *enjarradoras* in the documentary *Adelante Mujeres!* (National Women's History Project, 1992). See Anita Rodriguez, "Las Enjarradoras: Women of the Earth," New Mexico, (February 1980) 46-47. Also, from Ramon

Gutierrez, *When Jesus Came the Corn Mothers Went Away: Marriage, Sexuality and Power in New Mexico, 1500-1846*: "The role men played in the construction of homes was rather limited. 'Women mix the plaster and erect the walls; the men bring the [roof and support] timbers and set them in place, observed Pedro de Castaneda in 1540.'" (Stanford: Stanford UP, 1991) 15.

[18] Denise Riley, *Am I That Name? Feminism and the Category of 'Women' in History*, (Minneapolis: U Minnesota P, 1988) 47.

[19] Key essays in feminist theory debates on cultural feminism include: Linda Alcoff, "Cultural Feminism vs. Post-Structuralism:The Identity Crisis in Feminist Theory," *Signs: Journal of Women in Culture and Society* 13.3 (1988) 405-436 and Verta Taylor and Leila J. Rupp, "Women's Culture and Lesbian Feminist Activism: A Reconsideration of Cultural Feminism," *Signs: Journal of Women in Culture and Society* 19.1 (1993) 32-61.

[20] The danger in such an approach is that culture would potentially be viewed as a static entity outside of the influences and determinations of political economy and history. So, as cultural nationalism's version of tradition constrained women in particular ways, so did the discourse of women as holders of superior cultural and moral values.

[21] At the same time, there was a generation gap in which younger Chicana activists questioned the limitations of a strategy in which Chicanas claimed their place within the family on the terms of cultural nationalism's return to traditions or to ancient cultural knowledges in a modern society that offered new freedoms. In "Soy Chicana Primero," Vasquez referred to forms of contraception control rooted in elder women's cultural knowledge of rhythm methods—a position that did not challenge the Catholic Church (which allowed the 'rhythm method') and attempted to work within a cultural nationalist paradigm which often constructed Western medicine as antithetical to Chicana/o culture. Given a context in which a Chicana's access to reproductive choice was limited by the state on one hand, and by religious taboos against contraception, on the other, Vasquez's statement inspired a response by Beverly Padilla who asserted, in an essay on abortion: "The moon-cycle birth control methods that our viejitas knew about may be well and good, but...how many Chicanas have known or know about this method? ...how good is it as a sure contraception method?" The acknowledgement of elder's knowledge and its conflict with the "modern" knowledge of birth control methods proved contentious to Padilla who was critical of the romanticization of culture if it meant that women would be kept within restricted cultural roles that would limit her reproductive rights. "Chicanas and Abortion," *Chicana Feminist Thought*, Ed. Alma M. García. (New York: Routledge, 1998) 120-121.

[22] Estelle Freedman, "Separatism as Strategy: Female Institution Building and American Feminism: 1870-1930," *Feminist Studies* 5.3 (Fall 1979) 512-529.

[23] *El Grito Del Norte*, August 20, 1971, p. 18.

[24] See Angie Chabram-Dernersesian "I Throw Punches for My Race, But I Don't Want to Be a Man: Writing Us-Chica-nos (Girl, Us)/Chicanas—into the Movement

Script" in Lawrence Grossberg, Cary Nelson, and Paula Treichler, eds. *Cultural Studies* (New York: Routledge, 1992), 83.

[25] I see this as a subversive move insofar as it constructs a theory of Chicana nationalist *hermana-dad*, but I also recognize the limitations of her subversion. Social groups are always embedded in a situation where there will be the potential for voyeurism or surveillance. According to Chantal Mouffe, while politics aims at constructing a political community and creating a unity, a fully inclusive political community and a final unity cannot be realized since there will permanently be a "constitutive outside," an exterior to the community that makes its existence possible," "Radical Democratic Citizenship," *The Miami Theory Collective Community at Loose Ends* (Minneapolis: U of Minnesota P, 1991), (78).

[26] See Carl Gutiérrez-Jones, *Rethinking the Borderlands* (Berkeley: U of CA P, 1995) 123-139 for a reading of the relevant passages in Acosta.

[27] See Emma Pérez, *The Decolonial Imaginary: Writing Chicanas into History,* for a psychoanalytic reading of Aztlán and cultural nationalism as a "return to the mother" in which Chicanas are not sexed beings, (Bloomington: Indiana UP, 1999) 122.

[28] The question of autonomy has been debated in the scholarship on women's movements as to whether it inherently expresses feminist consciousness. As women movements scholars, Maxine Molyneux argues in "Analysing Women's Movements," the organizational form that women's movements take does not necessarily express the existence of feminist interests as these interests may be achieved through multiple strategies. See *Development and Change* 29 (1998) 227.

[29] In interviews and subsequent writings, Vasquez suggested that there were cliques forming at the conference based on ideas about who was the "real" Chicana feminist as well as agitators who had been sent to disrupt the conference proceedings. I argue that the rift had several strands including different versions of how feminism and nationalism intersected as well as antifeminist strands.

[30] Accounts variously describe the walk-out as spurred by anti-feminism, "Chicano patriotism" (a.k.a. nationalism), working class politics, and outside agitation. A few sources include: Francisca Flores, "Conference of Mexican Women: Un Remolino," *Regeneración*, 1.10 (1971) 1-5; Anna Nieto-Gómez and Elma Barrera ,"Chicana Encounter," *Regeneración*, 2.4 (1975) 49-51; and Mirta Vidal, "Chicanas Speak Out," (New York: Pathfinder P, 1972) 132-140.

[31] Vasquez was also recognized by California-based feminist Ana Nieto-Gómez as a participant in the dialogue on feminism and gender equality. In her account of the First National Chicana Conference, Nieto-Gómez represented Vasquez as both a "loyalist" and a "feminist" within the same text—a seeming contradiction, yet an example of the emerging paradigms during this period. Anna Nieto-Gómez has formulated a useful paradigm for understanding different attitudes toward feminism Chicana activists: "loyalists" and "feminists." See "La Feminista," *Encuentro Femenil* 1.2 (1974): 34-47.

[32] "Chicanas of Today Say What They Want," *El Grito Del Norte,* Oct. 2, 1971, Volume IV, no. 9, p. 16.

[33] While she saw the overlap, the actual resolutions from "El Parque" were less strong on the topic of women's specific needs.

[34] "Soy Chicana Primero" initially appeared in *El Grito Del Norte*, April 26, 1971, 11, 14. It was reprinted in *El Cuaderno,* 1.1 (1972): 17-22 and *La Raza Habla*, Jan. 1976, 1-5.

[35] Garcia goes on to argue that is was not until the 1980s that Chicana feminism was able to "call for an analysis that stressed the interrelationship of race, class, and gender in explaining the conditions of Chicanas in American society." "The Development of Chicana Feminist Discourse, 1970-1980," *Gender and Society* 3.2 (1989) 228.

[36] Bernice Reagon, "Coalition Politics: Turning the Century," *Home girls: A Black Feminist Anthology*, ed. Barbara Smith (New York: Kitchen Table, Women of Color Press, 1982) 358 offers a definition of how nationalist "homes" operate as a social movement strategy that requires that a group close its doors to outsiders, so that coalition is not part of the initial gathering of people into safety.

[37] García, 232.

[38] *El Grito Del Norte*, Dec. 9, 1969, Vol. 2, no. 16, p. 7. Caren Kaplan, a scholar of transnational women's studies, shows how Adrienne Rich's politics of location glosses over racial inequality and Anglo feminist colonization of women of color within the feminist movement in the U.S. by shifting the focus of feminism to a global sisterhood that would mobilize against U.S. foreign policy. What is significant about Vasquez' statements is that she conjoins vocal resistance to foreign policy with a commitment to Chicana/o nationalism as a category of specificity. In other words, she does not advocate for a generalized "global sisterhood" without a statement of differences among feminists such that her connection to "third world women" is as a Chicana, rather than as a U.S. woman. For more on how Chicanas chose to affiliate with third world women beyond the U.S. rather than as American feminists, see Dionne Espinoza, "Chicana Feminisms and Women's Movements in Local, National, and Global Contexts, 1970-1975," delivered at the Berkshire Women's History Conference, June 2002.

[39] See "¡Que Linda es Cuba I!" *El Grito Del Norte*, Volume 2, No. 7, May 19, 1969, p. 8, and "¡Que Linda es Cuba II!" *El Grito Del Norte*, Volume 2, No. 8, June 14, 1969, p. 12.

[40] "Third World Women Meet," *El Grito del Norte*, Vol. 4, no. 1, Jan-Feb 1973, 12.

[41]"Chicana Feminisms: Their Political Context and Contemporary Expressions," in *Women: A Feminist Perspectives*, Ed. Jo Freeman (Mountain View, CA: Mayfield Publications, 1995) 620.

Additional titles in the Hispanic Civil Rights Series

La Causa: Civil Rights, Social Justice and the Struggle for Equality in the Midwest

Edited by Gilberto Cárdenas
2004, 176 pages, Clothbound
ISBN 1-55885-425-8, $28.95

In the first text examining Latinos in the Midwest, social science scholars evaluate the efforts and progress toward social justice, examine such diverse topics as advocacy efforts, civil rights and community organizations, Latina Civil Rights efforts, ethnic diversity and political identity, effects of legislation for Homeland Security, and political empowerment. *La Causa* fills a gaping void in the literature available about the Civil Rights Movement in the Midwest.

Hector P. García: In Relentless Pursuit of Justice

Ignacio M. García
2002, 416 pages, Clothbound
ISBN 1-55885-387-1, $26.95

This first definitive, superbly researched and documented biography of the founder of the American GI Forum is an objective appraisal of his successes and failures, as well as an analysis of the political, social and personal issues that he and the American G.I. Forum confronted during his lifetime.

Message to Aztlán

Rodolfo "Corky" Gonzales
Foreword by Rodolfo F. Acuña
Edited, with an Introduction, by Antonio Esquibel
2001, 256 pages, Trade Paperback
ISBN 1-55885-331-6, $14.95

Message to Aztlán is the first collection of Rodolfo "Corky" Gonzales' diverse writings: *I Am Joaquín* (1967); seven major speeches (1968-78); two plays, *The Revolutionist* and *A Cross for Malcovio* (1966-67); various poems and a selection of letters. Eight pages of photographs accompany the text.

Black Cuban, Black American: A Memoir

Evelio Grillo
Introduction by Kenya Dworkin-Mendez
2000, 224 pages, Trade Paperback
ISBN 1-55885-293-X, $13.95
Contains an eight page photo insert

A Chicano Manual on How to Handle Gringos

José Angel Gutiérrez
2003, 240 pages, Trade Paperback
ISBN 1-55885-396-0, $12.95

This manual penned by the founder of the only successful Hispanic political party, La Raza Unida, brings together an impressive breadth of models to either follow or avoid. This is a wonderful survey of the Chicano and Latino community on the move in all spheres of life in the United States on the very eve of its demographic and cultural ascendancy.

A Gringo Manual on How to Handle Mexicans

José Angel Gutiérrez
2001, 160 pages, Trade Paperback
ISBN 1-55885-326-X, $12.95

Originally self-published during the heat of the Chicano Movement, this tongue-in-cheek guide now expanded and revised, is a humorous and irreverent manual meant to educate grass-roots leaders in practical strategies for community organization, leadership and negotiation.

The Making of a Civil Rights Leader: José Angel Gutiérrez

José Angel Gutiérrez
2005, 160 pages, Trade Paperback
ISBN 1-55885-451-7, $9.95, Ages 11 and up

Gutiérrez grew up in a time when Mexicans and Mexican Americans in Texas and the Southwest attended separate schools and avoided public facilities and restaurants designated "Whites Only." Complemented by photos from his personal archives, Gutiérrez details his rise from being beaten down by racist political and agricultural interests in South Texas to his leadership role in the Chicano civil rights movement of the 1960s and 1970s.

We Won't Back Down Severita Lara's Rise from Student Leader to Mayor

José Angel Gutiérrez
2005, 160 pages, Trade Paperback
ISBN 1-55885-459-2, $9.95

On December 9, 1969, students of the local high school in Crystal City, Texas and their parents descended on the superintendent's office. Members of the school board fled to avoid the confrontation. As the students and their parents stood in front of the office, a cry rose from the crowd. "Walk out. Walk out."

Gutiérrez chronicles the life of Severita Lara, the little known female activist at the center of the Crystal City High School student walkout.

Additional titles in the Hispanic Civil Rights Series

The Struggle for the Health and Legal Protection of Farm Workers: El Cortito
Maurice Jourdane
2005, 192 pages, Trade Paperback
ISBN 1-55885-423-1, $16.95

The short hoe, known by Hispanic farm workers as *el cortito* (the short one), was the cause of severe and permanent crippling of hundreds of thousands of field laborers. The text and eight pages of photos from the period chronicle Jourdane's decade-long struggle to advocate for a ban of the short hoe and his efforts to protect other civil and human rights of California field workers.

Memoir of a Visionary: Antonia Pantoja
Antonia Pantoja
Foreword by Henry A.J. Ramos
2002, 218 pages, Trade Paperback
ISBN 1-55885-385-5, $14.95

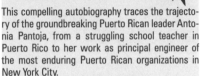

This compelling autobiography traces the trajectory of the groundbreaking Puerto Rican leader Antonia Pantoja, from a struggling school teacher in Puerto Rico to her work as principal engineer of the most enduring Puerto Rican organizations in New York City.

The American GI Forum
In Pursuit of the Dream, 1948-1983
Henry Ramos
1998, 224 pages
Clothbound, ISBN 1-55885-261-1, $24.95
Trade Paperback, ISBN 1-55885-262-X, $14.95

This book traces the stormy history of one of U.S. Hispanics' most important but least known civil-rights groups—the American G.I. Forum—from its controversial inception through the presidency of Ronald Reagan.

Chicano! The History of the Mexican American Civil Rights Movement
F. Arturo Rosales
1997, 304 pages, Trade Paperback
ISBN 1-55885-201-8, $24.95

Recipient of the Gustavus Myers Center for the Study of Human Rights in North America Book Award

This is the companion volume to the critically acclaimed, four-part documentary series of the same title, which is now available on video from the Corporation for Public Broadcasting.

Testimonio: A Documentary History of the Mexican-American Struggle for Civil Rights
F. Arturo Rosales
2000, 448 pages, Trade Paperback
ISBN 1-55885-299-9, $22.95

Beginning with the early 1800s and extending to the modern era, Rosales collects illuminating documents that shed light on the Mexican-American quest for life, liberty, and justice. Documents include petitions, correspondence, government reports, political proclamations, newspaper items, congressional testimony, memoirs, and even international treaties.

The Life and Times of Willie Velásquez
Su Voto es Su Voz
Juan A. Sepúlveda, Jr.
2005, 398 pages, Trade Paperback
ISBN 1-55885-402-9, $16.95

This critical biography of William C. "Willie" Velásquez, founder of the Southwest Voter Registration and Education Project (SVREP), features an introduction by Henry Cisneros, former Secretary of the Department of Housing and Urban Development. Former Rhodes Scholar and Velásquez protégé Juan A. Sepúlveda, Jr. chronicles Velásquez's influences, his landmark contributions to American civic culture, and his enduring legacy.

They Called Me "King Tiger"
My Struggle for the Land and Our Rights
Reies López Tijerina
English translation by José Ángel Gutiérrez
2000, 256 pages, Trade Paperback
ISBN 1-55885-302-2, $14.95

In this autobiography, Reies López Tijerina, writes about his attempts to reclaim land grants, including his taking up arms against the authorities and spending time in the federal prison system.

Eyewitness: A Filmmaker's Memoir of the Chicano Movement
Jesús Treviño
2001, 400 pages, Trade Paperback
ISBN 1-55885-349-9, $15.95

Coming of age during the turmoil of the sixties, noted filmmaker Jesús Salvador Treviño was on the spot to record the struggles to organize students and workers into the largest social and political movement in the history of Latino communities in the United States.